D0387573

SACRAMENTO PUBLIC LIBRARY
3 3029 04359 2765

SHAPERS OF THE GREAT DEBATE ON NATIVE AMERICANS

LAND, SPIRIT, AND POWER

Recent Titles in
Shapers of the Great American Debates

Shapers of the Great Debate on Immigration: A Biographical Dictionary
Mary Elizabeth Brown

SHAPERS OF THE GREAT DEBATE ON NATIVE AMERICANS

LAND, SPIRIT, AND POWER

A BIOGRAPHICAL DICTIONARY

Bruce E. Johansen

Shapers of the Great American Debates, Number 2
Peter B. Levy, Series Editor

Greenwood Press
Westport, Connecticut • London

Library of Congress Cataloging-in-Publication Data

Johansen, Bruce E. (Bruce Elliott), 1950–
Shapers of the great debate on Native Americans—land, spirit, and power : a biographical dictionary / Bruce E. Johansen.
p. cm.—(Shapers of the great American debates, ISSN 1099–2693 : no. 2)
Includes bibliographical references and index.
ISBN 0–313–30941–8 (alk. paper)
1. Indians of North America—Land tenure. 2. Land tenure—United States. 3. Land tenure—Europe. 4. Indians of North America—Biography. 5. United States—Biography. I. Title. II. Series.
E98.L3J65 2000
333.2—dc21 99–15383

British Library Cataloguing in Publication Data is available.

Library of Congress Catalog Card Number: 99–15383
ISBN: 0–313–30941–8
ISSN: 1099–2693

First published in 2000

Greenwood Press, 88 Post Road West, Westport, CT 06881
An imprint of Greenwood Publishing Group, Inc.
www.greenwood.com

Printed in the United States of America

The paper used in this book complies with the Permanent Paper Standard issued by the National Information Standards Organization (Z39.48–1984).

10 9 8 7 6 5 4 3 2 1

Copyright Acknowledgments

CONTENTS

SERIES FOREWORD

American history has been shaped by numerous debates over issues far ranging in content and time. Debates over the right, or lack thereof, to take the land of the Native Americans, and the proper place and role of women, sparked by Roger Williams and Anne Hutchinson, respectively, marked the earliest years of the Massachusetts Bay Colony. Debates over slavery, the nature and size of the federal government, the emergence of big business, the rights of labor and immigrants, were central to the Republic in the nineteenth century and, in some cases, remain alive today. World War I, World War II, and the Vietnam War sparked debates that tore at the body politic. Even the Revolution involved a debate over whether America should be America or remain part of Great Britain. And the Civil War, considered by many the central event in American history, was the outgrowth of a long debate that found no peaceful resolution.

This series, *Shapers of the Great American Debates*, will examine many of these debates—from those between Native Americans and European settlers to those between "natives" and "newcomers." Each volume will focus on a particular issue, concentrating on those men and women who *shaped* the debates. The authors will pay special attention to fleshing out the life histories of the shapers, considering the relationship between biography or personal history and policy or philosophy. Each volume will begin with an introductory overview, include several biographies of ten to fifteen pages, an appendix that briefly describes other key figures, bibliographical information, and a subject index. Unlike works that emphasize end results, the books in this series will devote equal attention to both sides, to the "winners" and the "losers." This will lead to a more complete understanding of the richness and complexity of America's past than is afforded by works that examine only the victors.

Taken together, the books in this series remind us of the many ways that class, race, ethnicity, gender, and region have divided rather than united the inhabitants of the United States of America. Each study reminds us of the frequency and variety of debates in America, a reflection of the diversity of the nation and its democratic credo. One even wonders if a similar series could be developed for many other nations or if the diversity of America and its tradition of free expression have given rise to more debates than elsewhere.

Although many Americans have sought to crush the expression of opposing views by invoking the imperative of patriotism, more often than not Americans have respected the rights of others to voice their opinions. Every four years, Americans have voted for president and peacefully respected the results, demonstrating their faith in the process that institutionalizes political debate. More recently, candidates for the presidency have faced off in televised debates that often mark the climax of their campaigns. Americans not only look forward to these debates, but they would probably punish anyone who sought to avoid them. Put another way, debates are central to America's political culture, especially those that deal with key issues and involve the most prominent members of society.

Each volume in the series is written by an expert. While I offered my share of editorial suggestions, overall I relied on the author's expertise when it came to determining the most sensible way to organize and present each work. As a result, some of the volumes follow a chronological structure; others clump their material thematically; still others are separated into two sections, one pro and one con. All of the works are written with the needs of college and advanced high school students in mind. They should prove valuable both as sources for research papers and as supplemental texts in both general and specialized courses. The general public should also find the works an attractive means of learning more about many of the most important figures and equally as many seminal issues in American history.

Peter B. Levy
Associate Professor
Department of History
York College

PREFACE

Land was the magnet that drew millions of people from crowded, rack-rented Europe to North America. Land—American Indian land—was the speculative fuel that stoked the economy of the westward drive across the continent, most of it during the nineteenth century, when the European-American "settlement frontier" surged from the Appalachian crest to the Pacific Ocean. Land was the single largest storehouse of wealth in this economy. Before the Civil War, slaves, human capital, were the second-largest class of capitalistic asset in the national economy.

This volume will examine ideological aspects of property—the ideas that were exchanged as a continent changed hands. The following chapters sketch how a selected group of Native American and European-American leaders perceived their relationship with the earth as home and source of sustenance.

Structurally, my intention is to provide eight "questions" within the large debate and to center each of these around two or more related major biographies, with additional material from other notable people who had opinions on the question at hand. The specific biographical figures whose lives I examine in this volume are outlined in the Introduction.

In this survey of ideas related to the acquisition and use of land, I have asked myself whether I could find more women, because most of the major figures are men. That is difficult because men were the main actors and keepers of records even in cases such as the Iroquois where women chose the leaders. Thus most of our history until recently has been men talking to men, since "Anglo" society was even more male oriented than today. Even in such a male-oriented record, however, some women stand out: Helen Hunt Jackson, for example, or the early feminists Matilda Joslyn Gage and Elizabeth Cady Stanton, both of whom drew inspiration from the matrilineal nature of Haudenosaunee (Iroquois) society.

The beginning of the "removal era" during the 1830s heralded an explosion of European-American expansion across the width of North America. Barely a decade passed between the Cherokees' Trail of Tears and the occupancy of Mexico's northern half during 1848, a year before the westward surge was accelerated by the discovery of gold in California. The speed with which a large part of the continent changed hands during the mid-nineteenth century can be gauged by the fact that Omaha and Seattle, 1,700 miles apart by road, started as urban areas at roughly the same time, during the mid-1850s.

One element that often perplexed Native Americans about the immigrant Europeans and their descendants was the mobile nature of European-American culture, which seemed able to sink its expanding roots in any soil. While the immigrants often supported their claims to the land by characterizing native peoples as rootless nomads, the distances Indians moved were small compared to the wholesale transplantation of Europeans (as well as Africans and, later, Asians) across world-girding oceans. From Tecumseh in the Ohio Valley to Chief Sea'thl in the Pacific Northwest, Native American leaders expressed amazement, dismay, and sometimes alarm at how easily the European-Americans wandered from the graves of their forebears, and at how easily and persistently they annexed the land and natural resources of other peoples.

Another European notion that perplexed Native Americans was the value the immigrants placed on exclusive personal ownership of the land itself, as well as of life's everyday implements. William Penn, in *A Description of Pennsylvania*, described many Indians' attitudes toward incidental property:

> Nothing is too good for their friends. Give them a fine gun, coat, or other thing, it may pass twenty hands before it sticks; light of heart, strong affections, but soon spent. . . . [T]hey never have much. nor want much. Wealth circulateth like the blood, all parts partake. (Black and Weidman, 52)

The immigrants soon learned that while Native Americans did not usually own land as individuals in the European sense, they exercised a collective title with identifiable boundaries. Every "Indian war" of roughly forty fought during the nineteenth century began as a contest over who should "own" the land, what ownership should mean, and to what purposes the land should be put. The native peoples were virtually always placed in a position of defending their lands (and, since land is central to life, their families and cultures) from invasion. Most of the 371 treaties negotiated with native nations and ratified by Congress to 1871, as well as several more negotiated and approved as "executive agreements" after that, aimed to acquire land for expanding European-American settlement. Conflict over land is the central element running through nearly four centuries of relationships between Native Americans and immigrant peoples and cultures in the land area that today comprises the United States of America.

Non-Indian attitudes toward native land tenure since the first sustained contact between the two groups of cultures may be divided into two rough categories: those who believed that Indians had a prior right to the land because of prior occupancy, and those who believed that European-Americans possessed a superior right to the land based on the assumption that they would make better use of it, according to the unquestioned assumptions of Anglo-American land tenure. During the years of westward movement—roughly from the landing of the *Mayflower* to the putative "closing" of the frontier in 1890—Native Americans most often were stereotyped in the immigrants' literature as wandering nomads, with little if any claim to the land. While it is true that, over time, many if not most native peoples in the eastern half of North America moved from one part of North America to others, they also usually stayed in one place long enough to cultivate the earth extensively. Many native peoples who did not cultivate the earth, such as Northwest Coast peoples, were not nomadic. The stereotype of the nomadic savage served to deny the original inhabitants' rights to the land.

The rationale for taking the land often was couched in a language of legal appropriation that propelled the frontier westward in land-use patterns still prevailing today. "Highest and best use" is the legal motor of the system today, a direct reflection, to a degree, of a set of ethnocentric assumptions that justified the taking of the continent from its native peoples. The central assumption, that European-Americans would make better use of the land than native peoples, was the primary intellectual rationalization for the ideology of "Manifest Destiny." Today, the same system spins suburban galaxies ("urban sprawl") over ever-larger landscapes. Peter Nabokov has commented on how strange Anglo-American concepts of land tenure seemed to many Native American peoples:

> Defining land as a commercial product like sugar or gunpowder, the whites measured it, bought it or stole it, fenced it, tilled or built upon it, with an abandon that horrified Indians. At the same time the colonists, whose society was founded on private ownership and consolidation of personal riches, looked disapprovingly at Indian customs of sharing land in common. (Nabokov, 70)

Similarly, the experiences of America's native peoples are commonly called "prehistoric" before the arrival of Columbus, as if Europeans had brought history to the Americas as well as their religions, political systems, economic assumptions, plants, animals, and diseases. This assumption rolls off the tongue so effortlessly that we sometimes forget what saying it assumes. It is a reflection of an erroneous belief that native peoples in the Americas had no methods of recording history other than uncannily accurate oral traditions. For a long time, most Europeans did not understand that many Native American peoples had written histories that they did not understand, from the carved stelae of the Mayas to the codices of the Aztecs, the writing of the Incas, the wampum belts of the Haudenosaunee (Iroquois), and the winter counts of many Plains peoples.

Ignorance of native peoples' historical faces, along with Eurocentric assumptions about land use, permitted the dehumanization necessary to make the conquest acceptable to the immigrants without impugning their self-image as decent people. It was much easier to dispossess native peoples who were imagined as having no systems of land tenure and no "reliable" histories. European religious assumptions also played a role, as in New England, where Puritan immigrants, finding the land depopulated, assumed that their God had cleared the way for their arrival in a new world. They had no knowledge at the time that European pathogens had killed many of the native inhabitants.

The land was never openly taken in the name of greed and profit, but against a background of grander, often-imaginary, rationalizations associated with a set of nationalistic beliefs under the rubric of "Manifest Destiny," an assumption that the Anglo-American acquisition of North America was preordained by Christian commandment accentuated by various economic and political imperatives. Manifest Destiny adapted the Calvinistic beliefs that caused the Puritans to assume that Native Americans had died in New England by God's will to make way for his people. The Calvinistic view that God helps those who help themselves, slightly secularized, fit hand-in-glove with the doctrine of Manifest Destiny.

Anyone who believes that this discussion is merely of historical interest may be surprised by the last chapter of this volume. The reader will find many of the assumptions of "manifest destiny" displayed as freshly as today's headlines in the biography of Senator Slade Gorton, Republican of Washington State, who still would like to wipe the treaties (and the Native American rights they protect) from our law. As with any other history, our assumptions about Native Americans' relation to the land informs present-day political and social debates.

REFERENCES

Black, Nancy B., and Bette S. Weidman, eds. *White on Red: Images of the American Indian*. Port Washington, NY: Kennikat Press, 1976.

Nabokov, Peter, ed. *Native American Testimony*. New York: Viking, 1991.

INTRODUCTION

> Wherever we went, the soldiers came to kill us, and it was *all our own country*. It was ours already when the *Wasichus* made the treaty with Red Cloud, that said it would be ours as long as the grass should grow and water flow. That was only eight winters before, and they were chasing us now because we remembered and they forgot.
>
> —Black Elk (Vogel, ii)

This is a volume in the Shapers of the Great American Debates series and, as such, will utilize biographies of several noteworthy individuals in an effort to illuminate a major debating point in American history. When I was asked by Peter Levy, series editor, and Cynthia Harris, senior editor at Greenwood Press, to propose a volume in Native American history for this series, I chose the nature of land relations between native peoples and immigrants (mostly from Europe) as my central theme. Land relations have been a common thread in nearly every interaction between native and immigrant cultures.

Each chapter of this volume groups several biographies around a common land-related theme. This format is designed to blend biographical detail with significant treatment of important issues in Native American history as they concern land relations. This approach combines biography and historiography in a manner not seen before (to my knowledge) in the Native American precincts of American history to produce a readable narrative with substantial detail regarding major events in American history as seen from the perspectives of several influential Native Americans, as well as non-Indians who helped shape the same aspects of history. The account includes excerpts from some of the greatest oratory in American history; it is presented in the participants' own words as often as possible.

Our journey begins with one of the earliest and most controversial immigrants to America from England, Roger Williams. Immigrating to the Puritan settlements in and near Boston within little more than a decade after the first arrivals, Williams came to America from England as a Puritan clergyman intent on proselytizing the native peoples. Errands in the wilderness changed the way Williams looked at his own culture and contributed to his dissent from Puritan doctrines. When Williams was asked by Puritan clerics to compose a treatise on who owned America, he contested Puritan assumptions that God had made the land available for the immigrants by striking many of the native inhabitants dead of disease. (The immigrants had no understanding of how they themselves were vectors for smallpox and other illnesses.) Williams held that the Indians owned the land by right of prior occupancy, and that the Puritans had no superior right to native land.

Soon thereafter, Williams was ordered deported from the Puritan colony. The Puritan authorities meant to ship Williams and his intellectual "infections" back to England. Instead, Williams, with significant aid from local native peoples, escaped Puritania to found Providence Plantations, later renamed Rhode Island. The land to which Williams and his followers escaped was donated to them by its native owners.

Williams became a major diplomatic negotiator between Puritan authorities and local native peoples and came to know most of the major native leaders of his day. Williams was able to communicate with most of these leaders in their own languages. One of the most notable was Williams' friend Metacom, whom the English called King Philip. Metacom led the remnants of several New England native nations in a final explosion of violence that ended with his own death in 1676. Before he was drawn and quartered by the colonists, Metacom described to Williams how the loss of land was destroying his people. He likened the land to a canoe in which his people were riding on stormy seas. Before the war was over, Williams and Metacom had reason to reflect on the cost of war to friendship: Metacom was unable to prevent Indians from burning much of Providence, including Williams' own home.

Three-quarters of a century after Metacom died, English and French enclaves were firmly established on most of the Atlantic seaboard and along the Saint Lawrence River, respectively. The major Native American power in the contest for the land between Britain and France was the Haudenosaunee (Iroquois) Confederacy, located in upstate New York along the future route of the Erie Canal. This volume's second chapter describes how the contest for the land initiated diplomacy by the likes of Benjamin Franklin, which provided him and other prominent Anglo-Americans with an opportunity to watch the Iroquois, an ancient confederacy of related native nations, transact political business. The treaty conferences of the time were the most important forums for agreement and disagreement on issues of who owned the land and how it should be used. Most of them were conducted according to Iroquois protocol.

Franklin at first was a printer. He started his distinguished diplomatic career as an envoy to the Iroquois for the Pennsylvania colony and met, in person or in treaty proceedings issued by his press, two of the Iroquois confederacy's best-known leaders, Canassatego, an Onondaga, and Hendrick (Tiyanoga), a Mohawk. Subsequent history weaves the lives of these three men at the beginning of a new chapter in American land relations, the birth of the United States of America, in ways that left an Iroquois imprint on the democratic evolution and revolution that created the political institutions of the new nation.

By the beginning of the eighteenth century, the "settlement frontier," that point at which Native American land use had been replaced by that of immigrants, was spilling over the Appalachian Mountains westward into the Ohio Valley. This volume's third chapter presents Tecumseh's idea of a native confederation in defense of the land and the application of similar ideas before him by Little Turtle, a Miami who inflicted on the U.S. Army its worst battlefield defeat of the Indian wars in 1791. A European-American counterpart is provided through the persona of General William Henry Harrison, Tecumseh's major military and diplomatic adversary.

In the Southeast, the contest for the land evolved into a series of "removals," in which native peoples were forced to leave their homelands for promised tracts of land in "Indian Territory" (later the state of Oklahoma). The debate over removal and its subsequent toll on the Cherokees is described in the fourth chapter of this volume with reference to the lives and defining thoughts of four major figures: President Andrew Jackson, Supreme Court Chief Justice John Marshall, the Cherokee Sequoyah (the only individual in human history to invent a national written language by himself), and the Cherokee chief John Ross, a prominent opponent of removal.

By midcentury, the homelands of the Cherokees and other native nations in the South had become strongholds of King Cotton. The Anglo-American settlement frontier was hurdling the Missouri River and racing westward on news of a large gold strike in California. Within one lifetime, the lives of Native Americans in the middle of the continent were turned upside down as land use changed around them. Chapter 5 of this study develops the lives of Native American leaders whose people became exiles in their own land: Chief Joseph the Younger, Sitting Bull, Red Cloud, and the Ponca Standing Bear.

The lives of Sitting Bull and Red Cloud extended from a time when their people rode as mounted masters of the plains to their last years on reservations that were little more than open-air concentration camps. In the course of their lives, Sitting Bull and Red Cloud had words for what was becoming of their land, as well as the staple of their lives, the massive buffalo herds that were all but exterminated within one lifetime. Sitting Bull's views are counterposed with those of George Armstrong Custer, and Chief Joseph's are compared with those of General Oliver Otis Howard, the general who had been charged with bringing Joseph's Nez Perce people to reservation life.

Standing Bear's Poncas had been deprived of their land along the Niobrara River on Nebraska's northern border because the United States had mistakenly signed it over to their enemies, the Sioux, in the Fort Laramie Treaty of 1868. The Poncas were exiled to Indian Territory, where many of them died of disease and destitution. In defense of their right to their homeland, Standing Bear twice led groups of Poncas 500 miles northward during the worst of a midwestern winter. On the second march, after they had eaten their food, the Poncas ate their mounts. On foot now, they subsisted on horsemeat until it was gone. Then they ate their moccasins. The Poncas were taken into custody near Omaha by General George Crook as their bare feet bled in the snow.

Manifest injustice to the Poncas became a national scandal with the help of an Omaha newspaperman, Thomas Tibbles, who heard Standing Bear's story after Crook had detained them. The Poncas' arrest led to a landmark legal case, *Standing Bear v. Crook*, in which the right of habeas corpus was applied to Indians for the first time, in 1879, by Omaha District Court Judge Elmer Dundy.

Chapter 6 develops Native American conceptions of the land through spiritual and ecological prisms. Its major biographical figures are Chief Sea'thl, the Lakota holy man Black Elk, and the Sioux author Luther Standing Bear. Contemporary debates regarding the authenticity of Sea'thl's speech are aired, along with similar questions about whether Native American leaders during the nineteenth century sketched an ecological metaphor of earth as mother or whether, as some of today's scholars assert, such metaphors have been dreamed up by white environmental activists and placed in the mouths of nineteenth-century native holy men such as Black Elk. I have tried to place their evocation of the mother-earth image in a historical context developed in earlier chapters, noting that the message arrives in our time with increasing urgency as industrial man's ability to subdue the earth threatens ecological damage beyond the imaginings of Tecumseh, Sea'thl, or Black Elk.

When the Ponca Standing Bear was in Boston on a fund-raising tour, he met Helen Hunt Jackson, who was known at the time as one of America's foremost woman poets (unlike her childhood playmate Emily Dickinson, whose poetry was largely unappreciated at the time). Jackson was so moved by the story of the Poncas that she set out to write what became arguably the most important book in a policy-reform movement, *A Century of Dishonor*. In Chapter 7, Jackson's life and works are portrayed against a background of national debate in the late nineteenth century over what was to become of the native peoples who had survived the Indian wars. Jackson was representative of a reform movement that sought to preserve native peoples from extermination through assimilative measures such as allotment of land and industrial education. General Richard Henry Pratt, who founded the first Indian boarding school at Carlisle, Pennsylvania, also is profiled in this context, in which the best of intentions on the part of the reformers often produced the worst results for Native Americans. A counterpoint to the reformers' vision is provided by a sampling of nineteenth-century household names who advocated extermination, among them Horace Greeley, the abolitionist newspaper editor, and Lyman Frank Baum, one-time newspaper editor in Aberdeen, South Dakota, who, in 1900, published the first of several *Oz* books.

Chapter 8 ties the themes in the previous chapters to present-day figures and issues, with biographies of Felix Cohen, author of the *Handbook of American Indian Law*, Onondaga faithkeeper Oren Lyons, and Sioux writer and social critic Vine Deloria, Jr. A counterpoint to contemporary Native American points of view is provided through the legal practice and legislative agenda of U.S. Senator Slade Gorton of Washington, who has campaigned his entire adult life to abrogate Indian treaties that he contends make Indians "supercitizens."

In *Indian Atrocities: Narratives of the Perils and Sufferings of Dr. Knight and John Slover among the Indians*, a book first published in 1782, author H. H. Brackenridge gave voice to his own rationale for taking Indian land, one that he shared with both orthodox Puritans and Senator Gorton: "I am so far from thinking the Indians have a right to the soil, that not having made a better use of it for many hundred years, I conceive they have forfeited all pretence to claim, and ought to be driven from it" (Vogel, 105). To Brackenridge, the immigrants had no need to ask the permission of Indians to traverse the land. One might as well, in his opinion, ask the buffalo and the birds. A Eurocentric spin could even be cast on the often-voiced Native American observation that the earth teemed with the spirits and ashes of Native American ancestors. Thomas Farnham, a lawyer living in Vermont, turned that image on its head in 1839 by writing in a travel narrative from the Oregon Country that "Indians' bones must enrich the soil" to "fatten the corn hills of a more civilized race" (Vogel, 138).

Today one may find remnants of century-old attitudes in unexpected places. The following verse was engraved atop an outside door at Omaha's Joslyn Art Museum early in the twentieth century, within a lifetime of Omaha's urban origins:

They entered the land
to discover it.
Iron was in their hands.
They entered the land
to redeem it.
Love was in their hearts.

"Iron" could have meant several things: the iron of firearms, the iron of railroad tracks, or the iron of the plow, all of which were employed across the continent as one system of land tenure replaced another. The weaving of themes related to discovery and redemption through the use of machine-age iron in an act of ethnocentric love springs from the rhetoric of Manifest Destiny.

Some early New England colonists assumed that Native American peoples had no land-tenure ethic because they did not fence land or raise domestic animals on it. Native Americans did not issue each other deeds or trade in real estate, but they did use the land. William Cronon reminds us to consider the differences between individual ownership of land, which most Native Americans did not practice, and their collective use of an area:

> European property systems were much like Indian ones in expressing the ecological purposes to which a people intended to put their land; it is crucial that they not be oversimplified if their contributions to ecological history are to be understood. The popular idea that Europeans had private property, while the Indians did not, distorts European notions of property as much as it does Indian ones. (Cronon, 68–69)

According to Cronon, both European and Native American property systems involved distinctions between individual ownership and community property. Both "dealt in bundles of culturally defined rights that determined what could and could not be done with land and personal property" (Cronon, 69). Customs of land tenure varied greatly in detail across New England and the rest of North America; generally, however, Native Americans individually owned the implements of their work, their clothing, and other items used in their daily lives. The extended family that shared a lodging usually exercised a sense of ownership over it. Land, however, was usually held collectively. America was not a "Virgin Land" when Europeans arrived. Large tracts were under intensive management for hunting and agriculture by Native Americans.

Because attitudes toward land tenure varied, negotiations that Europeans thought gave them exclusive property rights were not interpreted this way by Native Americans. Differing land-tenure systems afflicted many treaty negotiations with a high degree of intercultural misunderstanding. When the English colonists of New England thought that they were buying land, Native Americans often took the same agreements to mean that they were agreeing to share it (Cronon, 70).

This volume combines detailed biographies with analysis of the ways in which cultural orientations toward land tenure differed between Native American and European-American leaders during nearly four centuries from the first English immigration to North America to the present day. I hope that this combination will provoke intellectual sharing that will increase our understanding of American history.

REFERENCES

Cronon, William. *Changes in the Land: Indians, Colonists, and the Ecology of New England*. New York: Hill & Wang, 1983.

Vogel, Virgil J. *This Country Was Ours: A Documentary History of the American Indian*. New York: Harper & Row, 1972.

SHAPERS OF THE GREAT DEBATE ON NATIVE AMERICANS

LAND, SPIRIT, AND POWER

1
WHO "OWNS" THE WILDERNESS?

Roger Williams and Metacom (King Philip)

Roger Williams was the "first rebel against the divine church-order" (Parrington, 1:6), "morning star in the galaxy of the American great" (Savelle, 51). During his life, Williams was excoriated as a spreader of intellectual "infections." Afterwards, he was hailed as the first flower of the Enlightenment's spring. Roger Williams was the first North American revolutionary, or at least the first of European extraction.

Although Williams' ideas were couched mainly in a religious context, they also engaged debates regarding political liberty that would fire the American Revolution more than a century later. Like many of the founders of the United States, Williams also often used his perceptions of American Indians and their societies as a reference point on which to hone his preexisting desires for an alternative to the European status quo. Williams tried to implement his ideas of "soul liberty," political freedom, and economic equality. His experiment presaged the later revolution of continental scope.

Williams was remarkable in his time because of his camaraderie with Native Americans. He seemed to be naturally drawn into the making of peace between immigrant Anglo-Americans and the native inhabitants of the land the immigrants came to call New England. He was probably the only European trusted at all by the fiery native leader Metacom (King Philip), who led a desperate last-gasp revolt in defense of Indians' vanishing land base. The conflict was called King Philip's War by the English; it ended with Metacom's death in 1676. Williams found it difficult to hate Metacom, but war can come between the best of friends. Both Metacom and Williams may have paused to reflect on this fact after rebelling Indians surged over Providence Plantations, Williams' colony, and burned his own home to the ground.

Roger Williams (c. 1603–1683)

Educated at London's Charterhouse School and Cambridge University, Roger Williams was one of the Puritans' best and brightest when he emigrated to America. Having asserted liberty of the soul among the native peoples of America, as well as dissident colonists, Williams was cast out of Puritania and founded Providence Plantations, which became Rhode Island, a refuge for freethinkers, at least at its inception.

Like many another Puritan, Williams originally came to America "longing after the natives' soules" (Chupack, 63). More than most, his errand in the wilderness helped shape Williams' predispositions toward freedom. He engendered a passionate debate on both sides of the Atlantic that began to hone the definitions of political and religious liberty that would frame the ideology of the American Revolution.

Within a few months of Williams' arrival in Boston during 1631, he was learning the Algonquian language. He would master the dialects of the Showatuck, Nipmuck, Narragansett, and others. Williams' oratorical flourish and compassion won him esteem from congregations at Plymouth and Salem, as well as among native peoples of the area, all of whom sought his "love and counsel" (Ernst, *Roger Williams; New England Firebrand*, 179).

Williams' quick mastery of native languages did not alarm the soul-

Roger Williams; portrait created by Arthur William Heintzelman in 1936 for the 300th anniversary of Rhode Island's founding. No likenesses of Williams from life are known to exist. Courtesy Roger Williams University Library Archives

soldiers of Puritania. What landed him in hot ecclesiastical water was that he learned other things from the Native American peoples as he picked up their languages. Asked by William Bradford to compose a paper on the compact that established the Puritan colony in America, Williams declared it invalid. How, he asked, could the Puritans claim the land by "right of discovery" when it was already inhabited? Furthermore, Williams argued that the Puritans had no right to deny the Indians their own religions, divine or secular. Soon the authorities were transferring Williams from pulpit to pulpit, fretting over how easily he won friends not only among the colonists, but also among the native peoples of the area.

Questions regarding who owns the land (and what is meant by "ownership") thus began to affect the relationship between Native Americans and European immigrants to North America within a few years of the Puritans' arrival in the land they called New England. As Williams sought to reconcile these questions in his own mind, other Puritans were wrestling with definitions of land tenure that differed markedly from their own.

In *Brave Are My People*, Frank Waters described a "purchase" by Miles Standish and two companions of a tract of land fourteen miles square near Bridgewater for seven coats, eight hoes, nine hatchets, ten yards of cotton cloth, twenty knives, and four moose skins. When native people continued to hunt on the land after it was "purchased" and were arrested by the Pilgrims, the Wampanoag sachem Massasoit protested:

> What is this you call property? It cannot be the earth. For the land is our mother, nourishing all her children . . . birds, fish, and all men. The woods, the streams, everything on it belongs to everybody and is for the use of all. How can one man say it belongs to him only? (Waters, 28)

While Standish and his companions thought that they had purchased an English-style deed, Massasoit argued that their goods had paid only for use of the land in common with Native Americans who were using the land when he "bought" it. Conflicts over concepts of land use elicited the term "Indian giver" among colonists who were unable or unwilling to accept American Indian concepts of shared land use.

Williams became friendly with Massasoit, who was described by Bradford in 1621 as "lustie . . . in his best years, an able body grave of countenance, spare of speech, strong [and] tall" (Covey, 125). Massasoit, the father of Metacom (who was called King Philip by the English), favored friendly relations with the English colonists when he became the Wampanoags' most influential leader about 1632. When Williams met Massasoit, he was about thirty years of age and, in Williams' words, became "great friends" with the sachem (Brockunier, 47). Williams also became close to Canonicus, born about 1560 and elderly leader of the Narragansetts, who regarded Williams nearly as a son. With both, Williams traveled in the forest for days at a time, learning what he could of their languages, societies, and opinions, drinking in experiences that, along with prior European experiences, would provide the intellectual groundwork for the model commonwealth Williams sought to establish in Providence Plantations on land given him by neighboring Native American peoples.

At their height, the Narragansetts, with Canonicus as their most influential leader, held sway over the area from Narragansett Bay on the east to the Pawcatuck River on the west. The Narragansetts were rarely warlike, but their large numbers (about 4,000 men of warrior age in the early seventeenth century) usually prevented other native nations from attacking them. William Wood, in *New England's Prospect*, characterized the Narragansetts as "the most numerous people in those parts, and the most rich also, and the most industrious, being a storehouse of all kinds . . . of merchandise" (Wood, 80). The Narragansetts fashioned wampum in bracelets and pendants for many other Indian nations. They also made smoking pipes "much desired by our English tobacconists for their rarity, strength, handsomeness, and coolness" (Wood, 80–81). According to Wood's account, the Narragansetts had never desired "to take part in any martial enterprise. But being incapable of a jeer, they rest secure under the conceit of their popularity, and seek rather to grow rich by industry than famous by deeds of chivalry" (Wood, 81). In this fashion, the Narragansetts built a confederacy in which they supervised the affairs of Indian peoples throughout most of present-day Rhode Island and eastern Long Island, about 30,000 native people in the early seventeenth century (Chapin, 7).

By 1635, having asserted that the immigrants had no God-given right to the land, Williams was also arguing that the church had no right to compel membership or contributions by force of law, the kernel of church-state separation. With such an argument, Williams struck at the assumption that the Puritan church subsumed the state. Taxes were levied to pay ministers; a law passed in 1631 required church membership to hold public office. Magistrates enforced the first four of the Ten Commandments. Williams contended that the church had no such right. Furthermore, Williams believed that civil authorities could not make an oath of allegiance to the church part of an oath of citizenship in the colony. He was defending the rights of the area's original inhabitants as well as those of Europeans who did not wish to conform to Puritan doctrine. "Natural men," as Williams called the Native American peoples, should not and could not be forced "to the exercise of those holy Ordinances of Prayers, Oathes, &c." (Giddings, 21).

Williams argued for a more personal religion much resembling the later conceptions of Benjamin Franklin, Thomas Jefferson, and others, who reacted to the state-church power alliances in Europe by seeking to separate ecclesiastical and secular authority in their designs for the United States. Williams argued for a religion that also was closer to Native American conceptions of spirituality than the Puritanism under which he had been raised. As early as 1624, Joseph Le Caron had reminded his Recollect brethren that no "savage" had ever killed a Christian for religious reasons (Axtell, 78–80). Native Americans held no Star Chambers, no Inquisitions to compel obedience to any particular sachem's version of the Great Spirit's wisdom. Indians sometimes fought with each other for many reasons, but none of them were religious. To Williams, there was nothing more absurd than killing in the name of eternal peace and love. Williams likened society to a ship carrying many kinds of people, each of whom valued his or her own opinions enough to debate, but not to fight. In this spirit, Williams argued against coercion of the soul and for beauty in diversity.

By January 1635, the Puritans' more orthodox magistrates had decided that Williams must be exiled to England, jailed if possible, and shut up. They opposed exiling Williams in the wilderness, fearing that he would begin his own settlement, from which his "infections" would leak back into Puritania. Not all Puritans wanted Williams shut up so quickly. Governor John Winthrop, for one, secretly aided plans by Williams and his confederates to establish a new colony. Winthrop's reasons were many. To begin with, the Puritans needed accurate intelligence about and diplomatic liaison with the Indians, both of which Williams could provide. On a more theoretical level, Winthrop was among those Puritans who wished to find out whether a colony established on principles of soul liberty and political democracy could work, or whether it would dissolve into atheistic anarchy. Later in his life, Williams recalled that "upon the express advice of your ever-honored Mr. Winthrop, deceased, I first adventured to begin a plantation among the thickest of these barbarians" (Dorr, 187–188).

Even so, a summons was issued for Williams' arrest, but he stalled the authorities by contending that he was too ill to withstand an ocean voyage. At the same time, Williams and his associates were rushing ahead with plans for their new colony, from which the worst fears of the orthodox magistrates would be realized. Williams already had arranged with Canonicus for a tract of land large enough to support a colony. Canonicus would not accept money in payment for the land. "It was not price or money that could have purchased Rhode Island," Williams wrote later. "Rhode Island was purchased by love" (Winslow, 133).

Williams was allowed to remain in Salem until the spring of 1636, provided he refrained from preaching. However, the magistrates learned that Williams was holding meetings of more than twenty people at a time in his house, and so, about January 15, 1636, Captain John Underhill was dispatched from Boston to arrest Williams and place him on board ship for England. Arriving at Williams' home, Underhill and his deputies found that Williams had escaped. No one in the neighborhood would admit to having seen him leave.

Aware of his impending arrest, Williams had set out three days earlier during a blinding blizzard, walking south by west to the lodge of Massasoit at Mount Hope, on a peninsula jutting into the northeastern side of Narragansett Bay, near the present-day town of Bristol, Rhode Island. Walking eighty to ninety miles during the worst of a New England winter, Williams suffered immensely and likely would have died without Indian aid. Nearly half a century later, nearing death, Williams wrote, "I bear to this day in my body the effects of that winter's exposure" (Guild, 20). Near the end of his trek, Williams lodged with Canonicus and his family. He then scouted the land that had been set aside for the new colony.

Week by week, month by month, Williams' family and friends filtered south from Plymouth and Salem. By spring, houses were being erected, and fields were being turned. The growing group also began to erect an experimental government very novel by European or Puritan standards of the time. For the first time among English-speaking people in America, they were trying to establish a social order based on liberty of conscience and other natural rights.

Very quickly, Williams' house became a transcultural meeting place. He lodged as many as fifty Indians at a time, including travelers, traders, and sachems on their way to or from treaty conferences. If a Puritan needed to contact an Indian, or vice versa, he more than likely did so with Williams' aid. Among Indian nations at odds with each other, Williams became "a quencher of our fires" (Ernst, *Roger Williams: New England Firebrand*, 252). When citizens of Portsmouth needed an Indian agent, they approached Williams. The Dutch did the same thing after 1636. Williams often traveled with Canonicus, Massasoit, and their warriors, lodging with them in the forest. The Narragansetts' council sometimes used Williams' house for its meetings.

Williams seemed happiest when he was making friends of old enemies, and unhappiest when former friends fought. On a cold, rainy Monday, September 16, 1638, he set out on a hundred-mile walk from Narragansett Bay to Hartford with Massasoit to cement an alliance with the Mohegans. A man who often lived on the run, Williams hardly ever detailed the events of his daily life. How fascinating it would have been to read what William[illegible] saw, heard, and said during that hundred-mile walk, camping three nigh[illegible] in woods thick with scrub, burnished by the rich colors of early autum[illegible]

For all the time Williams spent with his Native American friends [illegible] all that he learned from them, he retained his English physical habi[illegible] tastes. Unlike Thomas Morton before him or Sir William Johns[illegible] him, Williams never dressed the part. He adopted Native Ameri[illegible] solely on an intellectual plane. He never donned war paint [illegible] ceremonially. While Williams would lodge with Native Amer[illegible] and eat their food when called upon to do so, he did not [illegible] forsaking his English mattress for a bed of straw and blan[illegible] once called a smoky hole. Williams did not court Indian[illegible] last, Williams, this spreader of so many intellectual infections, was a Puritan Englishman in his manners, even as his mind wove the examples he saw before him with earlier, European experiences.

Even though Williams did not keep a personal journal, he did a great deal of writing: years of letters to Winthrop and others, tracts, and several books ranging in subject matter from descriptions of Indian languages to debates over fine points of theology. Williams only rarely injected himself into the rushing stream of events that propelled him through history. He seemed to have trouble finding time to write all that he felt he ought to commit to paper. Williams' writing often rushes on, full of grammar and spelling errors that stand out even in a time when English was not standardized. Williams' style seems to bespeak a man being carried along by events so quickly that he rarely had time to sit, much less consciously summon the muse.

Although he was never at home in war paint, Williams often was quick to defend the first inhabitants' rights to live and worship as they saw fit. Williams did his best, as well, to act as he thought everyone should and to accord every person equal respect no matter what he or she wore, or what manner of deity (if any) he or she believed in. Williams more than once pointed out that he personally detested professing Quakers, but they still were free to live and work in Providence Plantations at a time when the same people would at least have been locked in Boston's stocks, sent into exile, or hanged. Providence Plantations soon became a haven for dissenters from all of New England.

Puritania's dissidents were escaping from a place where religious orthodoxy was taken deadly seriously. "Blasphemy" (denial or cursing of the "true God") was made punishable by execution according to laws passed by the Puritans in 1646. There was no legal freedom of expression for religious opinion in the Puritan settlements; the laws explicitly stated that Indians also could be put to death for defaming the Puritan deity (Leach, 21).

When word reached Boston that the Pequots were rallying other Indian nations to drive the Massachusetts Bay settlements into the sea, the Massachusetts Council sent urgent pleas to Williams to use his "utmost and speediest Endeavors" to keep the Narragansetts out of it. Within hours after the appeal arrived in the hands of an Indian runner, "scarce acquainting my wife," Williams boarded "a poor Canow & . . . cut through a stormie Wind and with great seas, euery [*sic*] minute in hazard of life to the Sachim's [Canonicus'] howse" (Covey, 162). After traveling thirty miles in the storm, Williams put into port in a Narragansett town larger than most of the English settlements of his day, knowing that the success or failure of the Pequot initiative might rest on whether he could dissuade his friends from joining them in the uprising.

Canonicus listened to Williams with his son Miantinomo at his side. The younger sachem was assuming the duties of leadership piecemeal as Canonicus aged. The three men decided to seal an alliance, and within a few days, officials from Boston were double-timing through the forest to complete the necessary paperwork. Later, Williams also won alliances with the Mohegan and Massachusetts nations, swinging the balance of power against the Pequots and their allies. The Indians welcomed the Puritan deputies with a feast of white chestnuts and cornmeal with blackberries ("hasty pudding," later a New England tradition) as Williams translated for both sides, sealing the alliance.

The Puritan deputies were awed at the size of the Narragansett town, as well as the size of the hall in which they negotiated the alliance. The structure, about fifty feet wide, was likened to a statehouse by the men from Boston. Canonicus, so old that he had to lie on his side during the proceedings, surprised the Puritans with his direct questions and shrewd answers. The treaty was finally sealed, much to the relief of the Puritans, who thought the Narragansetts capable of fielding 30,000 fighting men. Although they had only a sixth of that number, the Narragansetts still were capable of swinging the balance of power for or against the immigrants, who had been in America only sixteen years at the time (Covey, 162).

The outcome of the Pequot War during the summer of 1636 radically altered the demographic balance in New England. Before it, the English colonists were a tiny minority. After it, they were unquestionably dominant. The atrocities of the war stunned Williams' conscience. He had been able to prevent a rout of the English, but at a profound moral cost. He could not prevent the war itself. Nor could he prevent the cruel retribution the Puritans took on the Pequots and their allies. Williams had put himself in the position of aiding those with whom he shared a birthright, although he disagreed with the rationale of their conquest. All during the war, Williams gleaned intelligence from Narragansett runners and traders, who knew far more about Pequot movements than any European. He was doubtless deeply grieved by the Pequots' deaths and the destruction of their culture and land base.

In some of his letters to Winthrop, Williams seems to be trying to answer repeated charges that he was "soft" on Indians. He seems to be a man straddling a knife-edged conscience, an extremely painful act when one has sympathies on both sides in a war. The very talents that made Williams' diplomacy effective produced an especially agonizing hell for him in times of war.

Williams was revolted by the Puritans' slaughter of their Indian enemies, which reached its apex with the burning of the Pequots' major fort at Mystic, Connecticut, on May 25, 1637, which was "a human horror" according to historian Russell Bourne (Bourne, 71). The Puritans set fire to the thatch fort with hundreds of Pequots trapped inside. Pequots who sought to escape the flames met the business end of Puritan muskets at point-blank range, and witnesses left descriptions of Pequot flesh sizzling as the strings on their bows melted in a holocaust of roaring fire.

The Puritan forces trapped as many as 600 Indian men, women, and children in a raging inferno that roared through the thatch fort. The few who managed to crawl out of this roaring furnace jumped back into it when they faced a wall of Puritan swords and muskets. Puritan soldiers and their Indian allies waded through pools of Pequot blood, holding their noses against the stench of burning flesh. The wind-driven fire consumed the entire structure in half an hour. A few Pequot bowmen stood their ground amid the flames until their bows singed and they fell backward into the fire, sizzling to death. The massacre even frightened some Puritans. Bradford recalled, "It was a fearful sight to see them thus frying" (Covey, 200). While a few Puritans remonstrated, many (Bradford included) soon placed the massacre in the category of God's necessary business, along with all sorts of other things, from smallpox epidemics to late frosts and early freezes.

Beginning about 1640 and continuing for most of his remaining years, Williams engaged major Puritan thinkers, especially John Cotton, in a series of published theological and political sparring matches. In these debates, Williams' image of American Indians and their societies, as well as his defense of their land rights, played a provocative intellectual role. To twentieth-century eyes, these arguments may seem unceasingly windy and irrelevant, full of the sort of biblical hairsplitting that today eludes all but religious scholars and a few stump preachers. In the Puritan world of the mid-seventeenth century, however, what might appear as so many angels dancing on so many pins was a vitally important debate that defined issues of secular and religious authority that later would animate the American Revolution.

Williams had collected material for an Indian grammar much of his adult life, but the press of events left him little time to write. It was not until 1643, on a solitary sea voyage to England, that Williams composed his *Key into the Language of America*, the first Indian grammar in English, as well as a small encyclopedia of his observations among Native Americans. In the *Key*, Williams also began to formulate a critique of European religion and politics that would be a subject of intense debate on both sides of the Atlantic for several generations to come.

In the *Key*, Williams indicates that the word "barbarian" had a more positive connotation to him than the same word would evoke three centuries later. Like Benjamin Franklin after him (among many other observers), Williams used the Indian as counterpoint to Europe, in words very similar to those that would be used by Franklin in the eighteenth century. Indians were hospitable to everyone, said Williams; they would offer whatever they had to a guest, even if it was not enough to feed themselves. "It is a strange truth," wrote Williams, "that a man can generally find more free entertainment and refreshing amongst these Barbarians than amongst the thousands that call themselves Christians" (Rider, 22).

Some of Williams' American lessons were offered in verse:

I've known them to leave their house and mat
To lodge a friend or stranger
When Jews and Christians oft have sent
Jesus Christ to the Manger.

Oft have I heard these Indians say
These English will deliver us
Of all that's ours, our lands and lives
In the end, they'll bereave us.
(Rider, 44)

Williams disputed notions that Europeans were intellectually superior to Native Americans, reasoning that God had given all peoples intellectual skills with which to deal with life. He rejected the widespread notion that the God of European Christians had given them more brains than non-Christians: "Nature knows no difference between Europeans and Americans in blood, birth, bodies, &c. God having of one blood made all mankind, Acts 17. . . . The same Sun shines on a Wilderness that doth on a garden" (Rider, 49, 53, 78).

Thus by implication, according to Williams' reasoning, the Puritans had no right to take land and resources from Native Americans by "divine right." Williams' was the first expression in English on American soil of a belief that would power the American Revolution a century and a half later: "All men are created equal, and endowed by their Creator with certain inalienable rights."

In some ways, Williams found what Europeans called "Christian values" better embodied in Native American societies: "There are no beggars amongst them, nor fatherless children unprovided for" (Rider, 29). The *Key* was more than a grammar. It also was a lesson in humility directed at the most pompous and ethnocentric of the English:

When Indians heare the horrid filths,
Of Irish, English men
The horrid Oaths and Murthurs late
Thus say these Indians' then:

We weare no Cloathes, have many Gods,
And yet our sinnes are lesse:
You are Barbarians, Pagans wild,
Your land's the wildernesse.
(Rider, 9)

And:

Boast not, proud English, of thy birth and blood;
Thy brother Indian is by birth as good.
(Brockunier, 141)

The *Key* became a standard text for English-speaking people wishing to learn the languages of New England's Native American peoples. The small book was printed in England and widely distributed there, but not in Puritania. Despite his diplomatic aid, which may have saved the Massachusetts Bay colony, Williams still was regarded as a dangerous radical by orthodox Puritans. Addressing Christian hypocrisy, using his image of the Indian as counterpoint, Williams minced no words:

> How often have I heard both the English and the Dutch[,] not only the civil, but the most debauched and profane say: "These Heathen Doggs, better kill a thousand of them than we Christians should be endangered or troubled with them; they have spilt our Christian blood, the best way to make riddance of them is to cut them all off and make way for Christians. (Ernst, *Roger Williams: New England Firebrand*, 251)

Indians provided Williams perspective in matters of religion, but he often learned from them in political matters as well. Williams called Indian governmental organizations "monarchies" (as did many Europeans in the earliest colonial days), then contradicted himself by catching the scent of popular opinion in them. In his *Key*, Williams described the workings of Indian government in ways similar to the structure he was erecting in the new colony: "The sachims . . . will not conclude of ought that concerns all, either Lawes, or Subsidies, or warres, unto which people are averse, or by gentle perswasion cannot be brought" (Williams, *Complete Writings*, 1: 224). When some Puritans asked whether a society based on individual choice instead of coerced consent would degenerate into anarchy, Williams found the Indians' example instructive: "Although they have not so much to restraine them (both in respect of knowledge of God and lawes of Men) as the English have, yet a man shall never heare of such crimes amongst them [as] robberies, murthurs, adultries &c., as among the English" (Williams, *Complete Writings*, 1:225).

Williams' reports of Indian attitudes toward liberty in New England resembled those of French Jesuits in the Saint Lawrence Valley at about the same time. The Jesuit Bressani refuted arguments that liberty would lead to anarchy by describing the Hurons' governance as "quite as effective as our own, since very few disorders appear in the midst of extreme liberty." He described Wyandot (Huron) leaders as "neither king nor absolute prince . . . certain as if [they] were heads of a republic." Bressani wrote that Wyandot leaders managed villages and tribes as fathers ought to manage their families, by power of persuasion, "obtaining everything . . . with eloquence [and] exhortation" and (would a Jesuit dare forget?) "prayer" (Kennedy, 264).

Among the colonists of Providence Plantations, as among the native peoples he knew, Williams envisioned a society where "all men may walk as their consciences perswade them" (Kennedy, 42–43). Williams' ideal society also shared with the Indian societies he knew a relatively egalitarian distribution of property, with political rights based on natural law: "All civil liberty is founded in the consent of the People"; "Natural and civil Right and Privilege due . . . as a Man, a Subject, a Citizen" (Ernst, *Roger Williams: New England Firebrand*, 276–277).

Establishing such a utopian society was easier said than done. As Williams watched, some of his fellow settlers set up land companies similar to those in other colonies in an attempt to hoard land that had earlier been set aside for future arrivals to prevent the growth of a landless underclass in the colony. In 1654, in a letter to the town of Providence, Williams showed how isolated he sometimes felt in his quest for a new way of life: "I have been charged with folly for that freedom and liberty which I have always stood for—I say, liberty and equality in both land and government" (Miller, 221–222).

Arriving in England during 1643, Williams was doing more than taking his *Key into the Language of America* to be printed. He also was seeking a charter for his colony and meeting with people who shared his opinions. Williams' observations and arguments provided raw observational material for the philosophers of Europe and, through them, to the authors of the Declaration of Independence and France's revolutionary rhetoric. Edwin Poteat commented that the enthusiasm and much of the political idealism of John Milton and Oliver Cromwell was derived from their personal contacts with Williams. Insofar as Thomas Hobbes, John Locke, Sir Henry Vane, and others were inspired by Milton and Cromwell, they too are intellectual heirs of Williams (Poteat, n.p.).

Williams' *Bloudy Tenent of Persecution* (1644), which advocated soul liberty independent of churches, became a virtual textbook among the Secretarians and Levellers during the English revolution of 1648 (Ernst, *Roger Williams and the English Revolution*, 2). Even before its publication, Williams met during his visit in 1643 with Seekers and other radical thinkers who spread his ideas across England and into Wales. On August 9, 1644, the House of Commons ordered the public hangman to execute a public burning of Williams' *Bloudy Tenent*. A few weeks later, another unauthorized edition appeared, along with a host of other tracts by other writers who picked up Williams' refrain of secular government and popular sovereignty.

Williams' ideas did not spread without opposition, of course. In the Massachusetts colony, as in England, tract writers busied presses with arguments against Williams' "contamination." In "The Shield Single against the Sword Doubled" (1654), Henry Niccols of South Wales decried "that seed that sprouts in this wild and bitter fruit, and that in such a season when the spirit of error is let loose to deceive many a thousand souls in the Nation, whose hearts are become tinder or gunpowder ready to catch and kindle at every spark of false light" (Ernst, *Roger Williams and the English Revolution*, 8). Niccols accused Williams and his associates of seeking to "take away all the Gospel . . . all instituted worship of God" (Ernst, *Roger Williams and the English Revolution*, 9). He embraced John Cotton's description of Williams as "the Prodigious Minister of Exorbitant Novelties" (Ernst, *Roger Williams and the English Revolution*, 9).

The debate became an impassioned one on both sides. "Forcing of conscience is soul-rape," Williams wrote, pointing out that even Jesus Christ "commands tolerance of anti-Christians." After citing Christ, Williams added his observations of the Narragansetts, among whom the "civil commonwealth" and the "spiritual commonwealth . . . are independent the one of the other. . . . The very Indians abhor to disturb any conscience at worship" (Straus, 139). Later in his life, Williams expanded on this theme:

> God requireth not an uniformity of religion to be enacted and enforced in any civil state; which enforced uniformity (sooner or later) is the greatest occasion of civil wars. . . . It is the will and command of God that . . . a permission of the most Paganish, Jewish, Turkish, or Anti-Christian consciences and worships be granted to all men in all nations and countries. (Davis, 603)

To Williams, the only way to prevent wars based on religion was to actively sanction tolerance. He argued vehemently against assertions that one had to be Christian to possess a conscience and a soul. If all peoples were religiously equal, religious crusades made little sense. Williams took this to be God's word and, like many preachers, often spoke for himself by invoking a deity. To Williams, religion seemed to be less a professed doctrine than possession of an innate sense of justice and morality. He saw this capacity in all people, Christian or not. From observing the Indians, Williams learned that such morality was endowed in humankind naturally, not by membership in a church or adherence to a doctrine: "It is granted, that nature's light discovers a God, some sins a judgement, as we see in the Indians" (Williams, *Complete Writings*, 4:441). In his extensive travels with the Narragansetts, Williams sensed "the conscience of good and evil which every savage Indian in the world hath" (Williams, *Complete Writings*, 4:443).

Williams became a peacemaker between races as well as religions, and he often expressed amazement at people in authority whose horizons were narrower and whose self-interest was more evident. When Williams returned again to England in the early 1650s, one of the items of his agenda was a petition from Native Americans in New England requesting the aid of the British government to preserve their religions against the Puritans:

> I humbly pray your consideration, whether or not it be only possible, but very easy, to live and die in peace with all the natives of this country. . . . Are not the English of this land, generally, a persecuted people from their native soil? And hath not the God of peace and father of mercies made these natives more friendly in this, than our native countrymen in our own land to us? . . . Are not our families grown up in peace amongst them? Upon which I humbly ask, how can it suit with Christian ingenuity to take hold of some seeming occasions for their destruction? (Williams, *Complete Writings*, 6:269–271)

Where Puritans often saw heathens and devils, Williams saw people, usually friends, with intelligence, moral sense, and a workable political system based on consensus. Such people had the intelligence and the right, Williams reasoned, to judge Christianity for themselves and to decide, without coercion, whether they preferred the Christian doctrine to their own traditions, making the decision "according to their Indian and American consciences, for other consciences it is not supposed they should have" (Williams, *Complete Writings*, 3:250).

Like the American Indians, societies in Arabia, the Far East, and elsewhere had managed to sustain themselves and even flourish without knowledge of or devotion to "a true Church of Jesus Christ," Williams argued (Williams, *Complete Writings*, 3:331). It was this notion of a common moral sense among all peoples that would play a role in arguments by Thomas Jefferson, Thomas Paine, Benjamin Franklin, and others that the state should not sanction religion. Williams' beliefs, based in part on his observations of native societies, came into the U.S. Constitution a century and a half later as separation of church and state.

Perhaps the greatest backhanded tribute of Williams' life was paid him by his master antagonist John Cotton, who wrote that Williams' "dangerous opinions subverted the state and government of this country, and tended to unsettle the kingdoms and commonwealths of Europe" (Ernst, *Roger Williams: New England Firebrand*, 445). While Cotton and other Puritan polemicists could have done without Williams' ideas, they needed his frontier diplomacy. Williams' yeoman efforts did much to maintain a shaky peace along the frontiers of New England for nearly two generations after the Pequot War. In 1645, Williams' efforts barely averted another Native American uprising against encroaching European-Americans. By the 1660s, however, the aging Williams was watching his lifelong pursuit of peace unravel yet again. This time, he felt more impotent than before: his English ancestry seemed to drive him to protect English interests as wave after wave of colonists provided Native American peoples with plentiful grievances by usurping their land without permission or compensation. In this matter, Williams had never changed his mind: neither the Puritans nor any other Europeans had any right, divine or otherwise, to take Indian land, "that we have not our land by Patent of the King, but that the Natives are the true owners of it; and that we ought to repent of such receiving it by Patent" (Williams, *Complete Writings*, 2:4). The final years of Williams' life were profoundly painful for a sensitive man who prized peace and harmony above all.

As Williams entered his sixties, his body grew old quickly. In 1663, he complained often of "old pains, lameness, so th't sometimes I have not been able to rise, nor goe [*sic*], or stand" (Winslow, 267). Williams found himself using his pastoral staff as more than a ministerial ornament.

Roger Williams died on January 27, 1683 in Providence, with the pain of the world bowing his creaking shoulders, likely realizing just how out of step he was with the temper of his time. He was a peacemaker in time of war, a tolerant man in a world full of ideologues; a democrat in a time of ecclesiastical and secular sovereigns, a dissenter wherever self-interest masqueraded as divinity. Williams had planted seeds in American soil that would not fully flower for more than another century. He would have relished the company of Thomas Jefferson, for example, at a time when his ideas were the common currency of revolution.

Williams also would have enjoyed meeting two Creek sachems who visited England in 1791, "where, as usual, they attracted great attention, and many flocked around them, as well to learn their ideas of certain things as to behold 'the savages.' " Asked their opinion of European religion, one said that the Creeks had no priests, or established religion, and that all people were not expected to agree on mere matters of opinion. "It is best that everyone should paddle his own canoe in his own way," the two Creeks told the assembled English—a simple American notion that had engaged England's public hangman a century and a half earlier when he burned Williams' *Bloudy Tenent* (Drake, 37–38).

Metacom (King Philip) (c. 1640–1676)

Mixanno, one of Massasoit's sons, was assassinated in 1643, and his murder never had been avenged. Rumors circulated that the English had plotted the murder and were harboring the assailant. When Alexander, another of Massasoit's sons, visited Boston in 1662, he fell gravely ill and died as a party of Wampanoag warriors rushed him homeward. When Alexander died, the warriors beached their canoes, buried his body in a knoll, and returned home with rumors that he, too, had been a victim of the English.

The mantle of leadership among the Pokanoket band of the Wampanoag confederacy then fell to Metacom, who was called King Philip by the English. John Josselyn, an English traveler, scribbled a word portrait of Metacom in his journal during 1663, when the chief was in his early twenties: "Prince Philip . . . had a coat on and buckskins set thick with these beads [wampum] in pleasant wild works and a broad belt of the same" (Bourne, 1). Wampum was usually convertible into English pounds in New England at the time, and Josselyn calculated in his head that Philip's personal adornments "were valued at twenty pounds [sterling]" (Bourne, 1), a considerable sum of money beyond the reach of most people.

Other than scattered impressions indicating that he was muscular and

---

Metacom, engraved by Paul Revere. It should be noted that Revere had no visual images of Metacom on which to base his portrayal. National Anthropological Archives, Smithsonian Institution

carried an air of authority, we know very little of Metacom's personal appearance. We are left to examine scraps of history that indicate his personal habits. It was said that when Metacom visited Boston, he acted like a prince and ran up substantial hotel bills. History has left us nearly nothing about Metacom's early life, except for his impressive lineage. No authentic portrait of Metacom has come to light, the closest in time being a full-figure engraving of him etched by Paul Revere a century later. Revere probably knew nothing of Metacom's actual physical profile. Historians with little concrete evidence with which to work have fallen back on portrayals of Metacom as an obstinate prince, a bloodthirsty demon, or a Robin Hood–like figure protecting the shrinking estate of his people. The factual context for detailed biography is scanty.

We do know that Metacom distrusted nearly all whites, Roger Williams being one of very few exceptions. He also was known as a man who did not forgive insults easily. It was once said that Metacom chased a white man named John Gibbs from Mount Hope to Nantucket Island after Gibbs had insulted his father. Throughout his childhood, Metacom had watched his people dwindle before the English advance.

By 1670, the native population in what is now eastern Massachusetts, Connecticut, and Rhode Island had fallen to about 20,000, reduced by roughly three-quarters since the landfall of the Pilgrims. The European population had risen to roughly 40,000 by 1670. European farms and pastures were crawling toward Mount Hope, driving away game and creating friction over land that the Indians had used without question for so many generations they had lost count of them. By 1675, the Wampanoags held only a small strip of land at Mount Hope, and settlers wanted it.

Metacom grew more bitter by the day. He could see his nation being destroyed before his eyes. English cattle trampled Indian cornfields; farming forced game animals further into the wilderness. Metacom was summoned to Plymouth to answer questions, and other people in his nation were interrogated by Puritan officials. Traders fleeced Indians, exchanging furs for liquor. The devastation of alcohol and disease and the loss of land destroyed families and tradition. These were Metacom's thoughts as he prepared to go to war against the English.

By 1670, Indian informants were providing the Puritans with unsettling rumors that Metacom was assembling an armed force and an impressive armory of rifles and other weapons. An alliance of Metacom and several native nations with the French was rumored to be in the works. From time to time, Puritans or their native allies glimpsed armed columns of guerrilla fighters in the wilderness, "marching up and down, constantly in arms" (Bourne, 99).

During this buildup, Metacom outlined the land-based nature of his motivations:

> The English who came first to this country were but a handful of people, forlorn, poor, and distressed. My father was then sachem; he relieved their distress in the most kind and hospitable manner. He gave them land to plant and build upon . . . they flourished and increased. By various means they got possession of a great part of his territory. But he still remained their friend till he died. My elder brother became sachem. . . . He was seized and confined and thereby thrown into illness and died. Soon after I became sachem, they disarmed all my people . . . their land was taken. But a small part of the dominion of my ancestors remains. I am determined not to live until I have no country. (Bourne, 107)

The following remark, attributed to Metacom during King Philip's War, was delivered by William Apees, a Pequot, in 1836:

> Brothers, these people from the unknown world will cut down our groves, spoil our hunting and planting grounds, and drive us and our children from the graves of our fathers, and our council fires, and enslave our women and children. (Calloway, 20)

As rumors of war reached Williams, he again tried to keep the Narragansetts out of it. This time, he failed. Nananawtunu, a son of Mixanno, told his close friend Williams that while he opposed going to war, his people could not be restrained. They had decided that the time had come to die fighting rather than to expire slowly. Williams' letters of this time were pervaded with sadness as he watched the two groups he knew so well slide toward war.

Shortly after hostilities began in June 1675, Williams met with Metacom, riding with the sachem and his family in a canoe not far from Providence. Williams warned Metacom that he was leading his people to extermination. He compared the Wampanoags to a canoe on a stormy sea of English fury. "He answered me in a consenting, considering kind of way," Williams wrote, " 'My canoe is already overturned' " (Giddings, 33).

Many Puritans thought of Metacom as an agent of Satan, "a hellhound, fiend, serpent, and dog" (Josephy, 35). To quell this "satanic" rebellion, the English brought a number of native allies into the fray with Philip and his allies. Most were recruited from neighboring Native American peoples who had historical grudges to settle with the Wampanoags, but the Mohawks also joined in the war as allies of the English. At one point, a brutal surprise attack by the Mohawks (the name means "man-eater" in the Algonquian language) killed about 350 of Metacom's warriors.

The Puritans and other European settlers suffered as well. Of ninety white settlements in the area scorched by the war, fifty-two were attacked and a dozen were destroyed completely. An Indian war party invaded the Puritan village of Dartmouth, burning thirty houses to the ground and flaying alive some whites who had been taken prisoner. Others were impaled on sharp stakes or "roasted over slow fires," according to one source (Bourne, 118). In Providence, despite Roger Williams' friendship with Metacom, eighty houses were burned to the ground in an Indian attack. Sixteen were similarly torched in Boston, and forty-two whites were killed in Plymouth (Josephy, 57).

When Indians painted for war appeared on the heights above Providence, Williams picked up his staff, climbed the bluffs, and told the war parties that if they attacked the town, England would send thousands of armed men to crush them. "Well," one of the sachems leading the attack told Williams, "let them come. We are ready for them, but as for you, brother Williams, you are a good man. You have been kind to us for many years. Not a hair on your head shall be touched" (Straus, 220).

Williams was not injured, but his house was torched on March 29, 1676, while he met with the Indians on the bluffs. Williams watched flames spread throughout the town. "This house of mine now burning before mine eyes hath lodged kindly some thousands of you these ten years," Williams told the attacking Indians (Swan, 14).

If the colony was to survive, Williams, for the first time in his life, had to become a military commander. With a grave heart, Williams sent his neighbors out to do battle with the sons and daughters of Native American people who had sheltered him during his winter trek from Massachusetts forty years earlier. As Williams and others watched from inside a hastily erected fort, nearly all of Providence burned. Fields were laid waste and cattle were slaughtered or driven into the woods (Ernst, *Roger Williams: New England Firebrand*, 500).

Colonists, seething with anger, caught an Indian, placing Williams in the agonizing position of ordering him killed rather than watching him tortured. The war was irrefutably brutal on both sides, and the English fought with their backs literally to the sea for a year and a half before going on the offensive. At Northfield, Indians hung two Englishmen on chains, placing hooks under their jaws. At Springfield colonists arrested an Indian woman, then offered her body to dogs that tore her to pieces (Howe, 40).

By August 1676, the war ended as the Mohawks and Mohegans opted out of their alliance with the Wampanoags, leaving after the English had exterminated the Narragansetts. Nearly all of Metacom's warriors, their families, and friends had been killed or driven into hiding. During the waning weeks of the war, and for a month or more afterwards, Boston Common became a killing ground on which as captured Indians accused of staining their hands with English blood were hung or shot to death. The executions continued for several weeks; as many as eight Indians were condemned in a single day.

As his alliance collapsed, Metacom himself fled toward Mount Hope, then hid in a swamp. A Pokanoket whom the English called Alderman, in retribution for Metacom's earlier murder of his brother, told the Puritans where to find him. When English soldiers found Metacom, they dragged him out of the mire, shot him dead, and then had his body drawn and quartered. Each of Metacom's limbs was tied to one of four horses, which were set running at the same time in opposite directions, tearing his body apart. His head was sent to Plymouth on a gibbet, where it was displayed much as criminals' severed heads were shown off on the railings of London Bridge. Historian Frank Waters described the scene:

> The citizens of Plymouth mounted King Philip's head on a pole set on Fort Hill. Reverend [Cotton] Mather later carried away as a trophy the jawbone of "that blasphemous leviathan." Thereafter for twenty years the surviving portion of the head remained on the pole—the bleaching skull of the Wampanoags' greatest war leader, son of the noble Massasoit who had helped the Pilgrim Fathers to establish here their first colony in New England. (Waters, 31–32)

Metacom's hands were sent to Boston, where a local showman charged admission for a glimpse of them. The remainder of Metacom's body was hung from four separate trees (Straus, 222).[1]

In terms of deaths in proportion to total population, King Philip's War was among the deadliest in American history. Of 80,000 European-Americans and Indians who took part in the Pequot War, about 9,000 died, roughly one-third English and two-thirds Native American (Bourne, 36). Thousands more European-Americans became wards of the state after they lost their farms, businesses, and other productive assets. Thousands more Indians were sold into slavery or otherwise exiled from their demolished homes.

Every native nation bordering the Puritan settlements was reduced to ruin—those whose members, in happier days, had offered the earliest colonists their first Thanksgiving dinner. Many of the survivors were sold into slavery in the West Indies, by which the colonists served two purposes: removing them from the area and raising money to help pay their enormous war debts (Labaree, 53). Philip's wife and nine-year-old son were auctioned off with about 500 other slaves following a brief, but intense, biblical debate over whether a family should be forced to atone for the sins of its father (Straus, 222). Canonchet, Metacom's ally, also was drawn and quartered.

By the end of the war, Metacom's people and their land base had been nearly obliterated. The residents of Providence and the Puritan settlements rebuilt their homes, buried their dead, and sent their sons and daughters westward, on occasion, to push westward the European-American settlement frontier, a contest for the land that had begun as soon as the first English immigrants debarked at Plymouth Rock.

NOTE

1. Straus, 222, says that the head of Metacom was sent to Boston and the hands to Plymouth. The version used in the text is adapted from Ernst, *Roger Williams: New England Firebrand*, 501.

REFERENCES

Axtell, James. *The European and the Indian: Essays in the History of Colonial North America*. New York: Oxford University Press, 1981.

Bourne, Russell. *The Red King's Rebellion: Racial Politics in New England, 1675–1678*. New York: Atheneum, 1990.

Brockunier, Samuel H. *The Irrepressible Democrat: Roger Williams*. New York: Ronald Press, 1940.

Calloway, Colin, ed. *The World Turned Upside Down: Indian Voices from Early America*. Boston: Bedford Books/St. Martin's Press, 1994.

Chapin, Howard M. *Sachems of the Narragansetts*. Providence: Rhode Island Historical Society, 1931.

Chupack, Henry. *Roger Williams*. New York: Twayne, 1969.

Covey, Cyclone. *The Gentle Radical: A Biography of Roger Williams*. New York: Macmillan, 1966.

Davis, Jack L. "Roger Williams among the Narragansett Indians." *New England Quarterly* 43:4 (December 1970): 593–604.

Dorr, Henry Crawford. "The Narragansetts." *Rhode Island Historical Society Collections* 7 (1885): 187–188.

Drake, Samuel G. *Biography and History of the Indians of North America*. 11th ed. Boston: Sanborn, Carter & Bazin, 1857.

Ernst, James. *Roger Williams and the English Revolution*. Rhode Island Historical Society Collections 24:1. Providence, 1931.

———. *Roger Williams: New England Firebrand*. New York: Macmillan, 1932.

Giddings, James L. "Roger Williams and the Indians." Typescript, Rhode Island Historical Society, [1957].

Guild, Reuben Aldridge. *Footprints of Roger Williams*. Providence: Tibbitts & Preston, 1886.

Howe, George. *Mount Hope: A New England Chronicle*. New York: Viking Press, 1959.

Josephy, Alvin, Jr. *The Patriot Chiefs: A Chronicle of American Indian Leadership*. New York: Viking, 1961.

Kennedy, J. H. *Jesuit and Savage in New France*. New Haven, CT: Yale University Press, 1950.

Labaree, Benjamin W. *America's Nation-Time, 1607–1789*. Boston: Allyn & Bacon, 1972.

Leach, Douglas E. *Flintlock and Tomahawk: New England in King Philip's War*. 1958. New York: W. W. Norton, 1966.

Miller, Perry. *Roger Williams: His Contribution to the American Tradition*. Indianapolis: Bobbs-Merill Co., 1953.

Parrington, Vernon Louis. *Main Currents in American Thought*. New York: Harcourt, Brace & Co., 1927.

Poteat, Edwin M. "Roger Williams Redivivus." Speech to the Northern Baptist Convention, Atlantic City, NJ, May 1940. Unpaginated typescript in the archives of the Rhode Island Historical Society, Providence.

Rider, Sidney S. *The Lands of Rhode Island As They Were Known to Caunounicus and Miantunnomu When Roger Williams Came in 1636*. Providence: the author, 1904.

Savelle, Max. "Roger Williams: A Minority of One." In *The American Story*, ed. Earl S. Miers. Great Neck, NY: Channel Press, 1956.

Straus, Oscar S. *Roger Williams: The Pioneer of Religious Liberty*. New York: Century Co., 1894.

Swan, Bradford F. "New Light on Roger Williams and the Indians." *Providence Sunday Journal Magazine*, November 23, 1969, 14.

Waters, Frank. *Brave Are My People: Indian Heroes Not Forgotten*. Santa Fe, NM: Clear Light, 1993.

Williams, Roger. *The Complete Writings of Roger Williams*. New York: Russell & Russell, 1963.

———. *A Key into the Language of America*. 1643. Providence: Rhode Island and Providence Plantations Tercentenary Committee, 1936.

Winslow, Ola Elizabeth. *Master Roger Williams*. New York: Macmillan, 1957.

Wood, William. *New England's Prospect*. 1635. Amherst: University of Massachusetts Press, 1977.

2

BALANCE OF POWER AND THE BIRTH OF THE UNITED STATES

Hendrick, Canassatego, Benjamin Franklin, and Red Jacket

By the mid-seventeenth century, the Haudenosaunee (Iroquois) were forced to define their relation to the land within the context of worldwide military power. Throughout the seventeenth and eighteenth centuries, the Haudenosaunee maintained a wide network of Native American alliances situated between French settlements in the Saint Lawrence and Ohio river valleys and English colonies along the Atlantic seaboard. The Iroquois crafted an adroit diplomatic strategy that balanced their own interests against those of their colonizing neighbors.

This chapter examines the consequences of this balance of power through three lives: Canassatego and Hendrick, Iroquois leaders at the confederacy's height, and Benjamin Franklin, arguably the most important single founder of the United States. We will be looking at issues of land tenure and heritage through the eyes of important individuals who shaped the Iroquois response to the colonial powers of Europe: Spain, France, and England.

The eighteenth century was a period of worldwide struggle between the empires of Spain, France, and England; the Iroquois and other native nations played a crucial role in this struggle. During the American Revolutionary War, the British colonists needed Iroquois support against the French.

The struggle for land had many social and political implications that influence our lives today. Ultimately, the Haudenosaunee sided with the English, one major historical reason why most of North America speaks

English today. With the ejection of the French from political power in North America after 1763, the Haudenosaunee lost their diplomatic leverage. In the meantime, colonial diplomacy had introduced some of the founders-to-be of the United States to the Iroquois way of doing political business.

At no time were Native American people more influential in the politics of Europe than during the seventeenth and eighteenth centuries. At that time, no confederacy was more influential than that of the Iroquois. The Iroquois Confederacy controlled the only relatively level land route between the English colonies and French settlements in the Saint Lawrence valley; it also maintained alliances with most of the native nations bordering both clusters of settlements.

In the service of British interests, future American revolutionaries were absorbing the Native American ideas that they would later use as a counterpoint to British tyranny in the colonies. The circumstances of diplomacy in eastern North America arrayed themselves so that opinion leaders of the English colonies and the Iroquois Confederacy were able to meet together to discuss the politics of alliance and confederation.

Beginning in the early 1740s, Iroquois leaders strongly urged the colonists to form a federation similar to their own. The Iroquois leaders' immediate practical objective was unified management of the Indian trade and prevention of fraud in land cessions. The Iroquois also believed that the colonies should unify as a condition of an alliance with them in the continuing "cold war" with France.

During the mid-eighteenth century, diplomatic and political roads crossed in Albany as Franklin prepared the first serious attempt at colonial union, the Albany Plan of Union. After the American Revolution, however, the Iroquois were largely written out of European politics despite their contributions to the democratic ideology that had helped forge a new nation on the anvil of America. The experiences of Red Jacket, the Seneca leader, are offered at the end of this chapter as an illustration of the increasingly desperate situation of the Iroquois after the Revolution.

This set of circumstances brought Franklin into the diplomatic equation. As a printer of Indian treaties, Franklin very likely read Canassatego's remarks at Lancaster during 1744 (to be discussed later) in galley proof. By the early 1750s, Franklin was more directly involved in diplomacy itself at the same time that he became an early, forceful advocate of colonial union. All of these circumstantial strings were tied together in the summer of 1754 when colonial representatives, Franklin among them, met with Iroquois sachems at Albany to address issues of mutual concern and to develop the Albany Plan of Union, a design that echoes both English and Iroquois precedents and would become a rough draft for the Articles of Confederation a generation later.

Hendrick (Tiyanoga, c. 1680–1755)

The Iroquois leader Hendrick (Tiyanoga) had become acquainted with England early in his life. He was probably about thirty years old when he became one of four Mohawks given a grand tour of Queen Anne's realm in 1710. He had caught the eye of British officials in Albany as a bright young man who had the wisdom (as they saw it) to study the Bible. He also was a leader among the Mohawks whose dramatic flair would enliven the colonial records of New York State for the next half-century.

Imagine standing on a street corner in London, near Buckingham Palace, on a spring day in 1710. Like most Britons of the time, you have only rarely traveled outside your home town or village. A trip even to London is an exotic experience. You marvel at the surge of humanity streaming after an elegantly painted and plated pair of carriages crawling through the excited mob. Elbowing your way through the crowd, you catch a fleeting glimpse of the passengers in the carriages: American kings! Tall, well muscled, black of hair and bronze of skin, they are clothed in a riot of color, a combination of their native dress and royal gifts that make them look even more exotic than you might have imagined.

The carriages carrying the "American kings" disappear into the palace, bound for the Court of Saint James, four Mohawk Indians on their way

---

Hendrick, depicted on a visit to England as a young man. National Anthropological Archives, Smithsonian Institution

to an audience with Queen Anne and her ministers, all taking part in an ongoing contest for North America and the rest of the world as Europe's mapmakers know it. English royalty has cast the four visiting Mohawks in its own image, believing that these four Mohawks can issue edicts to their nation and the other four Iroquois nations. It imagines in error, of course, since, in reality, only one of the four has any real influence at home, and he leads his fellow Mohawks not by edict, but by persuasion. This one "king" is a young man whom his people call Tiyanoga. The English called him Hendrick even in 1710, almost half a century before English colonists invited him to the Albany Congress of 1754 to describe for them how the Iroquois Confederacy operated.

Queen Anne had not invited Hendrick and his three companions to London for a lesson in democracy, however. She had invited them to see the grandeur and power of England, which was bidding for an alliance with the Iroquois in the contest with the French for North America. In Iroquois country—so the story went—Jesuit missionaries had been telling the Indians that Christ, the savior, was born in France and crucified in Protestant England. Not that the story mattered much to the Indians. It mattered a great deal to the English.

American Indians had visited England, France, Portugal, and Spain for at least a century before that spring day in 1710, but they had never before come as the guests of royalty. One of the most memorable visitors, Squanto, had visited England by the time the Pilgrims got to America, and he met them on the beach, speaking English. During these decades, European fishermen had taken a few American natives back to England—some willingly, some not. Traders had enslaved small groups in hopes of selling them as carnival attractions. Never before, however, had London risen to quite this degree of excitement over American visitors. Thus the carriages, the pomp, the mobs of gawkers and hawkers, and the columns of newsprint mixing reporting with imagination. With as much speed as the communication and transportation technologies of the early eighteenth century could muster, the four Mohawk "kings" became instant celebrities.

No Mohawk or Iroquois council had appointed the four "American kings" as ambassadors to Queen Anne's court. They had been chosen more or less at the convenience of Peter Schuyler, British Indian agent, from the Iroquois he knew. The fact that all four were Mohawks was not coincidental, for the Mohawks were the best-known of the five Iroquois nations to the English, the keepers of the eastern door of the league's symbolic longhouse, which opened at the British trading post of Albany. If Schuyler had known more about the Haudenosaunee political structure, he might have requested four ambassadors from the Grand Council at Onondaga.

The three Mohawks who accompanied Hendrick had very short historical careers. Oh Nee Yeath Ton No Prow's Christian name was John; during the royal visit, he was often called "King of Ganajahhore," which suggests that many English in 1710 were still struggling with Columbus' geographical error. He signed with the wolf, his clan. History has left us nothing more about him.

Sa Ga Yean Qua Prah Ton's Christian name was Brant, and he would later become known as the grandfather of Joseph Brant, a famous figure in Iroquois history late in the century. The elder Brant, who also signed with the wolf, died shortly after returning to America from London. During the visit, the English called him "King of the Maquas" (Bond, 40).

Elow Oh Kaom was Christianized Nicholas and called "King of the River Nation" during the visit. He may have been born a Schacook or Mohican, whom the English sometimes called "River Indians," and adopted as a Mohawk. He signed with the tortoise (Bond, 40).

Hendrick was the youngest of the four. His native name was Tee Yee Neen Ho Ga Prow, often shortened to Tiyanoga. Hendrick would become a key figure in the English alliance with the Iroquois and would die in 1755 at the Battle of Lake George, leading a force of Mohawks allied with the British against the French.

Hendrick became important not only as a historical figure, but also as an object of European and American literary imagination. A lifelong friend of Sir William Johnson,[1] Hendrick appeared often at Johnson Hall, near Albany, and had copious opportunities to rub elbows with visiting English nobles, sometimes arriving in war paint, fresh from battle. Well known as a man of distinction in his manners and dress, Hendrick visited England again in 1740. At that time, King George II presented him with an ornate green coat of satin fringed in gold, which Hendrick was fond of wearing in combination with his traditional Mohawk ceremonial clothing. By 1754, Hendrick was well enough known among the colonial English to earn a special invitation to the Albany Congress, a year before he was killed in battle. At the congress, he consulted with Franklin and other colonial delegates on a plan for intercolonial union that in some ways resembled the Iroquois system of government. Like two of the other three visitors to Queen Anne's court, Hendrick was a member of the Wolf Clan.

Riding around London in their carriages, the four "kings" doubtless looked at the flood of English people around them with as much awe as the English looked at the Native Americans. They, too, were drinking in the novelty of a "new world." The Mohawks first visited Buckingham Palace on April 19, 1710. In the Court of Saint James, the duke of Shrewsbury introduced the four "American kings" to Queen Anne. Abraham Schuyler, Peter's cousin, interpreted.

"GREAT QUEEN," Hendrick opened, with a sense of pomp enhanced by the creative capitalization of English printers, "we have undertaken a long and tedious Voyage, which none of our Predecessors could ever be prevailed upon to undertake." Hendrick reminded Queen Anne that the Mohawks had been "a strong wall [of] Security" for the English against the

French in North America, "even to the loss of our best men." Hendrick then told the queen that the Mohawks were tired of getting ready to do battle against the French with the English, only to have the engagements postponed, giving a sense that they were eager to reclaim for the Mohawks "Free hunting and a great Trade with our Great Queen's children" (Boyer, *History of the Reign of Queen Anne*, 189–191). The four Mohawks then punctuated the importance of their statements by presenting the queen with several large wampum belts.

The speech then became very nearly a warning: "We need not urge our Great Queen . . . that in Case our Great Queen should not be mindful of us, we must, with our families, forsake our Country and seek other Habitations, or stand Neuter, either of which would be very much against our inclinations." After Hendrick was finished speaking, the four Mohawks requested the queen's "most Gracious Consideration" and then left her with their words and wampum belts to begin a hectic, two-week tour of London and other nearby points in southern England (Boyer, *History of the Reign of Queen Anne*, 189–191).

Day by day, the four "American kings" were spirited from their lodgings at London's Two Crowns and Cushions to see the sights of southern England—to dinner with the duke of Ormonde near Richmond; by the queen's barge to visit Dr. Flamsteed, the astronomer royale, at Greenwich; to the Greenwich hospital and the dockyards of Woolwich; and to Whitehall. At every stop, their celebrity seemed to grow; crowds often followed their carriages.

By April 24, five days after the Mohawks' audience with Queen Anne, at least one theatre manager was using them as an advertising gimmick to upstage Shakespeare. In the *Daily Courant*, the Queen's Theatre in the Haymarket advertised a performance of *Macbeth* "For the Entertainment of the Four INDIAN KINGS lately arriv'd." On the 24th, as advertised, the four Mohawks appeared at the theatre wearing black waistcoats, stockings, and breeches. The curtain rose, and the performance began as scheduled until the audience stopped it, shouting for an eyeful of the Mohawks.

The same writer felt obliged to reconcile the celebrity status of the four Americans with what he assumed was their more humble life at home: "According to the custom of their Country, these princes do not know what it is to cocker and make much of themselves." The frenzied round of wining and dining in London was said to stand in stark contrast with the Indians' more wholesome fare at home, free of "those indispositions our Luxury brings upon us." Such abstinence earned the "kings" lifelong freedom from "Gout, Dropsy, or Gravel," as well as various fevers, the writer rhapsodized, as one of them, probably the elder Brant, laid on his bed at the Two Crowns and Cushions, groaning with illness from English overindulgence. Despite that fact, the anonymous writer could not help but use the Mohawks as a counterpoint to the rich, fat, stale life of English nobility. He said that they had offered to entertain the Queen by running down "a Buck or Stag . . . when she pleases to see them, in any of her Parks or Chaces. They are to tire down the Deer, and catch him without Gun, Speare, Launce, or any other weapon" (Bond, 7–8).

Meanwhile, the Mohawks remained on the stage of the Queen's Theatre until the audience had its fill of them, and then *Macbeth* continued. No trace remains of what the four Native American "kings" thought of the stage play, but, as Richmond P. Bond pointed out in *Queen Anne's American Kings* (1952), the reaction of the English to the Mohawks was obvious: "The kings proved to be a hit, and for the remainder of the week, the Haymarket tagged all its performances 'For the Entertainment of the Four INDIAN KINGS,' including *Hamlet, Otway*, two operas, and a one-act farce" (Bond, 5).

The use of the Mohawks as crowd bait was catching. They could not possibly have attended every event that was advertised in their honor. Drury Lane's Theatre Royal announced two plays in their name, and the Cockpit Royal on Cartwright Street offered a cockfight for their entertainment. The *Tatler* of April 27–29 advertised a concert of "Vocal and Instrumental Musick" sponsored by "Several Ladies of Quality" for them on May 1. On the same day, Powell the Puppeteer offered a show at Punch's Theatre in honor of the "kings," whose visages he sketched on a handbill advertising the event (Ashton, 1:294).

The *Daily Courant* of May 2 advertised a "Tryal of Skill to be fought in the Bear Garden in Hockley in the Hole." In this contest, John Parkes of Coventry and Thomas Hesgate, "a Berkshire Man," were to go at each other with "these following weapons, *viz.*: Backsword, Sword and Dagger, Sword and Buckler, Single Falchon, . . . and Quarter Staff" (Grinde and Johansen, 46). If the Mohawks had been in the audience, one can only wonder what might have crossed their minds had they watched these two warriors of the urban wilderness trying to slice each other up in front of a crowd of frenzied Londoners who were attempting, perhaps, to forget a new tax on bread that had been announced in the *Daily Courant* on May 3, when the promoter of the "Tryal of Skill" again advertised the event in honor of the four "kings," several hours after they had departed London for the last time.

Between attending royal audiences and public spectacles, the four Mohawks also asked English missionaries to counter the influence of French Jesuits among their people. The Society for Propagation of the Gospel was happy to oblige. Its members sent the four Mohawks home with copies of the Bible "bound handsomely in red Turkey leather" (Bond, 8). The Mohawks also got from the missionary society a pledge that it would help combat the sale of intoxicating liquor to Indians in America. In the meantime, speculation in the newspapers centered on the Mohawks' own drinking habits. The general consensus, quite without factual foundation, was that they much preferred English "pale ales" to French wines.

The Mohawks heard a sermon preached by the Lord Bishop of London at Saint James' Chapel and (according to *The Royal Strangers' Ramble*, a poem composed shortly after their visit) also visited Leadenhall Market to witness the bounty of English agriculture and industry. They also were shown the London Tower, as well as some of the military might the English were prepared to use against the French. They stared up at the dome of Saint Paul's Cathedral and attended innumerable receptions hosted by "persons of quality."

Following a short audience of leave-taking with Queen Anne, the Mohawks departed London by carriage early on May 3, arriving at Portsmouth the next day via the main road through Southampton. The dock beside their ship groaned under crates of gifts: clothing of linen, cotton, and wool (including forty-three linen shirts), razors, hair combs, jews' harps, two dozen large pairs of scissors, an equal number of magnifying glasses, hats, pistols, 400 pounds of gunpowder, lead bars, brass kettles, and portraits of the Queen. This, more of England's carefully strutted industrial produce, all was presented to convince the Mohawks that they would do better siding with the English than with the French.

On May 6, the Royal Navy had its turn to show off English power to the Mohawks. They were received on board the *Royal Sovereign*, the flagship of Admiral Matthew Aylmer, commander of the fleet, where they "tarry'd on board till the evening, and at their departure received the usual honours of the ship" (Grinde and Johansen, 48). Delayed by incessant socializing and contrary winds, the Mohawks did not set sail for the open ocean until May 19 on board the *Dragon*, a man-of-war accompanying a merchant fleet for Boston.

Hendrick knew both Iroquois and English cultures well. He converted to Christianity and became a Mohawk preacher shortly after 1700. In England, he was painted by John Verelst and called the "Emperor of the Five Nations." As he gained prominence around Albany, New York, Hendrick became increasingly interested in English life and manners. Hendrick was perhaps the most important individual link in a chain of alliance that prevented French invasion of the New York frontier during the initial stages of the Seven Years' War, which was called the French and Indian War (1754–1763) in North America.

Thomas Pownall, a shrewd observer of colonial Indian affairs, described Hendrick as "a bold artful, intriguing Fellow and has learnt no smell share of European Politics, [who] obstructs and opposes all [business] where he has not been talked to first" (Jacobs, 77). Another contemporary described Hendrick as a "man of spirit and striking force" (Bond, 118).

J. Hector St. John Crèvecoeur, himself an adopted Iroquois who had participated in sessions of the Grand Council at Onondaga, described Hendrick in late middle age, preparing for dinner at the Johnson estate, within a few years of the Albany Congress:

> [He] wished to appear at his very best. . . . His head was shaved, with the exception of a little tuft of hair in the back, to which he attached a piece of silver. To the cartilage of his ears . . . he attached a little brass wire twisted into very tight spirals. . . . A girondole was hung from his nose. Wearing a wide silver neckpiece, a crimson vest and a blue cloak adorned with sparkling gold, Hendrick, as was his custom, shunned European breeches for a loincloth fringed with glass beads. On his feet, Hendrick wore moccasins of tanned elk, embroidered with porcupine quills, fringed with tiny silver bells. (Crèvecoeur, 170)

Crèvecoeur indicates that Hendrick was seated at dinner next to a European duchess, who swooned over him. She asked Hendrick to escort her to the Mohawk country, which he did. She so impressed Hendrick and other Iroquois that they set aside 5,000 acres of choice land for her so, as Crèvecoeur put it, "she would have a place of her own where she could raise her wigwam, light her fire, and hang her kettle every time she came to see them" (Crèvecoeur, 170).

Hendrick often utilized his frequent meetings at Johnson Hall, William Johnson's mansion near present-day Albany, New York, to detail Mohawk complaints about illegal land seizures by immigrant Europeans and European-Americans. At times, these complaints also were raised during the proceedings of the Iroquois Grand Council. On September 10, 1753, Johnson was present at a council meeting when Hendrick spoke for the council. The wording indicates that while the immigrants' sources assert that Hendrick had been a practicing Christian most of his life, in 1753, two years before his death, he characterized Christians as invaders of Haudenosaunee land:

> We don't know what you Christians, English and French, intend. We are so hemmed in by you both that we have hardly a hunting place left. In a little while, if we find a bear in a tree, there will immediately appear an owner of the land to claim the property and hinder us from killing it, by which we live. We are so perplexed between you that we hardly know what to say or think. (Rosenstiel, 84)

Hendrick attended the Albany Congress during the last year of his life. He was drawn to Albany to instruct the colonists on the politics of union because the Iroquois desired unified management of trade with the English. He also wished to see his friend William Johnson reinstated as the English superintendent of affairs with the Six Nations.[2] Without him, Hendrick maintained that the covenant chain would rust.

The Albany Congress convened on June 19, 1754, five days after its scheduled opening, because most of the Iroquois and some of the colonial commissioners arrived late. Most of the sessions of the congress took place at the Albany Courthouse; many of the speeches to the Indians and their replies occurred in front of the governor's residence. Albany at the time straddled the border between colonial settlement and Iroquois country at the eastern door of the Six Nations' symbolic longhouse. The town was still dominated by the architecture of the Dutch, who had started Albany before the English replaced them.

On June 28, 1754, the day after Hendrick arrived with the Mohawks, Governor James DeLancey met with him. The 200 Indians in attendance sat on ten rows of benches in front of the governor's residence, with colonial delegates facing them in a row of chairs, their backs to the building. According to Theodore Atkinson's account of the conference, the gathering was held on a warm day, after morning rain. Governor DeLancey read a speech that had been approved by the delegates paragraph by paragraph, and New York's interpreter relayed his words to the Indians. The speechmaking also stopped briefly for the presentation of belts to the Indians, following Iroquois diplomatic protocol.

DeLancey's speech began with a condolence that also used the language of Iroquois protocol: "I wipe away your tears, and take sorrow from your hearts, that you may open your minds and speak freely" (O'Callaghan, *Documentary History*, 6:567). Then Governor DeLancey gave the Iroquois a string of wampum. This greeting ritual was very similar to what Franklin had witnessed a year earlier when he had attended a treaty conference at Carlisle, Pennsylvania. As DeLancey proceeded, the assembled Indians "Signifyed [*sic*] their understanding of each paragraph by a kind of Universal Huzzah," and "When the great Chain belt was Dil[i]vered on this occassion, they Signifyed their understanding or Consent by Such a Huzzah repeated Seven Times over for every Tribe" (McAnear, 736).

Holding the wampum belt given him by the colonial delegates, Hendrick made it a metaphor of political union when he advised DeLancey, "In the mean time we desire, that you will strengthen yourselves, and bring as many into this Covenant Chain as you possibly can" (O'Callaghan, *Documentary History*, 6:869). It is likely that Hendrick remarked on this subject several days later when the Indians and delegates assembled again in front of the governor's residence (McAnear, 736–737). In effect, Hendrick was repeating the advice to unite on an Iroquois model that Canassatego had given colonial delegates at Lancaster a decade earlier, this time at a conference devoted not only to diplomacy, but also to drawing up a plan for the type of colonial union the Iroquois had been requesting. The same day, at the courthouse, the colonial delegates were in the early stages of debate over the plan of union.

Hendrick was openly critical of the British at the Albany Congress and hinted that the Iroquois would not ally with the English colonies unless a suitable form of unity was established among them. In talking of the proposed union of the colonies and the Six Nations on July 9, 1754, Hendrick stated, "We wish this Tree of Friendship may grow up to a great height and then we shall be a powerful people" (Grinde and Johansen, 107). Hendrick followed that admonition with an analysis of Iroquois and colonial unity in which he said, "We the United Nations shall rejoice of our strength . . . and . . . we have now made so strong a Confederacy." In reply to Hendrick's speech, DeLancey said, "I hope that by this present Union, we shall grow up to a great height and be as powerful and famous as you were of old" (Grinde and Johansen, 105, 107). Franklin was commissioned to draw up the final draft of the Albany Plan of Union the same day. Franklin wrote that the debates on the Albany Plan "went on daily, hand in hand with the Indian business" (Bigelow, 236).

On September 8, 1755, Hendrick was killed at the Battle of Lake George as Sir William Johnson defeated the French Baron Dieskau. The elderly Mohawk was shot from his horse and bayoneted to death while on a scouting party.

NOTES

1. Sir William Johnson was Great Britain's principal Indian agent to the Iroquois during the 1750s, 1760s, and early 1770s.

2. The Five Nations became six early in the eighteenth century with the adoption of the Tuscaroras.

Canassatego (c. 1690–1750)

The Onondaga Canassatego, a contemporary of Hendrick, was Tadadaho (speaker) of the Iroquois Confederacy, as well as a major figure in diplomacy with the French and English colonists. His advice that the colonies should form a union on a Haudenosaunee model was published by Benjamin Franklin and later figured into Franklin's conceptions of colonial union. Later in the century, a fictional Canassatego became a figure in English social satire and other literature as a fictional critic of English class structure, religion, and other aspects of society.

In 1742, Pennsylvania officials met with Iroquois sachems in council at Philadelphia to secure an Iroquois alliance against the threat of French encroachment. Canassatego spoke to the officials on behalf of the Six Nations. He confirmed the "League of Friendship" that existed between the two parties and stated that "we are bound by the strictest leagues to watch for each other's preservation" (Colden, 2:18–24). During the same speech, Canassatego complained that the Iroquois were not being paid enough for their release of lands on the west bank of the Susquehanna River:

> We know our lands are now become more valuable; the white people think we do not know their Value; but we are sensible that the land is everlasting, and the few

---

Canassatego, from Donald A. Grinde, Jr., and Bruce E. Johansen, *Exemplars of Liberty* (Los Angeles: UCLA American Indian Studies Center, 1991). Courtesy of the artist, John Kahionhes Fadden

goods we receive for it are soon worn out and gone. In the future, we will sell no lands except when Brother Onas [William Penn] is in the country, and we will know beforehand the quantity of goods we are to receive. Besides, we are not well used with respect to the Lands still unsold by us. Your people daily settle on these Lands, and spoil our Hunting. We must insist on your removing them. (Armstrong, 14)

Richard Peters, a delegate from Pennsylvania, described Canassatego as "a tall, well-made man" with "a very full chest and brawny limbs, a manly countenance, with a good-natired [*sic*] smile. He was about 60 years of age, very active, strong, and had a surprising liveliness in his speech" (Boyd, "Dr. Franklin," 244–245). Dressed in a scarlet camblet coat and a fine, gold-laced hat, Canassatego was described by historical observers such as Peters as possessing an awesome presence that turned heads whenever he walked into a room. Given his personal magnetism and his position as speaker of the Iroquois Grand Council, Canassatego was one of the most influential leaders of the Iroquois and an important figure in the eighteenth-century struggle for control of eastern North America.

One of the more important treaty councils between the Iroquois, their Native American allies, and delegates of the Middle Atlantic colonies, including Pennsylvania and Virginia, took place at Lancaster, Pennsylvania, during the summer of 1744. Lancaster was a frontier settlement at the time. This meeting was one of a number of significant diplomatic parleys between British colonists, the Iroquois, and their allies that helped shape the outcome of the French and Indian War. At the meeting, Canassatego and other Iroquois complained that the colonies, with no central authority, had been unable to restrain invasion of Indian lands by English settlers. (The French government, which had been all but begging its subjects to move to America, did not have this problem.) In that context, Canassatego advised the colonists to form a union emulating that of the Iroquois:

Our wise forefathers established Union and Amity between the Five Nations. This has made us formidable; this has given us great Weight and Authority with our neighboring Nations. We are a powerful Confederacy; *and by your observing the same methods, our wise forefathers have taken*, you will acquire such Strength and power. Therefore whatever befalls you, never fall out with one another. (Boyd, 75; emphasis added)

Canassatego's admonition of colonial union echoed throughout the colonies for over a generation, and it would be used later not only as a rallying point against French colonial designs but also, by the middle 1770s, when colonists along the eastern seaboard began to develop their own political identity, as propaganda to ally Iroquois and patriots against the British. In 1747, George Clinton, the royal governor of New York, observed that most American democratic leaders "were ignorant, illiterate people of republican principles who have no knowledge of the English Constitution or love for their country" (O'Callaghan, *Documents*, 6:670–671). Clearly, these unread Americans were gaining a new identity and a sense of freedom from the American environment and its native peoples long before the outbreak of the American Revolution.

Virginia delegates got Canassatego's consent for their own version of empire building. Canassatego signed a deed of cession that obtained for Virginia, at least on paper, rights to the present-day United States north of Virginia's southern boundary, except the lands explicitly claimed by the Haudenosaunee. Canassatego clearly did not understand the scope of the agreement he was signing.

In addition to advising the colonial representatives on political union at the Lancaster Treaty Council, Canassatego declined a colonial offer to educate Haudenosaunee young people. "We are convinced therefore that you mean to do us good by your Proposal, and we thank you heartily," he said, as recorded by Franklin. However, continued Canassatego,

> Several of our Young People were formerly brought up at the Colleges of the Northern Provinces; they were instructed in all your sciences, but when they came back to us, they were bad Runners, ignorant of every means of living in the Woods, unable to bear either Cold or Hunger, knew neither how to build a Cabin, take a Deer, or kill an Enemy, spoke our Language imperfectly, therefore were neither fit for Hunters, Warriors, or Counsellors; they were totally good for nothing. (Franklin, 969–970)

Canassatego concluded his thought: "To show our grateful sense of it [the offer], if the Gentlemen of Virginia will send us a dozen of their Sons, we will take Great Care of their Education, instruct them in all we know, and make Men of them" (Franklin, 970).

Speaking at the Lancaster Treaty Council on June 26, Canassatego defended Iroquois rights to the land vis-à-vis more recent claims by the French and English:

> When you mentioned the affair of the Land Yesterday, you went back to old Times, and told us, you had been in Possession of the Province of *Maryland* above One Hundred Years, but what is One Hundred Years in Comparison with the Length of Time since our Claim began? Since we came out of this Ground? For we must tell you, that long before One Hundred Years our Ancestors came out of this very Ground, and their children have remained here ever since. (Venables, x)

> You came out of the ground in a country that lies beyond the Seas, there you may have a just Claim, but here you must allow us to be your elder Brethren, and the lands to belong to us long before you knew any thing of them. (Calloway, 101)

Canassatego died in 1750; a contemporary source says that he was poisoned by the French (Jennings, 363). After his death, Canassatego became a British literary figure, the hero of John Shebbeare's *Lydia, or Filial Piety*, published in 1755. With the flowery eloquence prized by romantic novelists of his time, Shebbeare portrayed Canassatego as something more than human—something more, even, than the Noble Savage that was so popular in Enlightenment Europe. Having saved the life of a helpless English maiden from the designs of a predatory English ship captain en route, Shebbeare's fictional Canassatego, once in England, became judge and jury for all that was contradictory and corrupt in mid-eighteenth-century England.

The images of Canassatego and other Native Americans were a godsend to British novelists and satirists who were prohibited by punitive libel laws from denigrating members of the royal government. Charges of criminal libel (defamation of the state) could be utilized against authors who criticized people in power. Presses could be shut down and authors locked up in the Tower of London.

Canassatego, as a fictional figure, was used to describe the property relations of the various social classes in Britain. Disembarking, Shebbeare's Canassatego meets with a rude sight: a ragged collection of dwellings "little better than the Huts of Indians" (Shebbeare, 2:7) and men rising from the bowels of the earth, dirty, broken, and degraded. Asking his hosts for an explanation, Canassatego is told that the men have been digging coal. The Iroquois sachem inquires whether everyone in England digs coal for a living, and reflects that he is beginning to understand why so many English have fled to America.

By Shebbeare's fictional account, Canassatego arrived in England not merely as a tourist, but also to present a petition of grievances on behalf of his people. Continually frustrated in his efforts to do so, he finds England's leaders to be persons of small measure. The prime minister, in particular, strikes Canassatego as "ungrateful, whiffling, inconsistent, [a man] whose words included nothing to be understood . . . the farce and mockery of national prudence." Exasperated, Canassatego asks, "Can it be . . . that this man can direct the business of a people?" (Shebbeare, 3:264).

By and by, Canassatego meets Lady Susan Overstay, a woman of rank and breeding who is overly conscious of her lofty station in society. Faced with a windy exposition by Lady Overstay on the quality of her breeding, Canassatego replies that in his country no one is born any better than anyone else, and that wisdom, courage, and love of family and nation, as well as other virtues of the mind and body, are the only qualities that give authority and esteem among the Indians.

The character of Canassatego that Shebbeare created says much about what addled Europe late in the age of monarchy. It says as much about what people yearned for: freedom from oppressive taxation and the falseness of social convention, from a caste system that enriched a few and impoverished many. It would be less than a century from the needling of a fictional Canassatego during the 1750s to the first publication of *The Communist Manifesto* in 1848.

Benjamin Franklin (1706–1790)

A reader of Benjamin Franklin's papers cannot help but be awed by the ravenous curiosity of his intellect. Whether he was exploring the fundamental principles of electricity, designing a wood stove, composing pithy aphorisms about the nature of life, or designing a federal political union, Franklin's appetites for knowledge and experience propelled him to make his own life a feast of creative thinking and invention.

From his earliest days as a printer's devil (apprentice or assistant) in Boston to his later years as the United States' best-known diplomat, Franklin's mind struck sparks. From his first career move (escaping from Boston to Philadelphia as a young man), Franklin was a person who combined practical genius with hard work, whether as a scientist, a founder of fire companies and hospitals, or a designer of wood stoves. Like few other individuals, the animus of Benjamin Franklin defined America's character in his day. Today, bits of his character have become part of our everyday lives: a penny saved is a penny earned; no pain, no gain.

Franklin at first was a printer. His press issued printed proceedings of Indian treaties (including Lancaster's 1744 council) in small booklets that enjoyed a lively sale throughout the colonies. Beginning in 1736, Franklin published Indian treaty accounts on a regular basis until the early 1760s,

---

Benjamin Franklin held a copy of Pennsylvania's Constitution as he sat for this portrait in 1778. '46-51-243, Nee, Francois, Denis, *Benjamin Franklin*, Philadelphia Museum of Art: Given by Mrs. John D. Rockefeller

when his defense of Indians under assault by frontier settlers cost him his seat in the Pennsylvania Assembly. Franklin subsequently served the colonial government in England.

Franklin became an advocate of colonial union by the early 1750s, when he began his diplomatic career as a Pennsylvania delegate to the Iroquois and their allies. As mentioned earlier, Franklin had very likely read Canassatego's remarks at Lancaster, including his advice on colonial union, in galley proof. Franklin urged the British colonies to unite in emulation of the Iroquois Confederacy when he drew up his Albany Plan of Union in 1754. Using Iroquois examples of unity, Franklin had sought to shame the reluctant colonists into some form of union in a 1751 letter to his printing partner James Parker in New York City. In this letter, Franklin engaged in a hyperbolic racial slur (actually, subsequent evidence will show that Franklin had a healthy respect for the Iroquois):

> It would be a strange thing . . . if Six Nations of Ignorant savages should be capable of forming such an union and be able to execute it in such a manner that it has subsisted for ages and appears indissoluble, and yet that a like union should be impractical for ten or a dozen English colonies, to whom it is more necessary and must be more advantageous, and who cannot be supposed to want an equal understanding of their interest. (Smyth, 3:42)

On May 9, 1753, Franklin wrote a long letter to his friend Peter Collinson detailing the manners and customs of American Indians and how they appealed to colonial Americans. Franklin wrote that Indian children brought up in colonial society readily returned to their people after making only "one Indian ramble with them." However, Franklin observed that "when white persons of either sex have been taken prisoners young by Indians, and lived a while among them, tho' ransomed by their friends . . . [they] take the first good opportunity of escaping again into the woods, from whence there is no reclaiming them" (Labaree, *Papers*, 4:481).

During October 1753, Franklin began his distinguished career as a diplomat by attending a treaty council at Carlisle, Pennsylvania. At this treaty council with the Iroquois and Ohio Indians (Twightees, Delawares, Shawnees, and Wyandots), Franklin absorbed the rich imagery and ideas of the Six Nations at close range. On October 1, 1753, he watched an Oneida leader, Scarrooyady, and a Mohawk, Cayanguileguos, condole the Ohio Indians for their losses against the French. Franklin listened while Scarrooyady recounted the origins of the Great Law to the Ohio Indians:

> We must let you know, that there was a friendship established by our and your Grandfathers, and a mutual Council fire was kindled. In this friendship all those then under the ground, who had not yet obtained eyes or faces (that is, those

unborn) were included; and it was then mutually promised to tell the same to their children and children's children. (Labaree, *Autobiography*, 197–199)

Having condoled the Ohio Indians, Scarrooyady exhorted the assembled Indians to "preserve this Union and Friendship, which has so long and happy continued among us. Let us keep the chain from rusting" (Boyd, 1938, 128).

The next day, the Pennsylvania commissioners, including Franklin, presented a wampum belt that portrayed the union between the Iroquois and Pennsylvania. The speech echoed the words of Canassatego spoken a decade earlier at Lancaster. The speech to the assembled Indians recalled the need for unity and a strong defense:

Cast your eyes towards this belt, whereon six figures are . . . holding one another by the hands. This is a just resemblance of our present union. The first five figures representing the Five Nations . . . [and] the sixth . . . the government of Pennsylvania; with whom you are linked in a close and firm union. In whatever part the belt is broke, all the wampum runs off, and renders the whole of no strength or consistency. In like manner, should you break faith with one another, or with this government, the union is dissolved. We would therefore hereby place before you the necessity of preserving your faith entire to one another, as well as to this government. Do not separate; Do not part of any score. Let no differences nor jealousies subsist a moment between Nation and Nation, but join together as one man. (Boyd, 129)

Franklin and the other colonial delegates were engaged in practical diplomacy on one level; on another, they were observing Iroquois concepts of unity along with their advice to confederate in a manner similar to the Iroquois Confederacy. Scarrooyady took for granted that the Pennsylvanians had some knowledge of the Great Law's workings when he requested that "you will please to lay all our present transactions before the council at *Onondago*, that they may know we do nothing in the dark," (Boyd, 131). The three-cornered contest over the land between Britain, France, and the Iroquois thus played a role in helping to forge concepts of federalism and liberty in the aborning United States.

Franklin's knowledge of the Iroquois Confederacy appears in his letters to the noted scientist, political figure, and Iroquois scholar Cadwallader Colden in 1747, when Franklin requested and received copies of Colden's *The History of the Five Indian Nations*, which had just been published in a second edition. On January 27, 1748, Franklin mentioned to Colden in a letter that he had read the *History of the Five Indian Nations* and thought "that 'tis a well wrote, entertaining and instructive Piece" and must "be exceedingly useful to all those Colonies who have anything" to do with Indian affairs (Labaree, *Papers*, 5:272).

Colden wrote that Iroquois skill at oratory and statecraft resembled that of the Romans and Greeks, a popular conception in the eighteenth century that helped the colonists and European philosophers to integrate their observations of Native American societies with their own European histories. An engraving in Joseph-François Lafitau's *Moeurs des Sauvages Ameriquains* (1724) provided a striking graph illustration of this belief. Drawn by a French artist who had never been to America, the engraving purported to show an Iroquois council. The assembled Native Americans are wearing togas instead of their own native dress, have short, curly, Roman-style hair, and meet against a background of rolling, nearly treeless countryside that looks much more like Italy than the forests of northeastern North America.

In a letter to Colden on October 25, 1753, Franklin noted that he had seen extracts of his book "in all the magazines" (Labaree, *Papers*, 5:80). Shortly after attending the Albany Congress, Franklin stopped to see Colden and thank him for the notes that Colden had sent to him while he was at Albany. Upon his return to Philadelphia, Franklin wrote to Colden that he had journeyed "to meet and hold a treaty with the Ohio Indians." Franklin promised Colden a copy of the treaty and stated that he had left his copy of Colden's book with a friend in Boston (Labaree, *Papers*, 5:80–81).

In one of America's earliest editorial cartoons, Franklin advocated colonial unity in 1754 with the slogan "Join, or Die" under a disjointed snake, each piece of which contained the name of a colony. The drawing appeared in the *Pennsylvania Gazette* on May 9, 1754, just before the Albany Congress. The dissected-snake symbol (sometimes accompanied by the phrase "Don't Tread on Me") became a popular symbol of colonial unity a generation later.

Characterizations of native polities as "confederate republics" were part of intellectual discourse in the colonies when Franklin began to assemble plans for an intercolonial federation. Lewis Evans' "Brief Account of Pennsylvania," published while Franklin was at Carlisle, stated:

> They are all Republicks in the Strictest sense; every Nation has a general Council, whither deputies are sent from every village; & by a majority of votes everything is determined there. What is most singular in American Government is that there is no such thing as coercive power in any Nation. . . . the National Councils have Power of War and peace . . . [and] they can neither raise men nor appoint officers, but leave it to such as their own accord unite in a Company & chuse their war Captain, nor has this Captain any power to compel his men, or to punish them for neglect of duty & yet no officer on earth is more strictly obeyed, so strongly are they influenced by the principle of doing their Duty uncompelled. (Evans, 92)

According to Evans, the Six Nations, "the Mohocks, Onoyades, Tucaroras, Onondagoes, Cayugoes & Senecas . . . bear a universal dominion in North

America," and their colonial allies "need not fear any other nations" (Evans, 92).

On the eve of the Albany Congress, Franklin was already persuaded that Canassatego's words were good counsel, and he was not alone in these sentiments. In letters convening the conference from the various colonies, instructions to the delegates were phrased in Iroquois diplomatic idiom. From colonist to colonist, the letters spoke of "burying the hatchet"—a phrase that entered idiomatic English from the Iroquois Great Law—as well as "renewing the covenant chain" (O'Callaghan, *Documentary History*, 2:546–551).

On July 10, 1754, Franklin formally proposed his Plan of Union before the Congress. In his final draft, Franklin was meeting several diplomatic demands: the Crown's, for control, the colonies' desires for autonomy in a loose confederation, and the stated Iroquois advocacy of a colonial union similar but not identical to their own in form and function. For the Crown, the plan provided administration by a president-general, to be appointed by England. The individual colonies were to be allowed to retain their own constitutions, except as the plan circumscribed them. The retention of internal sovereignty within the individual colonies closely resembled the Iroquois system and had no existing precedent in Europe.

Franklin chose the name "Grand Council" for the plan's deliberative body, the same name generally applied to the Iroquois central council. The number of delegates, forty-eight, was close to the Iroquois council's fifty (O'Callaghan, *Documentary History*, 4:889), and each colony had a different number of delegates, just as each Haudenosaunee nation sent a different number of sachems to Onondaga. The Albany Plan was based in rough proportion to tax revenues, however, while the Iroquois system was based on tradition.

The Albany Plan of Union called for a "general Government . . . under which Government each colony may retain its present Constitution" (Labaree, *Papers*, 5:387). Basically, the plan provided that Parliament was to establish a general government in America, including all colonies, each of which was to retain its present constitution except for certain powers (mainly concerning mutual defense) that were to be given to the general government. The king was to appoint a president-general for the government. Each colonial assembly would then elect representatives to the Grand Council.

Under the Albany Plan, the president-general would exercise certain powers with the advice of the Grand Council, such as handling Indian relations, making treaties, deciding upon peace or war, raising troops, building forts, providing warships, and levying such taxes as would be needed for its purposes (Labaree, *Papers*, 5:387–392). Through this plan, colonial leaders embraced a plan for union that Indian leaders such as Canassatego and Hendrick had urged them to adopt for a decade.

Henry Steele Commager remarked that the Articles of Confederation "should be studied in comparison with the Albany Plan of Union and the Constitution" (Commager, 111). Awareness of the interrelatedness of the three instruments of government is an important part of understanding the path to union. According to Clinton Rossiter, "The Albany Plan is a landmark on the rough road that was to lead through the first Continental Congresses and the Articles of Confederation to the Constitution of 1787" (Rossitar, 179–180). The missing component in this analysis is the role of Iroquois political theory and its influence on the formation of American notions of government. Julian P. Boyd maintained two generations ago that Franklin "proposed a plan for the union of the colonies and he found his materials in the great confederacy of the Iroquois" (Boyd, "Dr. Franklin," 239).

According to Boyd, Franklin used the knowledge that he had absorbed from Canassatego, Hendrick, and other Iroquois to construct analogies about Indians whenever they suited his purposes. In Franklin's bagatelle *Remargues sur la politesse des sauvages de l'Amérique Septentrionale*, written for a French audience during the American Revolution, the spirit of the work was less an examination of Indian manners than it was a commentary on a civilized society that Franklin found artificial. In the beginning of the bagatelle, Franklin stated:

> Savages we call them because their manners differ from ours, which we think the perfection of civility: they think the same of theirs. The Indian men, when young, are hunters and warriors; when old, counsellors; for all their government is by counsel of the sages; there is no force, there are no prisons, no officers to compel obedience or inflict punishment. (Boyd, "Dr. Franklin," 238–239)

Franklin's interest in the Iroquois political system was practical. He needed a governmental system by which to unite the colonies, and the Iroquois had a workable example of a federal structure that allowed maximum internal freedom, a necessity for colonies that disagreed with each other more often than not. According to Boyd, "One of America's great contributions to the history of political thought has been its working out of the problem of federation." In the Iroquois, Franklin and other colonial and later revolutionary leaders could see a federation of American Indians maintaining a system of alliances that stretched from the Hudson to the James and Saint Lawrence rivers. "What he [Franklin] proposed [in 1754] came in part from the Iroquois . . . Here indeed was an example worth copying," wrote Julian Boyd, who edited Jefferson's papers and Franklin's Indian treaties (Boyd, "Dr. Franklin," 246).

New immigrants to the eastern seaboard of North America who settled in the fledgling cities or on frontier farms were affected by Indian power along the frontier since Indians inhibited unbridled westward movement.

The fur trade was a vital part of the economy for such places as Albany and Philadelphia. It was also one more focus of conflict between the English and the French. In fact, the whole commercial structure of the colonial economy was based on Indians supplying traders with furs and peltry. Franklin knew that Indians could subvert this commercial structure by simply refusing to trap and hunt. Hence Indians were an economic factor that influenced the nature of the economy from the wages of a Philadelphia countinghouse clerk to the decisions on taxation and defense policy that the British foreign ministers made at Whitehall in England.

The colonists figured into Whitehall's financial equation as well when England looked for ways to pay debts incurred in the long war with France. New taxes were being readied for the colonists, many of whom felt that they should bear no part of Britain's military burdens. They also were beginning to develop a distinctly American identity and to display it using the symbols of Native America as a symbolic prelude to revolution. The issue of taxes would kindle the rhetoric of liberty, which came dressed, as rebellion built to revolution, as a Boston Tea Party Mohawk.

Canassatego's words echoed to the eve of the American Revolution, amplified by Franklin's talents as author and publisher. In 1775, Canassatego's thirty-one-year-old advice was recalled as Franklin had printed it at a treaty council between colonial representatives and Iroquois leaders in New York State. The treaty commissioners told the sachems that they were heeding the advice that the sachems' Iroquois forefathers had given to the colonial Americans at Lancaster, Pennsylvania, in 1744 as they assembled in Philadelphia to sit around their own "grand council fire." Thus the politics of land brought the thoughts of Canassatego, Hendrick, and Franklin together at Independence Hall.

Red Jacket (c. 1755–1830)

Red Jacket became one of the Senecas' leading spokesmen in defense of what remained of their land base after the American Revolution when he witnessed the swelling tide of white immigration in upstate New York. Iroquois feelings toward the new United States became bitter when immigrants flooded into Iroquois lands near the end of the eighteenth century.

The predatory, punitive raids of General John Sullivan's revolutionary army during 1779, under orders from George Washington, also resonated in the memories of many Iroquois, especially the Senecas. The Seneca leader Cornplanter, who became something of a friend of President Washington, wrote him an unflattering letter during 1790: "When your army entered the country of the Six Nations, we called you 'town destroyer' [Canotaucarius]; to this day, when your name is heard, our women look behind them and turn pale, and our children cling close to the necks of their mothers" (Rosenstiel, 98).

Red Jacket was best known as an ally of the British in the American Revolution. Red Jacket's first name, given to him as a boy, was Otetiani, meaning "he is prepared." Later he took the name Sagoyewatha, meaning "he causes them to be awake." The name Red Jacket came from a scarlet coat given to him by the British for fighting with them during the American Revolutionary War.

Red Jacket. National Anthropological Archives, Smithsonian Institution

Red Jacket's skills lay more in diplomacy than in the waging of war. After he fled the Battle of Oriskany in 1777, avoided battle at Wyoming Valley in 1778, and made an early exit at the Battle of Newtown in 1779, Red Jacket got a reputation as a coward. At another point during the American Revolution, Red Jacket killed a cow and smeared his tomahawk with blood to convince other Iroquois that he had killed a white man. Instead, Joseph Brant and Cornplanter ridiculed Red Jacket as a "cow killer."

After the war, Red Jacket reconciled his differences with the Americans, unlike Brant and his supporters, who moved to Canada. In 1792, Red Jacket was one of a group of Iroquois chiefs invited to Philadelphia to parley with George Washington. In the War of 1812, he fought with the patriots against the British. Regardless of his shifting allegiances and lack of valor in battle, Red Jacket believed that Indians should retain their own lands and cultures. He sought and sometimes got extensive legal protection for reservation lands. Red Jacket's speeches in defense of native land and rights have been cited by generations of Iroquois. One famous speech, given in 1828, was addressed to a representative of the Boston Missionary Society named Mr. Cram, who was requesting approval to recruit Iroquois to his faith.

Brother, listen to what we say. There was a time when our forefathers owned this great island. Their seats extended from the rising to the setting sun. The Great Spirit had made it for the use of Indians. He had created the buffalo, the deer, and other animals for food. He had made the bear and the beaver. Their skins served us for clothing. He had caused the earth to produce corn for bread. All this he had done for his red children because he loved them. If we had some disputes . . . they were generally settled without shedding much blood. But an evil day came upon us. Your forefathers crossed the great water and landed on this island. Their numbers were small. They found friends and not enemies. They told us they had fled from their own country for fear of wicked men. . . . They asked us for a small seat. We took pity on them, granted their request, and they sat down among us. We gave them corn and meat; they gave us poison in return. (Hamilton, 236–238)

The white people had now found our country, and more came upon us; yet we did not fear them. We took them to be friends, they called us brothers, we believed them and gave them a larger seat. At length their numbers had greatly increased; they wanted more land; they wanted our country. Our eyes were opened and our minds became uneasy. Wars took place; Indians were hired to fight against Indians, and many of our people were destroyed. They also brought strong liquor among us . . . [which] . . . has slain thousands. (Rosenstiel, 112)

Brother, our seats were once large, and yours were very small; you now have become a great people, and we have scarcely a space left to spread our blankets. You have got our country, but you are not satisfied. You want to force your religion upon us. . . . [But] we also have a religion which has been given to our forefathers and handed down to us, their children. . . . Brother, we do not wish to destroy your religion or take it from you. We only want to enjoy our own. (Hamilton, 238–239)

Writing to De Witt Clinton, governor of New York State, in 1821, Red Jacket listed some of the Senecas' most frequent grievances: that whites were cutting down some of the most valuable timber on Indian lands, stealing horses and cattle, and then throwing Indians in jail when they were on white-owned lands for "the most trifling causes." The changes that immigrants were bringing to the land were making traditional native lifeways impossible, Red Jacket said. Iroquois hunting and fishing were being "greatly interrupted." Whites were stealing Indian catches of venison that had been hung from trees during hunting expeditions. Construction of dams and other waterworks was obstructing fish migrations. "We are almost entirely deprived of [our] accustomed sustenance," said Red Jacket. "The greatest source of all our grievances is, that the white men are among us" (Armstrong, 52).

An angry Red Jacket faced representatives of the Ogden Land Company who were seeking Seneca land in 1819, telling them: "Look back to the first settlement by the whites, and then look at our present condition." Red Jacket and other Iroquois spokesmen had watched the Indians "who extended to the salt waters" lose their land, their social cohesion, and, finally, their lives. Their numbers declined as immigrant settlements grew, spreading European land-use patterns. Now, the same thing was happening in New York. "Driven back and reduced as we are, you wish to cramp us more and more," Red Jacket complained (Jones, 57). On another occasion, Red Jacket sarcastically told a "black-coat" (clergyman): "If you white people murdered 'The Savior,' [stone for it] yourselves. We had nothing to do with it. If he had come among us, we would have treated him better" (Hamilton, 236).

In 1811, Red Jacket refused an offer to purchase Seneca land in a speech at Buffalo Creek, a site that would subsequently become known in connection with one of the most fraudulent land acquisitions in American history, the Buffalo Creek Treaty of 1838:

Brother!—We think it strange that you would jump over the lands of our brethren in the East, to come to our council-fire so far off, to get our lands. When we sold our lands in the East to the white people, we determined never to sell those we kept, which are as small as we can comfortably live on. . . .

Brother!—The white people buy and sell false rights to our lands, and your employers have, you say, paid a great price for their rights. They must have a plenty [*sic*] of money to spend it in buying false rights to lands belonging to Indians. The loss of it will not hurt them, but our lands are of great value to us, and we wish you to go back with our talk to your employers, and tell them . . . that they have no right to buy and sell false rights to our lands. (Moquin, 136)

Shortly before his death in 1830, Red Jacket penned his view of Anglo-American law and its relationship to the acquisition of other people's property:

> Among us we have no prisons, we have no pompous parade of courts, we have no written laws, and yet judges are revered among us as they are among you, and their decisions as highly regarded. Property, to say the least, is well guarded, and crimes are as impartially punished. We have among us no splendid villains above control of our laws. Daring wickedness is never suffered to triumph over helpless innocence. The estates of widows and orphans are never devoured by enterprising sharpers. In a word, we have no robbery under cover of law. (Rosenstiel, 113)

During his last years, Red Jacket became an alcoholic and was deposed as an Iroquois chief in 1827. The chieftainship was restored shortly before he died on January 20, 1830, in Seneca Village, New York. He was memorialized with a statue erected in 1891 by the Buffalo Historical Society near the graves of Cornplanter and Ely S. Parker, General U. S. Grant's secretary during the Civil War.

Cornplanter and Red Jacket had seen only the first advance guard of a wave of humanity that would propel European-Americans across North America during less than a century after Red Jacket's death. Within less than a decade after Cornplanter penned his letter to Washington, Native American peoples in the Ohio Valley would feel the tug of their frightened children as they too tried to organize in defense of their land against a roaring tide of European-American immigration.

REFERENCES

Armstrong, Virginia Irving. *I Have Spoken: American History through the Voices of the Indians*. Athens, OH: Swallow Press, 1984.

Ashton, John. *Social Life in the Reign of Queen Anne*. London: Chatto & Windus, 1882.

Atkinson, Theodore. "Memo Book of My Journey as One of the Commissioners to the Six Nations, 1754." Manuscript Division, Library of Congress.

Bigelow, John, ed. *Autobiography of Benjamin Franklin*. Philadelphia: Lippincott, 1868.

Bond, Richmond. *Queen Anne's American Kings*. Oxford: Clarendon Press, 1952.

Boyd, Julian P. "Dr. Franklin: Friend of the Indian." 1942. In *Meet Dr. Franklin,* ed. Roy N. Lokken, 239–245. Philadelphia: Franklin Institute Press, 1981.

———, ed. *Indian Treaties Printed by Benjamin Franklin, 1736–1762*. Philadelphia: Historical Society of Pennsylvania, 1938.

Boyer, Abel. *The History of the Reign of Queen Anne, Digested into Annals: Year the Ninth*. 189–191. London: Thomas Ward, 1711.

Calloway, Colin, ed. *The World Turned Upside Down: Indian Voices from Early America*. Boston: Bedford Books/St. Martin's Press, 1994.

Colden, Cadwallader. *The History of the Five Indian Nations of Canada*. 1765. New York: New Amsterdam Book Co., 1902.

Commager, Henry Steele. *Documents of American History*. 7th ed. New York: Appleton-Century-Crofts, 1963.

Crèvecoeur, J. Hector St. John. *Letters from an American Farmer*. 1782. New York: E. P. Dutton & Co., 1926.

Evans, Lewis. "Brief Account of Pennsylvania." In *Lewis Evans*, ed. Lawrence B. Gipson. Philadelphia: Historical Society of Pennsylvania, 1939.

Franklin, Benjamin. "Remarks Concerning the Savages of North-America." In *Franklin Writings*, ed. Lemay, 969–970. Cited in Robert W. Venables. "The Founding Fathers: Choosing to be Romans." *Northeast Indian Quarterly* 6: 4 (Winter, 1989); pp. 30–55.

Grinde, Donald A., Jr., and Bruce E. Johansen. *Exemplar of Liberty: Native America and the Evolution of Democracy*. Los Angeles: UCLA American Indian Studies Center, 1991.

Hamilton, Charles, ed. *Cry of the Thunderbird*. Norman: University of Oklahoma Press, 1972.

Jacobs, Wilbur R. *Wilderness Politics and Indian Gifts*. Lincoln: University of Nebraska Press, 1966.

Jennings, Francis. *The Ambiguous Iroquois Empire: The Covenant Chain Confederation of Indian Tribes with English Colonies from Its Beginnings to the Lancaster Treaty of 1744*. New York: W. W. Norton, 1984.

Jones, Louis Thomas. *Aboriginal American Oratory: The Tradition of Eloquence among the Indians of the United States*. Los Angeles: Southwest Museum, 1965.

Labaree, Leonard W., ed. *The Autobiography of Benjamin Franklin*. New Haven, CT: Yale University Press, 1964.

———. *The Papers of Benjamin Franklin*. New Haven, CT: Yale University Press, 1959–1998.

McAnear, Beverly. "Personal Accounts of the Albany Congress of 1754." *Mississippi Valley Historical Review* 39:4 (1953): 727–746.

Moquin, Wayne, ed. *Great Documents in American Indian History*. New York: Praeger, 1973.

O'Callaghan, E. B., ed. *The Documentary History of the State of New-York*. 4 Vols. Albany: Weed, Parsons & Co., 1849–1851.

———. *Documents Relative to the Colonial History of the State of New-York*. Vol. 6. Albany: Weed, Parsons, 1853–1887.

Rosenstiel, Annette. *Red and White: Indian Views of the White Man, 1492–1982*. New York: Universe Books, 1983.

Rossiter, Clinton. "The Political Theory of Benjamin Franklin." In *Benjamin Franklin: A Profile*, ed. Esmond Wright. New York: Hill & Wang, 1970.

Shebbeare, John. *Lydia, or Filial Piety*. 3 acts. 1755. New York: Garland Publishing, 1974.

Smyth, Albert H., ed. *The Writings of Benjamin Franklin*. Vol. 3. New York: Macmillan Co., 1905–1907.

"To Our Great Queen, April, 1710," and "The Four Indian Sacheme Letter to Rt. Honourable Lord's of Her Majesty's Council" [April 1710]. Schuyler Indian Papers, Box 13, Manuscript Division, New York Public Library.

Venables, Robert W., ed. *The Six Nations of New York: The 1892 United States Extra Census Bulletin*. Ithaca, NY: Cornell University Press, 1995.

3

ALLIANCES TO PRESERVE LAND BASE

Little Turtle, Tecumseh, William Henry Harrison, and Black Hawk

For seventy-five years, from the "conspiracy" of Pontiac during the early 1760s to the defeat of Black Hawk during the 1830s, Native Americans in the "Old Northwest" (roughly, the Ohio Valley north and westward to the Great Lakes) formed confederations to protect their land base against the rising tide of European-American immigration. The best-known alliance builder was Tecumseh, who maintained that Indian estate was owned in common and could not be sold or traded by individuals. Little Turtle also advocated alliance in the Ohio Valley and at one point, during 1791, inflicted on the U.S. Army the largest battlefield defeat of the Indian wars. After much suffering and struggle, both Little Turtle and Tecumseh were forced to surrender and sign away much of the Ohio Valley.

As European-American immigration began to explode across the Appalachians into the Ohio Valley and Great Lakes shortly after 1790, Native American resistance expressed itself in attempts at confederation along lines of mutual interest. A confederation that included elements of the Shawnees, Delawares, Wyandots, Miamis, and Ottawas told the United States in 1790 that settlers were not to transgress beyond the Ohio River. Thousands of settlers were surging into the area, ignoring governmental edicts. The settlers, who were squatters in the Indians' eyes, sought military help after members of the Native American confederacy began attacking their settlements.

The new United States actively sought to goad alliances led by Little

Turtle and Tecumseh into battle in the Ohio Valley because proceeds from sale of the land could be used to lighten the financial load of the federal government, which was still struggling with debts incurred during the American Revolution. The land could be sold to speculators and settlers and given as payment to veterans of the Revolution (Edmunds, 27). A major agent of United States expansion in the Ohio Valley was William Henry Harrison, territorial governor and high-ranking military officer, whose defeat of Tecumseh became so well known that he would campaign for president on it almost three decades later. Harrison's campaign slogan, "Tippecanoe and Tyler Too" refreshed national memory as he ran for office. Tippecanoe was the site of the battle; Tyler was his running mate.

The speed of European-American expansion following the defeat of Tecumseh is illustrated at the end of this chapter by the life of Black Hawk (c. 1770–1838). A generation after Tecumseh's death, the European-American settlement frontier had raced from the Ohio country to the Mississippi Valley, where Black Hawk waged a brief, unsuccessful war to protect Sauk and Fox lands in Illinois. Black Hawk often defended the land in terms that Tecumseh had used.

Little Turtle (c. 1747[or 1752]–1812)

Tecumseh's land-based ideology was his most notable achievement, but he never defeated the U.S. Army in a large-scale battle in defense of his land ethic. In militant defense of the land, Tecumseh was walking the path of the Miami/Mohican Little Turtle, who was called Michikinikwa by his own people. Little Turtle was the principal chief who united a coalition of Shawnees, Miamis, Delawares, Potawatomis, Ottawas, Chippewas, and Wyandots in the Old Northwest (Ohio country), which on November 4, 1791, defeated an army of 1,400 soldiers under General Arthur St. Clair.

Little Turtle's 1,200 warriors, aided by the element of surprise, killed roughly 900 of St. Clair's soldiers and a number of their wives, the largest single battlefield victory by an American Indian force in history. The victory was short-lived, however; in 1794, "Mad Anthony" Wayne's forces defeated Little Turtle and his allies at the Battle of Fallen Timbers. On August 3, 1795, the Indians gave up most of their land west of the Ohio River following the defeat by signing the Treaty of Greenville.

Very little is known of Little Turtle's early life. He was probably born in 1747 (although a few accounts maintain that he was born in 1752); controversy attends the place of his birth, but the location was probably in present-day Whitley County in northeastern Indiana. The name of Little Turtle's mother is unknown, but she was probably part Mohican. Little

Little Turtle. National Anthropological Archives, Smithsonian Institution

Turtle's father, Michikinikwa (a name by which Little Turtle also was called after his father's death), was a renowned war chief among the Miamis who had played a large part in organizing his people in battles against the Iroquois to the east and the Sioux to the west during the eighteenth century. Some accounts say that Little Turtle inherited from his father a network of alliances that covered much of present-day Indiana and western Ohio. The elder Michikinikwa was the first Miami to meet with European immigrants when he traveled to Lancaster, Pennsylvania, during 1748 to attend a treaty council.

Little Turtle was a military tactician of superior talents and intuition. He also was a sensitive man and a gentleman. He was revolted by the slaughter of St. Clair's forces and sought a negotiated peace after the battle, reasoning that the immigrant Americans would eventually overpower the Miamis and their allies because of their larger numbers and advantages in war-making technology. Little Turtle advocated negotiating from strength, but the majority of the Miamis whom he was leading disagreed with him. Little Turtle became a war chief of the Miamis because of his extraordinary personal abilities; under ordinary circumstances, the matriarchal nature of the culture would have prohibited a leadership role for him because his mother was not Miami.

In 1787, the hunting grounds of the Miamis and their allies had been guaranteed "in perpetuity" by the U.S. Congress. The act did not stop an invasion of settlers, and by the early 1790s, Little Turtle had cemented an alliance that foreshadowed later efforts by Tecumseh. Little Turtle's principal allies in this effort were the Shawnee Blue Jacket and the Delaware Buckongahelos. This alliance first defeated a 1,000-man force under Josiah Harmer during October 1790. Harmer dispatched an advance force of 180 men, who were drawn into a trap and annihilated. Harmer then dispatched 360 more men in an attempt to punish the Indians. This force was drawn into a similar trap, in which about 100 of them were killed. The remainder of Harmer's force then retreated to Fort Washington, on the present-day site of Cincinnati.

Harmer's defeat stunned the army, whose commanders knew that the Old Northwest would remain closed to legal settlement as long as Little Turtle's alliance held. General Arthur St. Clair, who had served briefly as president of the Continental Congress during the middle 1780s, gathered an army of 2,000 men during the summer of 1791 and marched into the Ohio Country. About a quarter of the men deserted enroute. To keep the others happy, St. Clair permitted about 200 soldiers' wives to travel with them.

St. Clair's army was plagued by problems from the start, including low quality of recruits (many of them were local militia and untrained volunteers), shoddy equipment, roughly 900 desertions, and consistently wet weather. Tecumseh and other Native American scouts spotted St. Clair's force long before the U.S. forces spotted the Indians. Little Turtle's forces obtained support from several other native nations in the area and were well supplied by British traders. "Impatient with St. Clair's progress," wrote R. David Edmunds, "on October 28, 1791, the Indians broke camp and moved south to meet the Americans" (Edmunds, 32–33).

On November 4, 1791, Little Turtle and his allies lured St. Clair's forces into the same sort of trap that had defeated Harmer's smaller army near St. Mary's Creek, a tributary of the Wabash River. Thirty-eight officers and 598 men died in the battle; 242 others were wounded, many of whom later died. Fifty-six wives also lost their lives, bringing the total death toll to about 950, the largest defeat of a U.S. Army force during a single battle in all of the Indian wars, a death toll higher than any inflicted on the United States by the British in the American Revolution. After the battle, St. Clair resigned his commission in disgrace.

Little Turtle's allies refused his advice to deal from strength and settle with the United States after the defeat of St. Clair. Instead, when Blue Jacket assumed the primary leadership role in Little Turtle's place, they refused to cede land. In 1794, "Mad Anthony" Wayne was dispatched with a fresh army that visited the scene of St. Clair's debacle. According to Wayne, 500 skull bones lay in the space of 350 yards. The woods were strewn with skeletons, knapsacks, and other debris for five miles, artifacts of St. Clair's forces' pell-mell retreat. In one of his letters, Wayne described the abundance his troops had found before they destroyed it:

> The margins of these beautiful rivers, the Miami of the Lake and Auglaize, appear like one continued village for a number of miles, both above and below this place. Nor have I ever before beheld such immense fields of corn in any part of America, from Canada to Florida. (Manypenny, 84)

Little Turtle had more respect for Wayne than for Harmer or St. Clair, calling him "the chief who never sleeps." On August 29, 1794, Wayne's forces defeated the Native American alliance at Fallen Timbers, and when the time to talk peace came a year later, the defeated Indians were forced to give up most of their lands. The native peoples of the region were left to poverty and disease, their economic base devastated.

For almost two centuries, local historians placed the site of the Battle of Fallen Timbers along the Maumee River floodplain adjacent to U.S. Highway 24, near Toledo, Ohio. A monument was erected at the site, even though Native Americans contended that the battle had occurred a mile away in what is today a soybean field. In 1995, to settle the issue, G. Michael Pratt, an anthropology professor at Heidelberg College, Tiffin, Ohio, organized an archaeological dig in the soybean field. Teams that included as many as 150 people excavated the site, which yielded large numbers of battlefield artifacts, indicating conclusively that the Native American account of the site was correct.

After the Treaty of Greenville (1795), Little Turtle visited George Washington during the waning days of his presidency. Washington presented Little Turtle with a sword and a gun and had his portrait painted by Gilbert Stuart (Winger, 8). After 1800, Little Turtle thought that his people would be best served by accepting the whites' advice to abandon the hunt and concentrate their economic energies solely on agriculture.

Thomas Jefferson appreciated Little Turtle's devotion to his ideal of the yeoman farmer when they met during January of 1802. Little Turtle himself was more concerned with acquiring Jefferson's help in an effort to ban the importation of liquor to his people:

> Father . . . Your children are not wanting in industry, but it is the introduction of this fatal poison, which keeps them poor. Your children have not the command over themselves which you have, therefore before anything can be done to advantage this evil must be remedied. (Carter, 162)

Little Turtle was described by his biographer Harvey Lewis Carter at negotiations leading to the Treaty of Greenville in 1795, when he was roughly forty-eight years of age. Carter's description is taken from an artist's sketch of Little Turtle made at about that time, but not at the treaty conference itself:

> Little Turtle, who wore white men's apparel in later years, now, in the hot weather of the Lightning Moon, wore no clothing but his breech cloth and moccasins; he also had on a bear-claw necklace, metal armlets on his upper arms, large metal ear hoops, a large medallion suspended by a second neck chain, and a headpiece of thirteen eagle feathers fastened in his hair by means of three snake rattles. (Carter, 149)

Little Turtle addressed the legislatures of Ohio and Kentucky during 1802, urging both to pass laws forbidding traders to supply Indians with whiskey. He said that whiskey traders had "stripped the poor Indian of skins, guns, blankets, everything—while his squaw and the children dependent on him lay starving and shivering in his wigwam" (Hamilton, 67). Neither state did anything to stop the flow of whiskey, some of which was adulterated with several other substances, from chili peppers to arsenic.

Little Turtle spent the last years of his life in a house built for him by the U.S. government near the Eel River Trading Post. He died on July 14, 1812, at the Fort Wayne home of William Wells, near the junction of the St. Joseph River and St. Mary Creek. During his official life as a leader of the Miamis, Little Turtle was often accompanied by Wells, a white man who had been captured as a youth and adopted by the Miamis. Wells also married into Little Turtle's family.

Little Turtle was buried with full military honors by army officers who knew his genius. William Henry Harrison, who had been an aide to Wayne, and who later defeated Tecumseh in the same general area, paid Little Turtle this tribute: " 'A safe leader is better than a bold one.' This maxim was a great favorite of [the Roman] Caesar Augustus . . . who . . . was, I believe, inferior to the warrior Little Turtle" (Porter, 51).

Tecumseh (c. 1768–1813)

Native resistance surged again shortly after the turn of the nineteenth century under the aegis of Tecumseh, which means "crouching tiger" in his native Shawnee language. Tecumseh was born near present-day Oldtown, Ohio. He fought with Turkey Foot at Fallen Timbers. Tecumsehs influence grew rapidly as he came of age after the American Revolution, not only because of his acumen as a statesman and a warrior, but because of his personal integrity. He forbade torture of prisoners, for example. European-American immigrants and his Native American allies trusted Tecumseh.

Tecumseh was raised from birth to make war on the encroaching whites by his mother, Methoataske, whose husband, the Shawnee Puckeshinwa, had been killed in cold blood by white immigrants when Tecumseh was a boy. Tecumseh and his mother found Puckeshinwa as he was dying. As he watched his father writhe in pain, Tecumseh vowed to avenge his death. A few years later, his hatred for the immigrants was deepened by the murder of Cornstalk, a Shawnee chief who had been a mentor to the young Tecumseh.

Tecumseh led a scouting party under Little Turtle preceding the Indian defeat of St. Clair in 1791. He probably took no part in the fighting. In the battle with "Mad Anthony" Wayne at Fallen Timbers (1794), Tecum-

Tecumseh. National Anthropological Archives, Smithsonian Institution

seh and his allies were in the forefront of the fighting. Wayne's forces were much better trained and provisioned than St. Clair's had been, and much less inclined to cut and run during battle. Tecumseh's contingent maintained its position until his rifle jammed. Tecumseh found another weapon and rallied his troops to take refuge in undergrowth until they stole horses belonging to an American artillery squad and escaped the battlefield (Edmunds, 41). By the turn of the century, as the number of immigrants grew, Tecumseh began to assemble the Shawnees, Delawares, Ottawas, Ojibwas, Kickapoos, and Wyandots into a confederation with the aim of establishing a permanent Native American state that would act as a buffer zone between the United States to the east and English Canada to the north.

Tecumseh was said to have been "a muscular man of great physical vigor" (Edmunds, 43). He was a skilled hunter who often provided for several families other than his own with a legendary generosity. Tecumseh was described as being a compact, muscular man who was known for his physical endurance. He had a full, high forehead, a slightly aquiline nose, and penetrating black eyes nestled under prominent eyebrows. The seriousness of his demeanor and his commanding personal presence were noted by European-American observers. Tecumseh was described in 1812, when he was perhaps about fifteen years of age, by army officer John B. Glegg as

> prepossessing, his figure light and finely proportioned . . . in height, five feet nine or ten inches; his complexion light copper; countenance oval, with bright hazle [*sic*] eyes, beaming cheerfulness, energy, and decision. Three small silver crowns or coronets were suspended from the lower cartilage of his aquiline nose. (Edmunds, 178)

General Sam Dale described Tecumseh as follows:

> [Words] fell in avalanches from his lips. . . . His eyes burned with supernatural lustre, and his whole frame trembled with emotion. His voice resounded over the multitude—now sinking in low and musical whispers, now rising to the highest key, hurling out his words like a succession of thunderbolts. . . . I have heard many great orators, but I never saw one with the vocal powers of Tecumseh. (Josephy, 158)

Tecumseh's adversary in battle William Henry Harrison respected him deeply:

> The implicit obedience and respect which the followers of Tecumseh pay to him is really astonishing and more than any other circumstance bespeaks him [as] one of those uncommon geniuses, which spring up occasionally to produce revolutions and to overturn the established order of things. If it were not for the vicinity of the United States, he would, perhaps, be the founder of an Empire that would rival in glory Mexico or Peru. No difficulties deter him. (Hamilton, 159)

Tecumseh was known all his life as being sober, except for one drunken escapade in his youth. He had the reputation of being "hospitable, generous, and humane . . . kind and attentive to the aged and infirm, looking personally to their comfort" (Drake, 225). For Shawnees who could not provide for themselves, Tecumseh repaired homes at the onset of winter and shared with them skins for clothing and the best of his food. By these acts, as well as his prominence as an orator and thinker, Tecumseh became a leader among the Shawnees and their allies. "Nor were these acts of kindness bestowed exclusively on those of rank or reputation," a Shawnee associate of Tecumseh is said to have recalled. "On the contrary, he made it his business to search out the humblest objects of charity, and in a quick, unostentatious manner, relieve their wants" (Drake, 225).

Tecumseh was a studious man who could read English and had something of a passion for books. He surprised some Anglo-American observers with his knowledge of Shakespeare and the Scriptures, as well as other aspects of European history and culture. Hannibal and Alexander the Great seem to have been particular objects of Tecumseh's intense curiosity (Tucker, 15). Transcribed versions of his speeches probably convey only a portion of what Tecumseh actually said, in large part because his eloquence in the Shawnee language confounded most interpreters. Tecumseh could speak imperfect English, but did not believe himself competent to address a large audience in the European language. His pride in being Shawnee also forbade communication in English when he could speak in Shawnee.

Because his father had been killed by whites, and because most of his associations with the immigrants had been a result of a lifetime of warfare, Tecumseh distrusted most non-Indians. Shabbona, his aide in later life, said that Tecumseh's "enmity was the most bitter of any Indian I ever knew" (Tucker, 27). Tecumseh himself was once overheard to say that he could not look at the face of a white man "without feeling the flesh crawl on his bones" (Tucker, 27). Tecumseh expressed his feelings regarding European-Americans when he summoned the Creeks to alliance:

> Let the white race perish! They seize your land, they corrupt your women, they trample on the grass of your dead. Back whence they came, upon a trail of blood, they must be driven. Back, back, aye, into the great waters whose accursed waves brought them to our shores. Burn their houses, destroy their stock! The red man owns the country and the palefaces must never enjoy it. War now, war forever! War upon the living, war upon the dead. Dig their bones from the grave. Our country must give no rest to a white man's bones. (Tucker, 209)

Despite his enduring enmity for the immigrants, Tecumseh was demonstrably opposed to torture or assassination of captives, even white ones. He once violently upbraided some of his men for killing a European-

American captive named McIntyre, demeaning them as cowards for shooting a man whose hands were tied behind his back (Tucker, 63).

Tecumseh absolutely refused to make war in such a manner that it threatened women and children (Edmunds, 42–43). His adversary, General William Henry Harrison, called Tecumseh "the Moses of the family" (Edmunds, 132). Ethnologist James Mooney characterized him as "abstemious in habit, charitable in thought and action, brave as a lion, but humane and generous withal—in a word, an aboriginal knight—his life . . . given to his people" (Edmunds, 223).

Tecumseh's oratory centers on the idea of common landownership and its relation to Native American identity. He traveled widely, especially to the south and east among the Choctaws, Chickasaws, and other native nations who were facing waves of immigration as the nineteenth century opened. Recalling the defeat and dispersion of native nations to the north and east of the Ohio Valley, Tecumseh said that if Indians did not combine their efforts in defense of a common estate, they would lose it to "our faithless invaders and heartless oppressors" (Vanderwerth, 64).

> Where today are the Pequot? Where are the Narraganset, the Mohican, the Pocanet, and other powerful tribes of our people? They have vanished before the avarice and oppression of the white man, as snow before the summer sun. . . . Will we let ourselves be destroyed in our turn, without an effort worthy of our race? Shall we, without a struggle, give up our homes, our lands, bequeathed to us by the Great Spirit? The graves of our dead and everything that is dear and sacred to us? . . . I know you will say with me, never! Never! (Armstrong, 45)

> Are we not being stripped day by day of the little that remains of our ancient liberty? Do they not even kick and strike us as they do their black-faces? How long will it be before they will tie us to a post and whip us, and make us work for them . . . ? Shall we wait for that moment or shall we die fighting before submitting to such ignominy? (Vanderwerth, 64)

Tecumseh's statements regarding his relationship with the land, like those of Sea'thl, Black Elk, and other Native American leaders, often were couched in a religious context. Tecumseh's speeches are filled with the specter of ancestors' bones being turned over by whites' plows. Tecumseh told General Harrison in person that he had "organized a combination of all the Indian Tribes in this to put a stop to the encroachments of the white people and to establish a principle that the lands should be considered common property and none sold without the consent of all" (Edmunds, 132). Tecumseh told Harrison at the same meeting that annuities were worthless without a land base on which his people could live.

Letters passing through the Fort Wayne Indian Agency at the time indicate that pressure on the land by white squatters was driving Indians into the camp of Tecumseh and his brother, Tenskwatawa, also known as the

Prophet. A speech at the Fort Wayne Indian Agency by Five Medals, a Potawatomi, indicated that after Indians sold one parcel of land, pressure soon built to cede yet another. "This alarmed us, and alarmed our young men and Warriors more—they said their chiefs would sell their land and ruin them" (Thornbrough, 121). According to Five Medals, "This destroyed the influence of the chiefs; since then, our young men have refused to obey us. It is now the young Shawanoe [*sic*] began to preach, and by this he gained his influence" (Thornbrough, 121). The agents at Fort Wayne sometimes displayed dismay at their inability to control the infiltration of the immigrants' seedier habits into Indian country. One agent at Fort Wayne remarked during July 1813 that whiskey merchants were setting up shop "immediately before the front gate of the fort" (Thornbrough, 197). The same observer watched a number of whites line up to buy liquor that later would be resold to the Indians.

Tecumseh was particularly galled by the fact that Harrison had chosen as his territorial capital the village of Chillicothe, the same site (with the same name) as the Shawnees' former principal settlement. The name itself is taken from the Shawnee expression meaning "principal town." Tecumseh also was angered by Harrison's treaty of September 30, 1809, with the Delawares, Potawatomis, Miamis, Kickapoos, Wea, and Eel River peoples. For $8,200 in cash and $2,350 in annuities, Harrison had laid claim for the United States to roughly three million acres of rich hunting land along the Wabash River in the heart of the area in which Tecumseh wished to erect his Native American confederacy. When Tecumseh and his brother, who also was a Shawnee war chief, complained to Harrison that the treaty terms were unfair, Harrison at first rebuked Tecumseh by saying that the Shawnees had not even been part of the treaty. The implicit refusal to recognize Tecumseh's alliance angered the Indians even more. Realizing that Tecumseh's influence made it politic for him to do so, Harrison agreed to meet with him. At a meeting on August 12, 1810, each side drew up several hundred battle-ready warriors and soldiers. Harrison agreed to relay Tecumseh's complaints to the president, and Tecumseh said that his warriors would join the Americans against the British if Harrison would annul the treaty.

Facing Harrison in 1810 at a meeting to which he had arrived with about 300 warriors in eighty canoes, Tecumseh protested land cessions made in alcohol-lubricated treaties beginning during 1805. According to later accounts, Tecumseh refused to enter Harrison's territorial governor's mansion, which had been designated for treaty making by the white men. Various accounts of this now-famous incident say that Tecumseh refused a chair and sat on the ground, telling Harrison that he would rather sit on the bosom of mother earth than on a white man's bench or chair. According to other accounts, Tecumseh took a seat on a bench next to Harrison and pushed the governor off of it, telling him that his people were being squeezed off their homelands in a like manner. Tecumseh has been said to have made an ecological and spiritual metaphor of his refusal, rejecting the very notion that land could have individual owners who could buy or sell it.

Questions have been raised about Tecumseh's declaration to Harrison that are similar to those that confound an accurate telling of Chief Sea'thl's "farewell speech" (see Chapter 6). Tecumseh's exchange with Harrison was not recorded in any official way; like Isaac Stevens' meeting with Sea'thl, it was not an official treaty council, but an informal meeting called to consider a request by Tecumseh to annul treaties signed several years earlier. No mention of the incident appears in Harrison's papers, just as no trace of the "farewell speech" is contained in Stevens' papers. As with Dr. Henry Smith's account of Sea'thl's speech, several years passed between the date of the event and the first appearance in published form of the anecdote concerning Tecumseh, Harrison, the bench (or chair), and its symbolic relation to the earth.

Tecumseh's now-famous anecdote was published eleven years after the meeting with Harrison in 1810. The May 12, 1821, edition of a popular magazine, the *National Recorder*, included a brief article. In this hundred-word piece, an unidentified non-Indian at the parley is said to have offered Tecumseh a chair with these words: "Warrior, your father General Harrison offers you a seat." Tecumseh seems to have taken offense first at the assumption that Harrison was his "father." The reporter says that his "dark eye flashed" as he exclaimed, "indignantly," that "the sun is my father and the earth is my mother; she gives me nourishment, and I repose on her bosom" (Gill, 14).

This anecdote reached a broader and more enduring public through Henry Rowe Schoolcraft, who in 1821 was traveling the Ohio Valley collecting his impressions of the land and Native American life there. The account appears nearly verbatim in an account of Schoolcraft's travels published in 1825. Schoolcraft even duplicated an error in the original piece that placed the meeting in 1811, not 1810 (Schoolcraft, 144–145).

Another variation of this story surfaced in the January 8, 1889, edition of the *Vincennes Commercial*, a newspaper published near the site of the meeting between Harrison and Tecumseh, during which the main stage prop is not a chair, but a bench. The *Commercial*'s version of this story was published in great detail, even listing the names of interpreters; it has been said to have been the product of Felix Bouchie, who reportedly was about seventy years of age in 1889. Bouchie said that the story was told in his family. In this account, Tecumseh asked that a bench be placed in the area being used for negotiations so that he could sit on it. A pew was taken out of a nearby Catholic church, the only bench available. Tecumseh then sat on the bench and invited Harrison to do likewise.

When they sat down together, Tecumseh sat close to Harrison, even crowding him. Harrison moved away a little, but Tecumseh followed him up, and still crowded him. Not a single word was said. . . . At last, Harrison reached the end of the seat, and then he said to the interpreter, "tell him he is about to crowd me off." . . . Tecumseh . . . straightened up in his seat, saying to the interpreter: ". . . Ask the Big Man how he would like for me to crowd him clear off. Ask how he would like for me to crowd him clear out of the country, as he is crowding my people." (Gill, 25)

Despite the fact that both of these accounts have spread through a network of secondary sources during the ensuing years, Sam Gill, author of *Mother Earth: An American Story* (1987), states flatly that "I do not believe that he made statements even approximating the one so often attributed to him. Belief that he made the statement doubtless emerged in the explosion of legend, lore, and literature that, after his death, transformed Tecumseh from an obstacle of settlement into a heroic figure" (Gill, 29). Gill writes that he scoured the literature and came up with only two historical references to "mother earth," one in this account and another by the Nez Perce Smohalla. (The severe limits of Gill's evidence will become obvious to even the most superficial reader in Chapter 6.) Gill tries to dismiss even the two references to "mother earth" he did find by insisting that whites imagining noble savages made them up. In the case of Tecumseh, Harrison, and the symbolic chair (or bench), Gill believes that the entire incident was made up as part of a hero-worship cult of Tecumseh that somehow sprang up within a decade of his death.

Whatever the specific details of this particular incident, the historical circumstances indicate that Tecumseh was in the mood to make a point to Harrison about his people's right to the land. The subject matter of the meeting was, at its basis, who should own the land.

Houses are built for you to hold councils in; Indians hold theirs in the open air. . . . The way, the only way to stop this evil [land sales] is for the red men to unite in claiming a common and equal right in the land, as it was at first, and should be now—for it was never divided, but belongs to all. No tribe has the right to sell, even to each other, much less to strangers. . . . *Sell a country! Why not sell the air, the great sea, as well as the earth?* Did not the Great Spirit make them all for the use of his children? (Armstrong, 44)

Tecumseh told Harrison that Indian leaders who sold portions of the native common estate would be made to answer for their actions, which would be treated as crimes. He was criticizing the frequently used tactic of treaty negotiators by which they signed treaties with a fraction of the people whom "treaty chiefs" were said to represent. For many years, Harrison had tried to undermine the growing strength of Tecumseh's Indian alliance by negotiating treaties of cession with individual tribes. Since only a portion of each tribe or nation's warriors elected to follow Tecumseh, Harrison found "treaty Indians" among those who did not elect to fight with him.

By 1811, Harrison had negotiated at least fifteen treaties, all of which Tecumseh repudiated.

Tecumseh told Harrison that Native Americans had just as much of a right to form a confederacy in their mutual interest as did the European colonies of the Atlantic seaboard: "The states have set the example of Tecumseh forming a union among all the fires [councils]—why should they censure the Indians for following it?" Tecumseh then asked Harrison, "What is your determination about the land?" (Josephy, 155–156). Harrison replied to Tecumseh with irritation in his voice, telling him that Tecumseh had no right to contest treaties already signed regarding Shawnee land in Indiana, because Georgia, not Indiana, was their original home. Harrison then asserted that the United States always had been fair in its dealings with Indians, at which Tecumseh jumped to his feet and yelled, "It is false! he lies!" (Josephy, 156). Harrison drew his sword and began to advance on Tecumseh as several army officers cocked their firearms. Several Indians standing behind Tecumseh drew their tomahawks. Harrison decided at that point to defuse the situation by adjourning the meeting.

Tecumseh and William Henry Harrison come nearly to blows in this nineteenth-century lithograph. From James A. Green, *William Henry Harrison: His Life and Times* (Richmond, VA: Garrett and Massie, Inc., 1941)

The next day, Tecumseh sent his apologies to Harrison, and the governor accepted them.

During 1811, bands of warriors allied with Tecumseh began ranging out of the settlement of Tippecanoe to terrorize nearby farmsteads and small backwoods settlements. Harrison said that he would wipe out Tippecanoe if the raids did not stop; Tecumseh said that they would stop when the Shawnees' land was returned. Tecumseh then journeyed southward to bring the Creeks, Chickasawe, and Choctaws into his alliance. Tecumseh carried the message that he had used to recruit other allies: that when the white men first set foot in North America, they had been hungry and feeble, with no place to spread their blankets or to kindle their fires. Tecumseh told potential allies that their fathers had commiserated with the immigrants and had shared freely with them whatever the Great Spirit had given his red children. They gave them food when they were hungry, medicine when they were sick, spread skins for them to sleep on, and gave them ground so that they might hunt and raise corn. Now that the whites had grown more numerous and much stronger, Tecumseh said that they had become like poisonous serpents: when chilled, they were feeble and harmless, but invigorate them with warmth, and they kill their benefactors.

Despite the eloquence and force of Tecumseh's message, he failed, for the most part, to bring new allies into the fight. While Tecumseh was traveling, the command of the existing alliance fell to Tenskwatawa. In the meantime, on September 26, 1811, Harrison departed Vincennes with more than 900 men, two-thirds of them Native American allies, from a fort named after himself on the present-day site of Terre Haute, Indiana. Harrison sent two Miamis to Tenskwatawa to demand the return of property Harrison alleged had been stolen in the raids, along with the surrender of Indians he accused of murder. The Miamis did not return to Harrison's camp. The governor's army marched to within sight of Tippecanoe and met with Tenskwatawa, who invited them to make camp, relax, and negotiate. Harrison's forces did stop, but set up in battle configurations as the Prophet's warriors readied an attack.

Within two hours of pitched battle, Harrison's forces routed the Indians, then burned the village of Tippecanoe as Tenskwatawa's forces scattered into the woods. Returning to the devastation from his travels, Tecumseh fled to British Canada, where, during the War of 1812, he allied with the British. Rumors that Tecumseh was appointed as a British brigadier general apparently are false, possibly a product of American propaganda. Glenn Tucker, biographer of Tecumseh, inspected the records of the British army during the 1950s and could find no evidence of such a commission (Tucker, 259).

Harrison's forces later met Tecumseh's forces at the Battle of the Thames in Kentucky. Tecumseh was killed during that battle, October 5, 1813. Shortly before his death, Tecumseh urged his British allies not to retreat from land his Indian confederacy had shed blood to defend: "As for us, our lives are in the hands of the Great Spirit. We are determined to defend our lands, and if it be his will we wish to leave our bones upon them" (Edmunds, 205). After the battle, some of the Kentucky militia who had taken part found a body they thought was Tecumseh's and cut strips from it for souvenirs. Tecumseh's warriors, who had dispersed in panic when Tecumseh was killed, said later that they had taken his body with them. Having committed 20,000 men and $5 million to the cause, the United States had effectively terminated armed Indian resistance in the Ohio Valley and surrounding areas.

William Henry Harrison (1773–1841)

William Henry Harrison was one example of a political genre during the nineteenth century: an army general whose road to the White House was paved with victories over Native American adversaries, as well as with treaties (usually negotiated as instruments of surrender) that added substantial parts of several soon-to-be states to the Union. Harrison was cast in the political mold of Andrew Jackson, but unlike Jackson, who served two full terms as president of the United States, Harrison died soon after assuming office. The success of both men illustrated the degree to which the politics of land acquisition permeated the economic culture of the fledging nation.

During his campaign for the presidency in 1840, Harrison's sloganeers waxed eloquent over Harrison's birth as a "child of the revolution," February 9, 1773, in the Berkeley manor house twenty-four miles east of Richmond, Virginia, downstream along the James River. His father, Benjamin Harrison, one of Virginia's largest landowners with several thousand acres, signed the Declaration of Independence when William Henry Harrison was three years of age. He also held a seat in the Continental Congress and served as governor of Virginia. William Henry was a child of almost nine years when the decisive Battle of Yorktown flared within a few miles of his home. British troops commanded by the traitor Benedict Arnold left

---

William Henry Harrison. Nebraska State Historical Society

their bootprints on his father's plantation. George Washington lodged at his father's house. Harrison's father also joined the Virginia militia during the war and fought at the Battle of Yorktown.

As a youth, William Henry was tutored privately at home, then sent to private school in Richmond. Early in his life, Harrison was described as a delicate child by his mother. He soon made up for his physical frailties with toughness and determination, however. With much effort, young William Henry learned to run and swim. The young Harrison attended college for a year at Hampden-Sydney College, on the eastern foothills of the Blue Ridge Mountains, where he seems to have enjoyed Greek and Roman history.

Harrison's father instructed him to train as a medical doctor, perhaps influenced by his physician friend Benjamin Rush, who also was serving in the Continental Congress at the time. Obeying his father's wishes, William Henry enrolled in the medical college of the University of Pennsylvania at Philadelphia. The entire medical curriculum consisted of a program of lectures during each of two sixteen-week semesters.

Benjamin Harrison died in 1791, after which William Henry discontinued his medical education and enlisted with General "Mad Anthony" Wayne's army to conquer Little Turtle's alliance in the Ohio Valley. At that point, Harrison made conquest of the Ohio country a career goal, a path that would bring him into conflict with Tecumseh. Harrison's political fortune was built on his victory over Tecumseh. One may juxtapose Tecumseh's view of Native American land tenure with that of Harrison, who, like Tecumseh, invoked his own conception of "the Creator":

> Is one of the fairest portions of the globe to remain in a state of nature, the haunt of a few wretched savages, when it seems destined by the Creator to give support to a large population and to be the seat of civilization, of science, and of true religion? (Vecsey and Venables, 68)

The war for the land in the Ohio Valley was not always fought in matches between armed men. Much of the ebb and flow of more than a decade of antipathy between Harrison and Tecumseh was psychological, the day-by-day incidents of a decades-long cold war. During April 1806, Harrison sent a message to the Delawares, whom Tecumseh was recruiting as allies, denouncing his brother, the prophet Tenskwatawa, as a fraud.

> Who is this pretend Prophet who dares to speak in the name of the Great Creator? Examine him. . . . Demand of him some proof at least of his being the messenger of the Deity. If God really employed him, He has doubtless authorized him to perform miracles that he may be known and received as a prophet. If he is really a prophet, ask him to cause the sun to stand still, the moon to alter its course, the

rivers to cease to flow, or the dead to rise from their graves. If he does these things, you may then believe he has been sent from God. (Tucker, 99)

The Prophet, accepting Harrison's challenge, announced that the sun would darken during daylight on June 16. The Prophet, along with numerous scientists and readers of some popular magazines, had long known that a solar eclipse was predicted for that date, but Harrison had somehow missed the news. Scientists from Harvard set up an observation station at Springfield, Illinois, in the path of the total eclipse of the sun. Harrison's aides complained that British intelligence had slipped Tenskwatawa the date to make Harrison look like a fool.

Following his victory over Tecumesh, Harrison became the commander in chief of the Army of the Northwest during the War of 1812. By 1816, he had been elected to Congress. Defeated for reelection in 1820. Harrison ran for the office of U.S. senator from Ohio in 1824 and won. He resigned in 1828 to become an envoy to Colombia, where he stayed until 1831. For most of the decade of the 1830s, however, Harrison's life was dominated by his growing popularity as a candidate for president of the United States.

William Henry Harrison never forgot Tecumseh. He was elected to the presidency during 1840, winning with a slogan eulogizing the site of his victory over the great native chieftain almost three decades earlier: "Tippecanoe and Tyler [his vice president] too." Harrison insisted on giving his inaugural address in a cold drizzle, wearing neither a hat nor an overcoat. Having contracted pneumonia from this dramatic illustration of his legendary toughness, Harrison died a month later at the age of sixty-eight.

Black Hawk (c. 1770–1838)

Black Hawk, who was called Makataimeshekiakiak by his own people, was a member of the Thunder Clan of the Sauk Nation. Black Hawk won renown as a warrior from the time he carried home his first scalp at the age of fifteen to his leadership of a Native American rebellion that bears his name in the early 1830s.

Black Hawk was capable of murderous hatred as well as acts displaying a most intense, personal sense of compassion. In one battle with the Osages, he personally killed nine people, but on another raid, against the Cherokees, he found only four people—three men and a woman. He took the woman captive and then freed the three men, figuring that it was dishonorable to kill so few. During the siege of an American fort during the War of 1812, as an ally of the British, Black Hawk found two white boys hiding in a bush. He thought of his own children and passed on without harming them. During the same war, Black Hawk learned that some of his Indian allies, also British allies, were torturing white prisoners. He halted the practice and poured his scorn on Col. Henry Procter, the British commander, for permitting torture.

About 1820, the Fox and Sauk divided over whether to resist European American expansion into their country in what is now southern Illinois. Keokuk and a number of his supporters decided to accommodate the ex-

---

Black Hawk. National Anthropological Archives, Smithsonian Institution

pansion and moved into Iowa. Black Hawk and his supporters remained at their principal village, Saukenuk, at the confluence of the Rook and Mississippi rivers, the site of present-day Rock Island. The land provided abundant crops, and the river was a rich source of fish. Black Hawk consulted with the spiritual leaders White Cloud and Neapope, who advised him to seek allies in defense of the land.

In the meantime, George Davenport, the Indian agent in the area, had what he believed to be a valid deed to the site on which Saukenuk was built, including Black Hawk's own lodge and his people's graveyard. Settlers began to take land around the village. Illinois governor John Reynolds ordered the state militia to march on Saukenuk. Black Hawk and his band moved west across the Mississippi, but pledged to return. When they did, they found white men in their lodges, getting ready to plant their cornfields. Black Hawk's people found themselves dispossessed of their homeland and all its improvements in a most personal fashion. Black Hawk cast his eyes upon cornfields

> which the Sauks have . . . cultivated for so many winters that our memory cannot go back to them. . . . They [white men] are now running their plows through our graveyards, turning up the bones and ashes of our sacred dead, whose spirits are calling to us from the land of dreams for vengeance on the despoilers. Will the descendants of Nanamakee and our other illustrious dead stand idly by and suffer this sacrilege to be continued? (Vanderwerth, 89)

Black Hawk recalled how the Great Spirit had given his people a homeland of 700 miles along the Mississippi River, "composed of some of the finest and best land," which "teemed with buffalo, moose, elk, bear, and deer. . . . Our children were never known to die of hunger, and no stranger, red or white, was permitted to enter our lodges without finding food and rest" (Vanderwerth, 86).

> We always had plenty; our children never cried from hunger, neither were our old people in want. . . . The rapids of Rock River furnished us with an abundance of excellent fish, and the land being very fertile, never failed to produce good crops of corn, beans, pumpkins, and squashes. . . . Our village was healthy and there was no place in the country possessing such advantages, nor hunting grounds better than the ones we had in possession. If a prophet had come to our village in those days and told us that the things were to take place which have since come to pass, none of our people would have believed them. (Stone, *The Life and Times*, 53)

In 1832, Black Hawk's band recrossed the Mississippi westward and sought Winnebago support. Contrary to the prophecies of Neapope and White Cloud, only a few Winnebagos joined them in arms. Black Hawk, his warriors, and their homeless families then attacked some frontier settlements in the area of their former homes in Illinois. In response, the Illinois militia was called out again. One of the new recruits was Abraham Lincoln, a young man at the time. Lincoln's unit was later disbanded after its members took a vote over whether to fight Black Hawk. The vote was a tie. Lincoln later reenlisted, but saw no fighting.

Regular army troops also were brought in to pursue Black Hawk's band, whose members had been forced to subsist on roots in the swamplands near the Mississippi. Several army and militia units caught Black Hawk and his people with their backs to the river. The Indians hoisted a flag of truce, but Gen. Winfield Scott and other officers ignored the appeal for a truce and engaged in a one-sided slaughter that became known as the Battle of Black Ax. General Scott later apologized for the large number of women and children killed by his men. He complained that they could not be distinguished from warriors in the heat of battle.

Black Hawk, Neapope, and other survivors of the battle fled north to a Winnebago village, where they were betrayed for a bribe of twenty horses and $100. Black Hawk was defiant in surrender:

> He has done nothing for which an Indian ought to be ashamed. He has fought for his countrymen . . . against the white men who came, year after year, to cheat them and take away their lands. You know the cause of our making war. It is known to all white men. They ought to be ashamed of it. The white men despise the Indians, and drive them from their homes. But the Indians are not deceitful. . . . The Indian does not tell lies; the Indian does not steal.
>
> An Indian who is as bad as a white man could not live in our nation; he would be put to death and eaten up by the wolves. The white men are bad schoolmasters; they carry false looks, and deal in false actions; they smile in the face of the poor Indian to cheat him; they shake them by the hand to gain their confidence, to make them drunk, to deceive them, and ruin our wives. . . . We lived in danger. We were becoming like them, hypocrites and liars, adulterers, lazy drones, all talkers, and no workers. (Rosenstiel, 118–119)

Black Hawk was led away in chains by Jefferson Davis, who would later become president of the Confederate States of America. After several months' imprisonment, Black Hawk was taken on a tour of several eastern cities; he met with President Andrew Jackson at the White House. Jackson gave Black Hawk a military uniform and a sword, but the aging chief was not mollified. He told Jackson that he had made war to avenge injustice against his people.

Behind Black Hawk's back, Jackson recognized Keokuk as principal chief of the Sauk and Foxes. The news came to Black Hawk and Keokuk as they stood together with army officers. Angry and frustrated, Black Hawk removed his breechclout and slapped Keokuk across the face with it. Black Hawk's body was still lean and firm at the age of sixty, his "hawk-like face with its long nose, luminous dark eyes, and firm mouth. . . . All the hair above his high forehead had been shaved off except for a scalp lock, and by this one knew he was a warrior" (Waters, 69).

Eventually, Black Hawk settled on land governed by Keokuk near Iowaville on the Des Moines River. Shortly before his death, in 1838, Black Hawk acknowledged his defeat without lingering bitterness, telling a Fourth of July gathering near Fort Madison, "A few winters ago, I was fighting against you. I did wrong, perhaps, but that is past; it is buried; let it be forgotten. Rock River is a beautiful country. I liked my towns, my cornfields, and the home of my people. I fought for it. It is now yours. Keep it as we did; it will produce you good crops" (Johansen and Grinde, 40).

REFERENCES

Armstrong, Virginia Irving. *I Have Spoken: American History through the Voices of the Indians*. Athens, OH: Swallow Press, 1984.

Carter, Harvey Lewis. *The Life and Times of Little Turtle: First Sagamore of the Wabash*. Urbana: University of Illinois Press, 1987.

Drake, Benjamin F. *Life of Tecumseh and His Brother the Prophet with a Historical Sketch of the Shawanoe Indians*. Cincinnati, OH: E. Morgan & Co., 1841. Reprint. New York: Arno Press and New York Times, 1969.

Edmunds, R. David. *Tecumseh and the Quest for Indian Leadership*. Boston: Little, Brown, 1984.

Gill, Sam. *Mother Earth: An American Story*. Chicago: University of Chicago Press, 1987.

Hamilton, Charles, ed. *Cry of the Thunderbird*. Norman: University of Oklahoma Press, 1972.

Johansen, Bruce E., and Donald A. Grinde, Jr. *The Encyclopedia of Native American Biography*. New York: Henry Holt, 1997.

Josephy, Alvin, Jr. *The Patriot Chiefs: A Chronicle of American Indian Leadership*. New York: Viking, 1961.

Manypenny, George W. *Our Indian Wards*. Cincinnati: Robert Clarke & Co., 1880.

Porter, C. Fayne. *Our Indian Heritage: Profiles of 12 Great Leaders*. Philadelphia: Chilton, 1964.

Rosenstiel, Annette. *Red and White: Indian Views of the White Man, 1492–1982*. New York: Universe Books, 1983.

Schoolcraft, Henry Rowe. *Travels in the Central Portions of the Mississippi Valley: Comprising Observations on Its Mineral Geography, Internal Resources, and Aboriginal Population*. New York: Collins & Hannay, 1825.

Stone, Jana, ed. *Every Part of This Earth Is Sacred: Native American Voices in Praise of Nature*. San Francisco: HarperCollins, 1993.

Stone, William L. *The Life and Times of Sa-go-ye-wat-ha, or Red-Jacket*. Albany, NY: Munsell, 1866.

Thornbrough, Gayle. *Letter Book of the Indian Agency at Fort Wayne, 1809–1815*. Indianapolis: Indiana Historical Society, 1961.

Tucker, Glenn. *Tecumseh: Vision of Glory*. Indianapolis: Bobbs-Merrill, 1956.
Vanderwerth, W. C., ed. *Indian Oratory*. Norman: University of Oklahoma Press, 1971.
Vecsey, Christopher, and Robert W. Venables, eds. *American Indian Environments: Ecological Issues in Native American History*. Syracuse, NY: Syracuse University Press, 1980.
Waters, Frank. *Brave Are My People: Indian Heroes Not Forgotten*. Santa Fe, NM: Clear Light, 1993.
Winger, Otho. *The Last of the Miamis: Little Turtle*. North Manchester, IN: Lawrence W. Shultz, 1968.

4
THE CHEROKEES, EXILES FROM THEIR OWN LAND

Andrew Jackson, Sequoyah, John Ross, and John Marshall

Mention Andrew Jackson to most Americans, and the phrase "Jacksonian democracy" may spring to mind. To the descendants of Native Americans who survived the period, however, the first comparative analogy may be the Bataan Death March of World War II. Comparisons to Joseph Stalin also spring to some Native American minds when Jackson's name is mentioned. There was very little that was democratic about Jackson's handling of relations with native nations.

President Jackson, Supreme Court chief justice John Marshall, and Cherokee chief John Ross became the three most influential leaders in the debate over removal of the Cherokees from their homeland in present-day Georgia, Alabama, the Carolinas, and Tennessee. I have added Sequoyah as an illustration of the Cherokees' intellect, as the only human being in history to invent an entire written language on his own. He invented it as those who would have his land said that civilization was marching into Cherokee country in their boots, that they would put the land to a higher and better use.

Removal of the Cherokees and several other native nations during the 1830s allowed expansion of Anglo-American populations south and west through parts of Georgia, Alabama, Mississippi, and neighboring states. At roughly the same time, industrial application of Eli Whitney's cotton gin created a mass market in moderately priced cotton clothing. Within a decade after the Trail of Tears, the Cherokees' homeland had been replaced, in large part, by King Cotton and a revival of slavery.

Between one-fourth and one-third of the 16,000 Cherokee people who were removed during 1838 died on the march to "Indian Territory" (now Oklahoma) or shortly thereafter. The Cherokees' name for the march, *nuna-daa-ut-sun'y* "the trail where they cried," provided its English name, the Trail of Tears.

President Jackson, having retired from his army career of Indian fighting, avidly supported the Removal Act of 1830, which led to the Cherokees' Trail of Tears. Ross was the Cherokees' foremost advocate against removal, the man most responsible for taking two major cases to the Supreme Court. Marshall worked the facts of the conflict into legal doctrine that has shaped law regarding Native Americans for more than a century and a half.

The removal of the "civilized tribes" from their homelands is one of the most notable chapters in the history of American land relations. Jackson's repudiation of John Marshall's rulings, which supported the Cherokees' rights to their homelands, comprised contempt of the Supreme Court, an impeachable offense under the Constitution. The subject of impeachment was not seriously raised, however. During the conflict over removal, which continued through most of Jackson's presidency, the entire United States debated assertions of "states' rights" vis-à-vis the federal government and the Cherokees in a prelude to the coming dissolution of the Union during the Civil War less than three decades later. Had Jackson followed Justice Marshall's rulings, the Civil War might have started during the 1830s.

Andrew Jackson (1767–1845)

The explosion of westward migration after roughly 1800 generated enormous profits in land speculation. Fortunes were made in early America not usually by working the land, but by buying early and holding large parcels for sale after demand increased dramatically because of non-Indian immigration. As a frontier lawyer in Tennessee, Andrew Jackson often took his fees in land rather than money, which was as scarce along the frontier as land was plentiful. As a lawyer, Jackson acquired "immense holdings" with which he "began a mercantile establishment and bought a plantation. . . . He built an expensive frame house at a time when most wealthy Tennesseeans still lived in log cabins, and spent large sums on whiskey, horses, and expensive home furnishings imported from Europe" (Rogin, 55).

Jackson quickly acquired more than a hundred slaves, making him one of frontier Tennessee's largest owners of human capital. He traded actively in slaves and occasionally wagered them on horse races in a display of expendable wealth that established power relationships on the frontier. In the realm of intellect, Jackson was not a subtle man. He admired Napoleon Bonaparte to the point of nearly totally ignoring the French emperor's tendencies toward tyranny. Perhaps yielding to the aftertaste of the War of 1812, Jackson sincerely believed that "a republic would spring from the wreck" if Napolean's army would invade England and topple British royalty (Rogin, 73).

Andrew Jackson. Nebraska State Historical Society

Land was the type of wealth with the largest value in the United States during Andrew Jackson's life. Slaves who worked the land of the South—human capital—were the second-largest widely held asset. The entire financial superstructure of stocks, bonds, and various forms of fungible cash so familiar in the late twentieth century lay largely in the future. Michael Paul Rogin wrote of the period:

> Land in America was not only a symbol of national identity, but also—in a more thoroughgoing fashion than anywhere else in the world—a commodity. Malcolm Rohrbough writes, "Land was the nation's most sought-after commodity in the first half-century of the republic, and the effort of men to acquire it was one of the dominant forces of the period." (Rogin, 79)

Andrew Jackson's slaves and plantation placed him squarely within the interests of the races and classes whose members benefited most from Indian removal. Rogin quotes a contemporary source: "Were I to characterize the United States, it would be by the appellation of the land of speculators" (Rogin, 80). Land, once ownership had been wrested from original native owners, became the largest "futures market" available at the time, its value determined by its hoped-for future use in a newly evolving non-Indian society. As a general, and later as president, Jackson represented the values and interests of the land-speculation industry.

Jackson did not seek the removal of the Cherokees and other "civilized tribes"—the Choctaws, Chickasaws, Creeks, and Seminoles—because they did not know how to make productive use of the land. On the contrary, four of the five (the exception being the Seminoles, who had escaped to Florida) were called "civilized tribes" by the immigrants precisely because they were making exactly the kind of progress the Great White Father desired of them: becoming farmers, educating their children, and constituting governments modeled on that of the United States. Immigrants, many of them Scots and Irish, had married into native families. Some of them owned plantations and slaves.

Removal had been proposed for the Cherokees as early as 1802, when Thomas Jefferson was president. During that year, the state of Georgia signed an agreement with the U.S. government (the Cherokees were not consulted) stating its intent to work toward extinguishment of all Cherokee land titles within state borders as early as the land could be "peaceably obtained, and on reasonable terms" (Moulton, 24). By the time President Jackson's Removal Act was passed by Congress, most white Georgians regarded the United States as "seriously delinquent in the bargain" (Moulton, 24).

Before he emerged as an advocate of Indian removal, President Jackson's name had scorched the memories of Native American peoples for decades as an Indian fighter. As a general in the U.S. Army, Jackson blazed a trail of fire throughout the South, refusing to retreat even when his superiors ordered him to relent.

In a battlefield confrontation with William Weatherford's Creeks at Horseshoe Bend, Alabama, Jackson imprisoned assistants who advised retreat. For those who retreated in battle without authorization, the penalty levied by General Jackson was harsher: "Any officer or soldier who flies before the enemy without being compelled to do so by superior force . . . shall suffer death" (Tebbel, 75).

The Creeks under Weatherford fought bitterly, but their clubs and tomahawks could not match the army's bayonets. One of the first soldiers to invade the Creek camp was Ensign Sam Houston, who later would become a hero to settlers in Texas. As Jackson's troops swarmed over the Creek camp, many of the native people ran for their lives. Those who leaped into the river were picked off by army sharpshooters. Jackson had held his initial attack while women and children were ferried across the river to a place that was supposed to spare them the worst of the battle. Several of them died anyway as the frenzy of battle spilled across the landscape. When the battle was over, Jackson's forces had sustained 49 killed and 157 wounded; Cherokees who had fought at his side sustained 18 killed and 36 wounded. The Creeks' original 900-man force suffered about 750 deaths. Weatherford himself was not among the dead. Not expecting Jackson to attack so quickly, he had been elsewhere that day. A few days after the battle, Weatherford surrendered to Jackson personally at the general's tent. By that time, word of Jackson's victory had spread eastward, and he was beginning to build the popular reputation that would later elect him president of the United States.

During July 1814, General Jackson returned to Horseshoe Bend for what was officially called a treaty conference with the defeated Creeks. The general, who never made a point of studying the cultures of the Indians he subjugated, probably did not know that he was compounding the Creeks' humiliation by holding the "treaty" on ground they regarded as sacred.

This meeting was not a treaty conference in a diplomatic sense. It contained none of the diplomatic equity that characterized eighteenth-century frontier diplomacy. The Creeks were summoned to this parley on pain of death by Jackson, who demanded 23 million acres—60 percent of the area that would later become Alabama, as well as nearly a quarter of Georgia. This was half the Creeks' motherland. When the Creek chiefs asked for time to seek concessions and to think the matter over, Jackson demanded an answer and hinted strongly that a negative reaction would be construed as a hostile act against the U.S. Army.

In the meantime, the Creeks were driven into the forests and swamps by white squatters. Their homes were taken, and many starved. A newspaper of the time described their destitution:

> To see a whole people destitute of food—the incessant cry of the emaciated creatures being *bread! bread!* is beyond description distressing. The existence of many of the Indians is prolonged by eating roots and the bark of trees . . . nothing that can afford nourishment is rejected, however offensive it may be. . . . They beg their food from door to door. . . . It is really painful to see the wretched creatures wandering about the streets, haggard and naked. (Brandon, 227)

Although he refused all concessions, Jackson himself wrote to his wife describing the poverty to which they had been reduced: "Could you only see the misery and the wretchedness of those creatures, perishing from want of food and picking up the grains of corn scattered from the mouths of horses" (Tebbel, 181). Alexis de Tocqueville, author of *Democracy in America*, who witnessed portions of the early removals, later told a story not much different from Jackson's:

> At the end of the year 1831, whilst I was on the left bank of the Mississippi, at a place named by the Europeans Memphis, there arrived a numerous band of Choctaws. These savages had left their country, and were endeavoring to gain the right bank of the Mississippi, where they hoped to find an asylum which had been promised them by the American government. It was in the middle of the winter, and the cold was unusually severe; the snow had frozen hard upon the ground, and the river was drifting huge masses of ice. The Indians had their families with them; and they brought in their train the wounded and the sick, with children newly born, and old men upon the verge of death. They possessed neither tents nor wagons, but only their arms and some provisions. I saw them embark to pass the mighty river, and never will that solemn spectacle fade from my remembrance. No cry, no sob was heard amongst the assembled crowd; all were silent. . . . The Indians had all stepped into the bark which was to carry them across, but their dogs remained upon the bank. As soon as these animals perceived that their masters were finally leaving the shore, they set up a dismal howl, and plunging all together into the icy waters of the Mississippi, swam after the boat. (Tocqueville, 435, 436, 448)

Having subdued the Creeks, General Jackson next received orders to quell what the War Department politely called "troubles" in Georgia, principally among the Seminoles. By 1818, Jackson's troops were chasing them into Florida, which was still under Spanish jurisdiction (the area would be ceded to the United States in 1821). Having seized several Spanish forts along the way, Jackson then withdrew. He then endured a debate in Congress over his extranational expedition. Jackson also reaped popular acclaim from expansion-minded Americans that swelled his ambitions for the presidency.

The Seminoles, most of whom were descended from Creeks, had elected to ally with the Spanish rather than the United States, an act of virtual treason to General Jackson. Furthermore, the Seminoles were giving shelter to runaway slaves. In some cases, the Seminoles and the escaped slaves had intermarried over generations. The pretext of Jackson's raid was recovery of "stolen property," runaway slaves. After Florida was purchased from Spain by the United States, slave-hunting vigilantes invaded the area en masse, killing Seminoles as well as blacks. During the 1830s, when President Jackson proposed to remove the Seminoles from Florida to Indian Territory, they refused. Moving deep into the swamps of southern Florida (an area that, ironically, would later be used as a removal destination for other native peoples), the Seminoles fought 1,500 U.S. Army troops to a bloody stalemate during seven years of warfare. They were never defeated and never moved from their new homeland.

After Spain ceded Florida to the United States, General Jackson and other U.S. officials lost any remaining motive for treating the Indians as allies. From then on, they were defined as subjects, to be moved out as Anglo-Americans rushed into the Southeast. Jackson's policy, "move the Indians out," became the national standard after his election as president in 1828. Alabama had already been created in 1819 from Creek and Cherokee territory; Mississippi had been created in 1817 from Choctaw and Chickasaw country. These two states, along with Georgia, passed laws outlawing tribal governments and making Indians subject to state jurisdiction, after which open season was declared on remaining native lands.

All of this violated Indian treaties with the federal government. Confronted with this fact, President Jackson told the Indians that he was unable to stand by the treaties because they raised nettlesome issues of states' rights, an emerging issue in the decades before the Civil War. Instead, Jackson proposed that the Indians be moved westward. At first, the moving of whole tribes was proposed as a voluntary act. In the meantime, land speculators and squatters closed a deadly vise on lands that had been home to the newly "civilized" tribes for thousands of years. One U.S. marshal said that land speculators in Georgia were "some of the most lawless and uncouth men I have ever seen." A federal agent wrote to President Jackson, "A greater mass of corruption, perhaps, has never been congregated in any part of the world" (Brandon, 227).

Because Indians no longer had federal protection from predatory state interests, Indian lands were thrown open to anyone, including dealers in alcohol, who had a heyday taking land in payment for strong whiskey and rum. Actions could be brought against Indians in state courts, and so their land and other belongings often were attached for debt. State laws were enacted barring courts from accepting an Indian's testimony against a white man in court. In practice, then, no claim by a white man, no matter how baseless, could be contested by Indians.

During the summer of 1829, a year after Jackson was elected to office, his advocacy of Indian removal received a boost from the discovery of gold on Cherokee land in the mountains of present-day northern Georgia. The Georgia state legislature quickly passed a law forbidding the Cherokees to prospect or mine gold on their own land, and 3,000 or more European-Americans quickly surged onto Cherokee territory, wrecking the farmsteads and villages that the Indians had so carefully built. As gold seekers swarmed into Cherokee lands, the *Cherokee Phoenix* warned against proposals to remove the Cherokees and the other "civilized tribes" westward to Indian Territory.

Within a few months, on December 19, 1829, the Georgia legislature passed a statute declaring the laws and constitution of the Cherokee Nation null and void. The Georgia statute was written to take effect on June 1, 1830. John Ross had been president of the Cherokee convention that drafted that constitution. In 1827, at about the same time, Jackson wrote, "The first original inhabitants of our forests are incapable of self-government by any of those rules of right which civilization teaches" (Rogin, 213).

When Jackson was finally forced by legal action to address the issue of the treaties, he refused to enforce them because of states' rights. When South Carolina nullified a federal tariff, however, Jackson sent troops into the state and a naval force to anchor off Charleston. He also vowed to execute John C. Calhoun, leader of the nullification movement, on a charge of high treason, along with any member of Congress from South Carolina who had taken part in the nullification proceedings. Even these threats turned out to be more bluster than substance. From President Jackson, however, the Indians got neither bluster nor substance to sustain treaties that had been signed with the stated intention of their being binding forever. These treaties were being trampled within living memory of their signing.

The first few articles of the Cherokee Constitution contained the phrases that Georgia wished to nullify—the Cherokees' right to hold their land inviolate against the federal and neighboring state governments. When it attempted to nullify the Cherokee Constitution, the Georgia legislature also took for granted its legal right to seize Cherokee land because the U.S. government had not fulfilled its promise, made in 1802, when Georgia relinquished its western land claims to the federal government, to remove the Cherokees from lands within Georgia's boundaries. The state legislature stated that it had the right to "extend her authority and laws over her whole territory, and to coerce obedience . . . from all descriptions of people, be they white, red, or black, who may reside within her limits" (Moulton, 33).

By about 1830, white squatters were swarming onto the lands of the five "civilized tribes." Many native people were dispossessed before the removals began. They had the choice of two untenable options: move or be pushed off the land anyway. Before their removal westward, many of the Cherokees, Choctaws, Chickasaws, and Creeks were driven out of their homes and into the forests and swamps by white squatters. Nearly a million

U.S. citizens lived in the Mississippi Valley by about 1830, and the area was acquiring increasing Anglo-American population and political leverage.

Jackson's political opinions reflected national demographics during his presidency. He made a small fortune by buying and selling land on the frontier. Between 1790 and 1840, roughly 4.5 million non-Indians surged across the Appalachians, more than the total population of the United States in 1790 (3.9 million). In 1790, two-thirds of those 3.9 million people lived within fifty miles of the Atlantic Ocean or watercourses leading to it; by 1850, the borders of the United States had reached the Pacific.

During all of Andrew Jackson's life, the explosion of westward migration was a central fact of national life among non-Indians (Rogin, 3–4). President Jackson called Indian removal "the most arduous of my duties" as president of the United States. "I watched over it [removal] with great vigilance," Jackson recalled after he left the presidency (Rogin, 206). Jackson somewhat understated his advocacy of the removals that opened millions of acres for many of the non-Indian voters who swept him into office after a career as a frontier lawyer, plantation owner, and U.S. Army general.

The Cherokees, who resisted removal until 1838, were among the last to be sent packing by Jackson. Between 1814 and 1824, before Jackson was elected president, he already had been the main agent for the United States in eleven treaties of cession. The land involved in these treaties included three-quarters of Alabama and Georgia, one-third of Tennessee, and one-fifth of Mississippi, as well as smaller areas of Kentucky and North Carolina (Rogin, 165).

Historian Ronald N. Satz argues that Jackson

> was not the merciless Indian-hater most historians have portrayed. . . . Old Hickory demonstrated great paternalism in his dealings with the Indians as territorial governor of Florida. He also openly sanctioned Indian-white marriages, adopted an Indian orphan, whom he treated as his own son, and counted hundreds of full-bloods as personal friends. (Satz, 9)

Donald B. Cole suggests in his history of the Jackson presidency that

> the old general did not hate Indians as some scholars have suggested; he had Indian allies in the battle of New Orleans, and he had adopted an Indian child. . . . Yet like many white Americans at the time he considered the Indians inferior and treated them paternalistically. (Cole, 68)

Whatever Jackson's personal feelings toward Native American peoples might have been, as a matter of military strategy and national policy he left little doubt where he was placing his bets for the future of the United

States. In a message to Congress during December 1830, in the midst of the nationwide debate over Indian removal, Jackson maintained:

> What good man would prefer a country covered with forests and ranged by a few thousand savages to our extensive republic, studded with cities, towns, and prosperous farms, embellished with all the improvements which art can devise or industry execute, occupied by more than 12 million happy people, and filled with the blessings of liberty, civilization, and religion? (Satz, 44)

Jackson, who as a general told his troops to root out Indians from their "dens" and kill Indian women and their "whelps," struck the same themes in a slightly more erudite tone as president. In his second annual message to Congress, Jackson reflected on the fact that some white Americans were growing "melancholy" over the fact that the Indians were being driven to their "tomb." These critics must understand, Jackson said, that "true philanthropy reconciles the mind to these vicissitudes as it does to the extinction of one generation to make way for another" (Stannard, 240). Jackson also liked to affect the rhetorical flourish of Native American speaking styles, and after the marching orders had been issued, he painted a verbal picture of an idyllic life for native peoples who were being removed westward:

> Your father has provided a country large enough for all of you. There your white brother will not trouble you. They will have no claim to the land, and you can live upon it, you and all of your children, as long as the grass grows, or the water runs, in peace and plenty. It will be yours forever. (Weeks, 35)

During the Jackson administration, the United States concluded nearly seventy treaties with Native American nations, more than any other presidential administration. The United States acquired more than 100 million acres of Native American land during the years Jackson was in office, in exchange for roughly $68 million (68 cents an acre) and 32 million acres west of the Mississippi River, much of which was subsequently taken as well. Forty-six thousand Indians were compelled to leave their homelands and move west of the Mississippi during the same years (Satz, 97). By such means, observed Tocqueville, "The Americans cheaply acquire whole provinces which the richest sovereigns in Europe could not afford to buy" (Satz, 98).

Jackson thought that Indian treaties were anachronisms, "an absurdity not to be reconciled with the principles of our government" (McNickle, 192). Before his election to the presidency, he elaborated on this opinion in a letter to President James Monroe (another advocate of Indian removal) in 1817:

> The Indians are the subjects of the United States, inhabiting its territory and acknowledging its sovereignty. Then is it not absurd for the sovereign to negotiate by treaty with the subject? I have always thought, that Congress had as much right to regulate by acts of legislation, all Indian concerns as they had of territories, are citizens of the United States and entitled to all the rights thereof, the Indians are subjects and entitled to their protection and fostering care. (McNickle, 1949, 193)

The confusions of convoluted grammar aside, it is not easy to decipher what General Jackson is saying. Is he declaring the Indians to be citizens? Legally, that was not widely the case until a century later. Is he personally abrogating the treaties, which were signed by parties who had addressed each other as diplomatic peers, nation to nation, barely two generations earlier? Whatever the nature of his rhetoric, the actions of the Jackson administration made clear, especially for the Native American peoples of the South, just what Jackson meant by "protection and fostering care."

Sequoyah (1776–1843)

While the state of Georgia and the Removal Act sought to destroy it, the Cherokee Nation was not only the scene of remarkable economic progress, but also the birthplace of the only written language in human history to have been developed by a single person. That person was Sequoyah (from *sikwaji*, meaning "sparrow" or "principal bird" in Cherokee). Sequoyah also was called George Gist, George Guess, and George Guest by some speakers of English.

Sequoyah was born in Taskigi, near Fort Loudon, Tennessee, of a Cherokee mother of the Paint Clan named Wurtee and (some say) the revolutionary soldier and trader Nathaniel Gist, although this lineage is not firmly attested. Clearly, Sequoyah is one of the most remarkable figures in American history. As a boy of twelve living with his mother near Willstown, Alabama, Sequoyah learned to tend dairy cattle and make cheese. He also broke horses, planted corn, and gained skills in hunting and trading furs. During a hunting trip, he sustained an injury to his leg that developed into arthritis. Consequently, Sequoyah walked with a limp and was given the nickname "the Lame One."

Perhaps out of frustration with his disability and its effects on his hunting, Sequoyah developed a drinking habit as a young man. Realizing what alcohol was doing to him, he turned away from drinking and sought a new

---

Sequoyah. Library of Congress, LC-USZC4-2566

way of life. As a result, Sequoyah became an excellent silversmith. In the Creek War of 1813–1814, he served under General Andrew Jackson. In 1815, he married Sarah (Sally), a Cherokee woman, and they had several children.

With a quick mind and active imagination, Sequoyah became intrigued by the "talking leaves," the written language of the whites. By 1809, he had started work on a written version of the Cherokee language using pictorial symbols, but he abandoned this method as untenable after he had created more than 1,000 symbols. Next, Sequoyah reduced the Cherokee language initially to 200 and then finally to 86 characters that represented all the syllables or sounds in the language. He derived the resulting syllabary in part from English, Greek, and Hebrew characters in mission-school books. At first he was thought by some to be engaging in witchcraft. Sequoyah's home was razed on one occasion, and his notes were destroyed.

Sequoyah came to believe that the European immigrants' ability to communicate in writing gave them great power. He looked at writing as a measure of equity with Europeans. Sequoyah completed his writing system during 1821. The same year, before an assembly of Cherokee leaders, he proved the viability of his system by writing messages to his six-year-old daughter that she understood and answered independently.

The Cherokee tribal council formally adopted Sequoyah's syllabary soon after this demonstration. By the mid-1820s, the written language had been taught in eighteen schools to thousands of people. The language invented by Sequoyah (after whom the giant redwoods in California were later named) had no silent letters or ambiguous sounds. Many Cherokees learned its system of writing in three or four days. In recognition of his accomplishments, a bust of Sequoyah was later placed in Statuary Hall of the U.S. Capitol. By 1824, white missionaries had translated parts of the Bible into Cherokee. In 1828, the Cherokee Tribal Council started in northern Georgia a weekly newspaper called the *Cherokee Phoenix and Indian Advocate*. The newspaper, printing bilingual editions in Cherokee and English, enjoyed great success until it was suppressed in 1835 by the state of Georgia for advocating Cherokee rights to their lands in Georgia.

John Ross (1790–1866)

Born along the Coosa River at Tahnoovayah, Georgia (near Lookout Mountain), John Ross also was called Coowescoowe or "the Egret." Ross, who would become the founder of a constitutional government among the Cherokees, was the third of nine children. His father was Daniel Ross, a Scot, and his mother, Mary (Molly) McDonald, was a Scot-Cherokee. As a youth, he was called Tsan-usdi or "Little John."

Although Ross was brought up with other Cherokees, he was educated at home by white tutors and then continued his education at Kingston Academy in Tennessee. Ross always identified himself as Cherokee, although he was only one-eighth native blood; he was married in 1813 to Quatie or Elizabeth Brown Henley, a full-blooded Cherokee. They had five children.

John Ross's association with Andrew Jackson predated the debate over removal. As a young soldier in the U.S. Army, Ross had served under Jackson during the War of 1812. Ross later recalled in a letter to Davy Crockett: "I have known Genl. Jackson from my boyhood—my earliest and warmest friends in Tennessee are generally his advocates—during the late war I held a rank in the Cherokee regiment & fought by his side . . . but it is with deep regret, I say, that his policy toward the aborigines, in my opinion, has been unrelenting, and in effect ruinous" (Moulton, 42).

John Ross. Nebraska State Historical Society

Ross began his political career in 1809 with a mission to the Arkansas Cherokees. By 1811, he was serving as a member of the Standing Committee of the Cherokee Council. In 1813–1814, he was an adjutant in a Cherokee regiment under the command of General Jackson and saw action with other Cherokees at Horseshoe Bend in 1813 against the Red Sticks commanded by Red Eagle (William Weatherford). Ross led a contingent of Cherokee warriors in a diversionary tactic and thus was an important factor in Jackson's victory over the Creeks.

In 1814, shortly after his marriage, Ross established a trading post. In 1817, he became a member of the Cherokee National Council; he served as president of the National Council from 1819 to 1826. In 1820, a republican form of government was instituted by the Cherokee people, similar in structure to that of the United States. As an advocate of education and missionization among his people, Ross thought that the Cherokees might become a state in the Union with its own constitution. When New Echota became the Cherokee national capital in 1826, he moved there with his family. In 1827, Ross became president of the Cherokee constitutional convention that drafted a new constitution. From 1828 to 1839, Ross served as principal chief of the Cherokee Nation under this constitution.

By the time the Removal Act was passed in 1830, the Cherokees had 22,000 cattle, 7,600 horses, 46,000 swine, 2,500 sheep, 762 looms, 2,488 spinning wheels, 172 wagons, 2,943 plows, 10 sawmills, 21 grist mills, 61 blacksmitheries, 18 schools, 8 cotton gins, and 1,300 slaves. All of these things indicated that they led prosperous lives very much like those of the European-American settlers who sought their land.

Removal was never popular among the Cherokees. The federal government's representatives disregarded the majority opinion and relied on the minority Treaty Party to negotiate removal treaties, largely ignoring John Ross's National Party. One proposed treaty, signed during February 1835, was voted down by a substantial number of Cherokees. The result (114 yes, 2,225 no) was a fair indication of the proposal's popularity. Despite the manifest unpopularity of removal, a minority of Cherokee leaders in the Treaty Party, including Elias Boudinot, John Ridge, and several others, journeyed to Washington, D.C., in 1835 to negotiate removal, an initiative that was not sanctioned by the Cherokee government. On December 29, 1835, Boudinot and nineteen other Cherokees signed the Treaty of New Echota, which ceded Cherokee lands as of May 23, 1836. This treaty, called the "Christmas trick" by its many opponents, was ratified by the U.S. Senate in 1836 by a one-vote margin (Cole, 116).

Although Ross continued to protest removal for two more years, the state of Georgia started to coerce the Cherokees into selling their lands for a fraction of their real value. Marauding whites plundered Cherokee homes and possessions and destroyed the *Cherokee Phoenix*'s printing press because the paper opposed removal.

Opposition to removal by a large proportion of the Cherokees continued until the Trail of Tears began. On March 10, 1838, with removal impending, the Cherokees assembled a petition opposing removal with more than 15,000 signatures. While some of the signatures may have been invalid (the entire Cherokee population at the time was about 16,000), the petition demonstrated widespread Cherokee opposition to the terms of the Treaty of New Echota.

John Ross was deeply disappointed by Jackson's unwillingness to enforce the law as interpreted by Chief Justice Marshall. When Ross faced removal from his own plantation-style home, he may have recalled words he had told a delegation of Senecas in 1834:

> We have been made to drink of the bitter cup of humiliation; treated like dogs; our lives, our liberties, the sport of whitemen; our country and the graves of our Fathers torn from us in cruel succession; until driven from river to river, from forest to forest, and thro [*sic*] a period of upwards of two hundred years, rolled back nation upon nation, we find ourselves fugitives, vagrants, and strangers in our own country, and look forward to the period when our descendants will perhaps be totally extinguished by wars, driven at the point of the bayonet into the Western Ocean, or reduced to . . . the condition of slaves. (Moulton, 55)

By 1838, the Cherokees had exhausted all their appeals. As they were being forced to leave their homes, the Cherokees passed a "memorial" that expressed the manifest injustice of their forced relocation:

> The title of the Cherokee people to their lands is the most ancient, pure, and absolute known to man; its date is beyond the reach of human record; its validity confirmed by possession and enjoyment antecedent to all pretense of claim by any portion of the human race.
>
> The free consent of the Cherokee people is indispensable to a valid transfer of the Cherokee title. The Cherokee people have neither by themselves nor their representatives given such consent. It follows that the original title and ownership of lands still rests with the Cherokee Nation, unimpaired and absolute. The Cherokee people have existed as a distinct national community for a period extending into antiquity beyond the dates and records and memory of man. These attributes have never been relinquished by the Cherokee people, and cannot be dissolved by the expulsion of the Nation from its territory by the power of the United States Government. (O'Brien, 57)

The U.S. Army forced Cherokee families into prison camps before their arduous trek westward. As a result of unhealthy and crowded conditions in these hastily constructed stockades, some Cherokees died even before the Trail of Tears began. James Mooney, an ethnologist, later described how the Cherokees were forced from their homes:

> Squads of troops were sent to search out with rifle and bayonet every small cabin hidden away in the coves or by the sides of mountain streams. . . . Families at dinner were startled by the sudden gleam of bayonets in the doorway and rose up to be driven with blows and oaths along the trail that led to the stockade. Men were seized in their fields or going along the road, women were taken from their wheels, and children from their play. (Van Every, 242)

A U.S. Army private who witnessed the Cherokee removal wrote:

> I saw the helpless Cherokee arrested and dragged from their homes, and driven by bayonet into the stockades. And in the chill of a drizzling rain on an October morning I saw them loaded like cattle or sheep into wagons and started toward the west. . . . Chief Ross led in prayer, and when the bugle sounded and wagons started rolling many of the children . . . waved their little hands goodbye to their mountain homes. (Worcester, 67)

More than 4,000 Cherokees died of exposure, disease, and starvation, about a quarter of the total Cherokee population. Quatie, Ross's wife, was among the victims of this forced emigration. After removal, the miserable conditions continued. Many Cherokees died after they arrived in Indian Territory as epidemics and food shortages plagued the new settlements. An observer in Kentucky described the Cherokees' midwinter march to Arkansas:

> Even aged females, apparently nearly ready to drop into the grave, were travelling with heavy burdens attached to their backs, sometimes on frozen ground, and sometimes on muddy streets, with no covering for their feet. (Collier, 124)

On the subject of the Cherokees' removal, Ralph Waldo Emerson weighed in solidly with John Ross. Emerson wrote to President Martin Van Buren on April 23, 1838, about the impending Trail of Tears:

> A crime is projected that confounds our understandings by its magnitude—a crime that really deprives us as well as the Cherokee of a country, for how could we call the conspiracy that should crush these poor Indians our government, or the land that was cursed by their parting and dying imprecations our country, any more? You, sir, will bring down that renowned chair in which you sit into infamy if your seal is set to this instrument of perfidy; and the name of this nation, hitherto the sweet omen of religion and liberty, will stink to the world. (Moquin, 105)

In his letter to Van Buren, Emerson seemed concerned less with Indian suffering or a sense of injustice than with a belief that their removal would stain his image of the presidency and the national history of the United States. Portions of the same letter to Van Buren contain assumptions that might have pleased Andrew Jackson, had Emerson's letter been addressed to him. Emerson spoke of the Cherokees' frame homes, grist mills, farms, government, and written language as "painful labors of these red men to redeem their own race from the doom of eternal inferiority . . . to borrow and domesticate in the tribe the arts and customs of the Caucasian race" (Black and Weidman, 272).

Despite the cruelty of the marches they were forced to endure, as well as the death, disease, and deprivation that dogged their every step, the surviving Cherokees, with Ross again in the lead, quickly set about rebuilding their communities. Much as they had in the Southeast, the Cherokees, Creeks, and others built prosperous farms and towns, passed laws, and set about rather self-consciously civilizing themselves once again. John Ross set about recreating a new Cherokee homeland with the same energy that had characterized his battle against removal.

John Marshall (1755–1835)

President Jackson's adamant support of Indian removal placed him on a direct constitutional collision course with Chief Justice John Marshall, who was in the process of evolving legal doctrines vis-à-vis Native American land rights on which he had been working before Jackson was elected. The "Cherokee cases" that came before Chief Justice Marshall's U.S. Supreme Court between 1823 and 1832 displayed in broad and emphatic relief how closely much of early-nineteenth-century American life was connected to the land-speculation machine that helped propel westward movement.

Marshall's legal opinions outlining Native Americans' status in the U.S. legal system took shape while he was defining the Supreme Court's place within U.S. political society as a whole. When Marshall became chief justice during 1801, the Supreme Court was little more than a clause in the Constitution. For thirty-four years as chief justice, Marshall played a major role in defining the Court as an institution. By the time Marshall wrote the Supreme Court's opinion in *Worcester v. Georgia* (1832), he had been chief justice since 1801, nearly a third of a century.

Marshall was born in a log cabin in the deep woods of the Blue Ridge foothills, the southern part of present-day Fauquier County, Virginia, on September 24, 1755. His father, Thomas Marshall, was a close friend of George Washington. Washington provided some of the books that Mar-

---

Chief Justice John Marshall. Prints File, Special Collections Department, University of Virginia Library

shall read as a young man who was being raised on a small, usually impoverished backwoods farm.

Thomas Marshall moved to a new farm when John was a boy, as the material circumstances of the family improved. Thomas loved books, and as soon as his circumstances allowed, he subscribed to the first American editions of the Blackstone law dictionaries, an outline of the growing legal infrastructure of the United States. Young John devoured the law books eagerly.

John admired his father's values, among them his patriotic fervor. Thomas was a supporter of Patrick Henry when the American Revolution began, and John marched away to join the Minutemen. By the age of nineteen, he was commanding a company of Minutemen, with the rank of lieutenant. Marshall's company endured the famous brutal winter of 1777 with George Washington at Valley Forge.

After the Revolution, Marshall began to prepare for a career in law, his intellectual passion since childhood. Marshall's career in public service spanned the birth of the United States as a nation. In 1782, at the age of twenty-seven, he was elected to the Virginia House of Delegates, six years after the Declaration of Independence was first posted. In 1801, weeks after his own installation as chief justice, Marshall swore in Thomas Jefferson as president. He served longer in the position of chief justice than any other person in the history of the United States. Charles F. Hobson wrote that Marshall "invented American constitutional law" (Hobson, 212).

In legal analysis, the term "Marshall Trilogy" is used to describe as a group Chief Justice John Marshall's rulings in *Johnson v. McIntosh, Cherokee Nation v. Georgia*, and *Worcester v. Georgia*. In these three cases, Marshall developed legal doctrines that defined the relationship of the United States, the individual states, and Native American nations. In these opinions, according to legal scholar Charles F. Wilkinson, "Marshall conceived a model that can be described broadly as calling for largely autonomous tribal governments subject to an overriding federal authority but essentially free of state control" (Wilkinson, 24).

The Marshall Trilogy is important in American Indian law because the key precepts of Marshall's three opinions have been interpreted by lawyers, judges, legal scholars, and government officials in many different ways. The Bureau of Indian Affairs, for example, used the words "dependent," "pupilage," and "ward" to construct a social and political control system in which Indians have been regarded legally as incompetents or children would be in other social and legal contexts.

Johnson v. McIntosh is notable as the first case to express a relationship between the Federal government and Indian nations.

In *Cherokee Nation v. Georgia*, the Cherokees sued in federal court under a clause in the Constitution (Article III, Section 2) that allows foreign citizens or states to seek legal redress against states in the Union. In this case, the Cherokees were suing as an independent nation seeking redress because the state of Georgia had extended its power over Cherokee territory, had extinguished the authority of the Cherokee government, and had executed one of its citizens.

Marshall found, without doubt, that the Cherokees had a legal relationship with the federal government through treaties; Georgia's assertion of unilateral control was said to be "repugnant to the said treaties, and . . . therefore unconstitutional and void" (Baker, 743). Writing for the majority in *Cherokee Nation v. Georgia*, Marshall skirted the issue by deciding that the Cherokees were not an independent country, but possessed a limited sovereignty: "They may, more correctly, perhaps be denominated domestic dependent nations. . . . Their relation to the United States resembles that of a ward to his guardian." Marshall thus threw the case out of court, deciding that the Cherokees had no grounds on which to sue under the Constitution. His phrases, interpreted by the Bureau of Indian Affairs, became the legal justification for the colonial system that was being imposed on Indians as Anglo-American settlement exploded across North America in the nineteenth century.

Marshall agonized over the proper legal relationship between the native peoples of America and the European-American regime that was pushing them aside. By 1832, the chief justice seems to have reconciled the situation in his mind by challenging the legal rationale of removal in favor of the Cherokees. In *Worcester v. Georgia*, Marshall held unconstitutional the imprisonment by Georgia of two missionaries, one of whom was Samuel Worcester, who had been active in defense of Cherokee rights.

Samuel Worcester, whose name became affixed to what is perhaps the best-known case in American Indian law, did more than establish a mission in Cherokee country. He also was something of a community activist among the Cherokees. Worcester collaborated on a translation of the Bible into Cherokee with Stephen Foreman and worked to procure type fonts and a press for the *Cherokee Phoenix*. He was the person who gave the newspaper its name. When the *Cherokee Phoenix* began publishing at New Echota on February 21, 1828, Worcester also was a major editorial force. The *Cherokee Phoenix* continued to publish as pressure for removal grew. It shared news reports with a hundred other newspapers, but shortages of ink and illnesses of printers and editors caused publication to become erratic. Georgia officials made obvious their desire to close the paper. The last issue of the newspaper was published on May 31, 1834. In 1835, the Georgia Guard confiscated its press.

The factual context of *Worcester v. Georgia* was established when three non-Indian missionaries living on Cherokee territory refused to swear an oath of allegiance to the state of Georgia. Georgia took its loyalty oath very seriously; the penalty for refusal was "not less than four years hard labor at the penitentiary" (Baker, 740). Worcester was one of ten white men indicted for what was called "a high crime . . . [of] residing within the limits of the Georgia Charter without taking the oath of allegiance" (Baker, 740). Eight of the men accepted pardons from the state. Two men refused the conditions of pardon: Worcester and another missionary, Elizur Butler, both of whom appealed to the Supreme Court.

State guards arrested the two men. They were chained to a wagon and forced to walk more than twenty miles to jail. Two Methodist preachers who objected to the brutality that accompanied the arrests also were chained and taken to jail. Worcester and Butler were tried, convicted, and sentenced to four years of hard labor at the Georgia state penitentiary. After the U.S. Supreme Court ordered the Georgia Superior Court to reverse its original decision and release Worcester, officials in Georgia flouted the ruling by holding Worcester in jail for a year after Marshall had ruled that he should be released.

By 1832, when he ruled in *Worcester*, Chief Justice Marshall was seventy-seven years of age and increasingly frail. Despite difficulties with his voice, he read the entire twenty-eight-page decision before the court. The renowned English feminist Harriet Martineau sketched the scene:

> I watched the assemblage when the Chief Justice was delivering the judgment . . . judges on either hand, gazing at him more like learners than associates. . . . These men absorbed in what they are listening to, thinking neither of themselves nor each other, while they are watched by the group of idlers and listeners. Among them the newspaper corps. The dark Cherokee chiefs, the stragglers from far West, the gay ladies in their waving plumes, and the members of either [H]ouse that have stepped in to listen; all these I have seen constitute the silent assemblage, while the mild voice of the aged Chief Justice sounded through the court. (Smith, 518)

If President Jackson did not actually say, "John Marshall has made his decision, now let him enforce it," his failure to protect Cherokee sovereignty with military force showed that "he certainly meant it," according to Leonard Baker, a biographer of Marshall (Baker, 746). When President Jackson ignored Chief Justice Marshall's opinion in *Worcester v. Georgia*, he also was showing his frontier constituencies that he supported a belief popular among states' rights advocates of the time: that the Supreme Court should be stripped of its power to review the rulings of state courts. Marshall repudiated the states' rights advocates' belief that Section 25 of the Judiciary Act of 1789 prohibited the Supreme Court from hearing the case because Section 25 was an invalid use of federal power over state courts. A bill that would have repealed Section 25 of the Judiciary Act, which gives the U.S. Supreme Court power to rule on appeals from state courts, was debated on the floor of the House of Representatives, voted on, and defeated on January 29, 1831.

Purported limits on the Supreme Court's authority based on states' rights stirred substantial controversy during the 1830s; when *Worcester v. Georgia* was heard before the Court on February 20, 1832, fifty members of the House of Representatives (about a quarter of that body) were in attendance. Marshall stepped into the maw of the states' rights firestorm by turning aside a ruling of the Georgia Superior Court. Jackson, in turn, all but created his own law by ignoring Marshall's ruling.

The state of Georgia, bolstering its case for removal of the Cherokees, pointed to a clause in the U.S. Constitution that says that a state may not be established within the borders of another state. Chief Justice Marshall's counterclaim, also based on the Constitution's own words, was that the founding charter of the United States

> confers on Congress the powers of war and peace; of making treaties; and of regulating commerce with foreign nations, and among the several states, and with the Indian tribes. These powers comprehend all that is required for the regulation of our intercourse with the Indians. They are not limited by any restrictions on their free actions; the shackles imposed on this power, in the confederation, are discarded.

The Constitution, Marshall ruled,

> by declaring treaties already made, as well as those to be made, to be the supreme law of the land, has adopted and sanctioned the previous treaties with the Indian nations, and, consequently, admits their rank among those powers who are capable of making treaties. (Baker, 744)

In *Worcester v. Georgia*, Marshall applied a standing rule of international law: "[T]he settled doctrine of the law of nations is that a weaker power does not surrender its independence—its right to self-government—by associating with a stronger, and taking its protection." Marshall concluded that Georgia's law interfered forcibly with the relations between the United States and the Cherokee Nation, "the regulation of which according to the settled principles of our constitution, are committed exclusively to the government of the United States."

The *Worcester* decision was one of the most emphatic rulings of Justice Marshall's judicial career. It was not at all equivocal. Marshall found that Worcester had entered the Cherokee Nation under protection of the federal government, and that the government had an obligation to protect him. The decision concluded:

> It is the opinion of this court that the judgement of the superior court for the county of Gwinnett, in the State of Georgia, condemning Samuel A. Worcester to hard labor in the penitentiary of the State of Georgia for four years, was pronounced by that court under color of a law which is void, as being repugnant to the Consti-

tution, treaties, and laws of the United States, and ought, therefore, to be reversed and annulled. (Baker, 745)

Chief Justice Marshall's opinions regarding the land rights of Native Americans were nearly the opposite of Jackson's. When the question of removal was raised in the Supreme Court in 1831 and 1832, Marshall was already on record in *Johnson v. McIntosh* as believing that Indians had a legal right to their homelands, protected by federal law. These rights included notions of property ownership that are familiar to non-Indians, as well as an as-yet-undefined right to national sovereignty. What remained was a definition of these rights within the context of a continent changing hands by legal and illegal means as non-Indians surged westward during the early nineteenth century. In 1828, Marshall had written in a private letter that the time had come to give full indulgence to those principles of humanity and justice which ought always to govern our conduct toward the aborigines when this course can be pursued without exposing ourselves to the most afflicting calamities. . . . oppression . . . of . . . a helpless people depending on our magnanimity and justice for the preservation of their existence, impresses a deep stain on the American character. (Hobson, 174)

While Marshall's opinions were ignored by President Jackson, they shaped the relationship of the United States to Native American nations within its borders to the end of the twentieth century. The 1934 Indian Reorganization Act and legislative efforts promoting self-determination after the 1960s were based in part on Marshall's opinion in *Cherokee Nation v. Georgia* that the rights of "discovery" did not extinguish the original inhabitants' "legal as well as . . . just claim to retain possession [of their land] and to use it according to their own jurisdiction."

Marshall, as has been previously noted, defined Indian nations not as totally sovereign, nor as colonies, but as "domestic dependent nations." Many of Marshall's actual definitions of these key words may have been lost in interpretation during subsequent decades. The concept of "dependency," for example, was explained by Henry Wheaton, a friend of Marshall and a longtime reporter of the Supreme Court, as relating to international law. According to Wheaton, Marshall did not imply Indian inferiority (or a need for social and political control) in his use of the phrase "domestic dependent nations." Instead, he meant to stress the semisovereign nature of Native American nations and the need to gain consent of both parties before fundamentally changing a treaty relationship.

The doctrine of wardship as it has been applied to Native Americans often is said to have grown out of Marshall's rulings, although he may not have intended such a conception. As Felix Cohen wrote:

[T]he doctrine of Indian wardship arose out of a misunderstanding of Chief Justice Marshall's holding, in 1831, that an Indian tribe was not a foreign nation but was

> rather a "domestic dependent nation," and that its position toward the United States resembles that of a ward toward a guardian. This did not mean that an Indian tribe is a ward; even less did it mean that an individual Indian is a ward. But the opinion and several later opinions popularized the term wardship. (Cohen, 331)

A concept of wardship has been used since the mid-nineteenth century to construct for American Indians a cradle-to-grave social and political control system that was described by Cohen:

> Under the reign of these magic words ["wardship" and "trust"] nothing Indian was safe. The Indian's hair was cut, his dances forbidden, his oil lands, timber lands, and grazing lands were disposed of by Indian agents and Indian commissioners for whom the magic word "wardship" always made up for lack of statutory authority. (Cohen, 131–132)

The Bureau of Indian Affairs was initially established to hold Indians' land and resources "in trust," following Marshall's phrasing in ways he may not have intended. Wardship status rationalized the establishment of Indian reservations and schools to assimilate Native Americans into mainstream U.S. culture.

There is in Marshall's rulings no prescription for a cradle-to-grave system to micromanage Indians' lives. Marshall was concerned with the rights of a body of people, a nation, to coexist with a stronger adjacent state. Marshall wrote that the Cherokees lived in "a distinct political society separated from others, capable of managing its own affairs and governing itself" (Hobson, 175).

The basic legal questions raised by Marshall have been fundamental to the relations of Native Americans and later immigrants since he considered them. The proper relations of state and native political power continue to be redefined with each subsequent Supreme Court. All of the decisions cite Chief Justice Marshall's rulings.

REFERENCES

Baker, Leonard. *John Marshall: A Life in Law*. New York: Macmillan, 1974.

Black, Nancy B., and Bette S. Weidman, eds. *White on Red: Images of the American Indian*. Port Washington, NY: Kennikat Press, 1976.

Brandon, William. *The American Heritage Book of Indians*. New York: Dell, 1964.

Cohen, Felix. *The Legal Conscience: Selected Papers of Felix S. Cohen*. Ed. Lucy Kramer Cohen. New Haven, CT: Yale University Press, 1960.

Cole, Donald B. *The Presidency of Andrew Jackson*. Lawrence: University Press of Kansas, 1993.

Collier, John. *Indians of the Americas*. New York: New American Library, 1947.

Hobson, Charles F. *The Great Chief Justice: John Marshall and the Rule of Law.* Lawrence: University Press of Kansas, 1996.

McNickle, D'Arcy. *They Came Here First: The Epic of the American Indian.* Philadelphia: J. B. Lippincott Co., 1949.

Moulton, Gary E. *John Ross: Cherokee Chief.* Athens: University of Georgia Press, 1978.

O'Brien, Sharon. *American Indian Tribal Governments.* Norman: University of Oklahoma Press, 1989.

Rogin, Michael Paul. *Fathers and Children: Andrew Jackson and the Subjugation of the American Indian.* New York: Alfred A. Knopf, 1975.

Satz, Ronald N. *American Indian Policy in the Jacksonian Era.* Lincoln: University of Nebraska Press, 1975.

Smith, Jean Edward. *John Marshall: Definer of a Nation.* New York: Henry Holt, 1996.

Stannard, David. *American Holocaust: Columbus and the Conquest of the New World.* Oxford: Oxford University Press, 1992.

Tebbel, John W. *The Compact History of the Indian Wars.* New York: Hawthorn Books, 1966.

Tocqueville, Alexis de. *Democracy in America.* Trans. Henry Reeve. New York: Century Co., 1898.

Van Every, Dale. *Disinherited: The Lost Birthright of the American Indian.* New York: William Morrow & Co., 1966.

Weeks, Philip. *Farewell, My Nation: The American Indian and the United States, 1820–1890.* Arlington Heights, IL: Harlan Davidson, 1990.

Wheaton, Henry. *Elements of International Law.* Boston: Dana, 1866.

Wilkinson, Charles F. *American Indians, Time, and the Law: Native Societies in a Modern Constitutional Democracy.* New Haven, CT: Yale University Press, 1987.

Worcester, Donald F., ed. *Forked Tongues and Broken Treaties.* Caldwell, ID: Caxton Printers, 1975.

5
REFUGEES IN THEIR OWN LAND

Chief Joseph, Oliver O. Howard, Sitting Bull, George Armstrong Custer, Red Cloud, and Standing Bear (Ponca)

After George Armstrong Custer's debacle at the Battle of the Little Bighorn during the middle of 1876, the U.S. Army wiped the boy general's shame from its collective brow by swiftly subjugating the last independent Native Americans. Any sign of independence, such as reluctance to report to Indian agencies to which the government had assigned them, invoked, for the army, a self-defined invitation to forceful subjugation on a wartime footing. During the five years after the Battle of the Little Bighorn, four native leaders—Chief Joseph, Sitting Bull, Red Cloud, and the Ponca Standing Bear—became refugees from their own lands rather than submit to authority they believed to be illegitimate. The long marches of the Hunkpapas, Nez Perces, and Poncas electrified the non-Indian public during the same years and energized a vibrant debate (which is described in Chapter 7) regarding the future of Native Americans after the Anglo-American conquest of the land was completed. I have chosen to counterpoise the lives of the four native leaders with reflections on the lives and thoughts of two of the military leaders charged with curtailing their freedom. One of them, George Armstrong Custer, was a no-holds-barred racist. The other, Oliver O. Howard, prized his friendships with native leaders, especially Chief Joseph.

Chief Joseph the Younger (1841–1904) and Oliver O. Howard (1830–1909)

The Nez Perce territory—central Idaho, northeastern Oregon, and southeastern Washington on present-day maps—was traversed by the Lewis and Clark expedition during the late summer of 1805. Stopped by mountain snows, Lewis and Clark spent several weeks in the Nez Perces' Wallowa Valley and found them to be excellent hosts and expert marksmen. "Nez Perce" ("pierced nose" in French) was a name given by French traders to a people whom they erroneously thought pierced their noses. The Nez Perces call themselves Ni Mii Pu, meaning "the people."

The Wallowa Valley and surrounding highlands, the homeland of the Nez Perce band led by Old Joseph and his son, whom the immigrating whites called Chief Joseph, covered about 3,000 square miles in present-day northeastern Oregon. Most of the area is high plateau that is very well suited for pasturing the Nez Perces' prized horse herds. As farming country, the Wallowa Valley left much to be desired:

> [L]ittle of it is good for farming. A large part of it is mountainous, and another large part is knifed by a network of lava-rimmed canyons that are among the deepest and most rugged in the world. Even its most habitable portion, the relatively

---

Chief Joseph (Younger). National Anthropological Archives, Smithsonian Institution; Oliver Otis Howard. Nebraska State Historical Society

flat valley drained by the meandering Wallowa River and its feeder streams has an altitude ranging from approximately 2,500 feet to above 4,000 feet, limiting the growth of crops to a short season. But the grasses in the canyons and along the great expanse of plateau that borders them are rich, and nowhere in the United States, perhaps, is there better natural grazing country. (Josephy, 437)

During the first decades of the nineteenth century, the Nez Perces experienced a flush of prosperity as the fur trade and horse-trading networks enriched them with a heretofore-unknown variety of imported manufactured goods. Measured in horses, the Nez Perces were among the richest of Native Americans.

By the late 1840s, a trickle of nonnative immigrants became a flood. Gradually, after 1850, the Nez Perces' prosperous economic system dissolved until, barely a quarter of a century later, they were reduced to widespread poverty and homelessness, their domestic, land-based economy having been destroyed.

The Nez Perces had occupied this valley as far into the past as their collective memory recalled. Like many Native American peoples in the Northwest, they had little organized agriculture and depended for their subsistence on hunting, fishing, and gathering. The Nez Perces' hunting and gathering range was extended by their utilization of horses, which had diffused north and westward from the provinces of New Spain during the seventeenth century. The horse enabled the Nez Perces to hunt buffalo on the high plains of eastern Montana. By the end of that century, guns had reached the Nez Perces, at about the same time that the fur trade began to unfurl its mercantilist fingers in the valley of the Wallowa.

The early life of Tuekakas, Chief Joseph's father, portended little of the turmoil that would engulf the Wallowa (Wallamwatkins) band of Nez Perces whom he led at his death. He was born near Wawawai on the Snake River. His father was a Cayuse chief, and his mother was a Nez Perce. During Tuekakas' childhood, his family migrated around the inland Northwest, living a generally peaceful life. In 1836, they greeted missionaries Henry Spalding and his wife. In 1839, Spalding gave Tuekakas the Christian name Joseph, which was passed to his son. As they aged, the two men came to be known to immigrants as Old Joseph (or Joseph the Elder) and Young Joseph (or Joseph the Younger).

The Nez Perces became steadfast U.S. allies as settlers moved into the Pacific Northwest in the face of opposition from Great Britain. They even rescued a body of U.S. troops from attack by other Indians in 1858. Nevertheless, during the same year, the United States signed a treaty with Nez Perce "treaty commissioners" who did not represent the entire nation. Without the consent of the Nez Perces who lived there, the treaty ceded the Nez Perces' Wallowa Valley to the United States and opened it for non-Indian settlement. The elder Joseph protested that the treaty was illegal, a violation of the Treaty of Walla Walla that had been signed with Washington territorial governor Isaac Stevens barely three years earlier.

This betrayal embittered Old Joseph. He tore up his copy of the agreement and his New Testament. The Nez Perces of Joseph's band remained in the valley despite the treaty. They continued to tend their large herds of prize horses as growing numbers of whites moved in around them. At first, the Nez Perces welcomed the settlers, figuring, as young Joseph remarked later, that there was plenty of land for all, and the Indians would learn useful things from the whites. The situation was complicated in 1860 by the discovery of gold in small amounts. This was not a large gold strike in a continental context, just large enough to bring to the Nez Perces' valley several thousand non-Indians with no enduring stake in the land, whose presence sparked several violent incidents.

Joseph the Elder died in 1871, passing leadership of the Wallowa Nez Perce band to Hin-mah-too-yah-laht-ket ("thunder rolling over the mountains"), whom English speakers later called Chief Joseph. The younger Joseph was about thirty years of age at the time. He was

> a large, heavily built man six feet, two inches tall, with handsome, noble features . . . [who] spoke intelligently and with moderation; he argued, but he was patient and kind; he seemed to believe that the day of Indian war against the whites was over, and that the two races must somehow try to find ways to settle their problems peacefully. (Josephy, 441, 443)

On his deathbed, Old Joseph asked his son never to sell the Nez Perces' homeland, an admonition that led the younger Joseph to resist removal to a reservation even when his dwindling band was being pursued about 1,500 miles through the northern Rockies and adjoining high plains during 1877.

As Young Joseph assumed leadership of his Nez Perce band, government emissaries continued to press the Nez Perces to move to a reservation where they would be allotted plots of land for each head of a household (defined in the European sense). The sizes of allotments (160 acres for a head of household; 80 acres for an individual) had been designed for farming in the humid east. Allotted lands were too small to run the prized blue Appaloosas that the Nez Perces used for hunting and war.

When General Oliver O. Howard told Old Joseph's band of Nez Perces that they had to move onto a reservation because other bands of the same people had signed a treaty, Young Joseph told a story:

> Suppose a white man should come to me and say, "Joseph, I like your horses and I want to buy them." I say to him, "No, my horses suit me, I will not sell them." Then he goes to my neighbor and says to him: "Joseph has some good horses. I want to buy them, but he refuses to sell." My neighbor answers, "Pay me the money and I will sell you Joseph's horses." The white man returns to me and says, "Joseph,

I have bought your horses, and you must let me have them." If we sold our land[s] to the government, this is the way they were bought. (Brown, 35)

Treaty negotiations grew testy as the government continued to pressure the Nez Perces to leave their valley. At a meeting with General Howard and several other Nez Perce leaders, Joseph expressed muted astonishment at Howard's arrogance in demanding that Joseph's band of Nez Perces move to a reservation designated by the government: "I do not believe that the Great Spirit gave one kind of men the right to tell another kind of men what they should do" (Moquin, 242). Howard absorbed that statement without complaint, but he bristled at a sharper retort by another Nez Perce, Tuhulkutsut, after Howard had told him to shut up and get on with the business at hand:

Who are you, that you ask us to talk, and then tell me I sha'n't [*sic*] talk. Are you the Great Spirit? Did you make the world? Did you make the sun? Did you make the rivers to run for us to drink? Did you make the grass to grow? Did you make all these things, that you talk to us as though we were boys? If you did, then you have the right to talk as you do. (Moquin, 242)

After Tuhulkutsut told General Howard that the earth could not be sold, he rejected the entire concept of ceding land for money and annuities: "You white people get together, measure the earth, and then divide it. . . . Part of the Indians gave up their land. I never did. The earth is part of my body, and I never gave up the earth" (Josephy, 489). Tuhulkutsut at about this time was described by one Anglo-American observer as "broad-shouldered, deep-chested, thick-necked, five feet ten in height [with] a heavy gutteral voice [who] betrayed in every word a strong and settled hatred of all Caucasians . . . an ugly, obstinate savage . . . [and] a cross-grained growler" (Brown, 83). Tuhulkutsut also was a *too-at* (priest, or holy man) in the Dreamer religion—the worst kind of heathen in General Howard's eyes.

Howard repeated his demand that Young Joseph's people move to the reservation set out for them at Lapwai, Idaho, by the government. His demand drew a look of contempt from Tuhulkutsut, who growled in a low voice, "What person pretends to divide the land and put me on it?" Howard straightened his back and demanded, in return, "Then you do not propose to comply with the orders of the government?" "So long as the earth keeps me, I want to be left alone," retorted Tuhulkutsut. "You are trifling with the law of the earth" (Josephy, 490).

Howard, losing his temper, said that if the Nez Perces did not move to the reservation peacefully, troops would compel them. Tuhulkutsut bristled at the hint of coercion and repeated, "I am not going to a reservation." Howard, appearing flustered, told Tuhulkutsut that if he did not move to the reservation, "You will have to be taken to Indian Territory. . . . I will send you there if it takes years and years." Howard then ordered a sentry to forcibly remove Tuhulkutsut to detention in an army guardhouse. Tuhulkutsut offered no resistance (Josephy, 490).

According to some reports, Anglo-American settlement pressure in the Wallowa Valley was waning when the army tried to force Joseph's Nez Perces out of it. The whole episode may have revolved more around the pride of a few high-ranking Anglo-Americans, Isaac Stevens in particular, than settlement pressure on the land, which remains sparsely populated even at the end of the twentieth century. In 1875, two years before the Nez Perces' Long March, Capt. Steven Whipple passed through the Wallowa Valley and later wrote to the secretary of war that no one seemed to want the land except its original inhabitants. "People were disappointed to learn that it was not to be taken for an Indian reservation," wrote Whipple. "One man regretted [this decision] because it would have given him a chance to sell his land to the government" (Chalmers, 27). Whipple found the Nez Perces in the valley to be "proud-spirited, self-supporting, and intelligent" (Chalmers, 27) and, given experience with the highland environment, better able to make use of the valley than outsiders. The land was capable of supporting horses, wrote Whipple, in an environment in which domesticated cattle would die.

Even General Howard, who put so much effort into pressuring the Wallowa Nez Perces to move, had expressed an attitude toward his assignment that was less than enthusiastic:

> So much for our ideas of justice. First, we acknowledge and confirm by treaty to Indians a sort of title to vast regions. Afterward, we continue, in a strictly legal manner, to do away with both the substance and the shadow of the title. Wiser heads than Joseph's have been puzzled by this manner of balancing the scales. (Brown, 42)

Howard also complained that some of the frontiersmen who had volunteered to serve in local militias actually had been thieves hatching plans to steal the Nez Perces' large herds of prized horses: "One band of men from Wash[ington] Terr[itory] who represented themselves as thirsting for Nez Perce gore turned out to be a gang of organized horse thieves" (Brown, 67).

Despite losing his temper with Tuhulkutsut, Howard was widely known as one of the army's more level-headed generals. Howard and Chief Joseph even cultivated a kind of friendship and appeared together, smiling, in photographs after the Long March.

Howard had been born on November 8, 1830, in rural Maine, northwest of Augusta, along the Androscoggin River. Young Oliver Otis Howard, who was named after his mother's father, lived his first nine years on a farm belonging to his father and grandfather. He attended local schools and did well in his studies. His father died when Howard was ten years of age.

Eliza Howard, Oliver O. Howard's mother, had three boys to raise and married another farmer in Leeds, Colonel John Gilmore, a year after her husband died. Oliver, who was called "Otis" by his friends, attended several schools in Maine, often in the care of different family members. One of his hosts was his uncle John Otis, a man of means who later was elected to represent Maine in the Thirty-First U.S. Congress. Oliver was admitted to the freshman class of Bowdoin College, near Leeds, in September 1846. Once more, young Howard excelled at academics, standing near the top of his class.

While attending Bowdoin, Howard accepted an offer to enroll in the West Point Military Academy. Thus began a life of service in the officer corps of the U.S. Army. After his graduation from West Point, Howard ascended ranks in the army before and during a distinguished career as a high-ranking battlefield officer of the Union Army in the Civil War, in which he earned a reputation for bravery and lost his right arm at the Battle of Fair Oaks.

From the end of the Civil War until 1872, General Howard was commissioner of the Bureau of Refugees, Freedmen, and Abandoned Lands, commonly called the "Freedmen's Bureau," a government agency designed to help former slaves make the transition to independent life. Like Richard Henry Pratt, also a high-ranking army officer, Howard was a fervent advocate of assimilative education for blacks and Native Americans. He played an important role in founding Howard University, which is arguably the most prominent black university in the United States. Howard served as its president from 1869 to 1874. After that, he was assigned by the army full-time to the dying embers of the Plains Indian wars as commander of the army's Department of the Columbia at Fort Vancouver.

Howard was a devoutly religious and intensely moral man, "the Christian general" in popular discourse. His long association with frontier campaigns from Florida to the Pacific Northwest taught him that the cause of conflicts over land most often rested with the transgressions of the immigrants, not the Native American inhabitants. The root cause of conflict, he said, was "the refusal of whites to recognize Indian occupancy of land" (Howard, xv). Like many other nonnative "friends of the Indian" at this time, Howard believed that native people would be best served by giving up their cultures and assimilating into the expanding United States as individuals, shorn of their tribal identities. He supported government-issue education, conversion to his beloved Christian ideology, and allotment of native land.

Heeding the advice of his father, Young Joseph continued to resist Howard's pressure to relocate the Wallowa Nez Perces from their homeland. On March 27, 1873, at one such council, Joseph said:

> I did not want to come to this council, but I came hoping that we could save blood. The white man has no right to come here and take our country. We have never accepted any presents from the Government. Neither Lawyer, nor any other chief, had authority to sell this land. It has always belonged to my people. It came unclouded to them from our fathers. And we will defend this land as long as a drop of Indian blood warms the hearts of our men. (Chalmers, 28)

After more pressure, and after some members of his band had moved to Lapwai, Joseph's replies assumed a taut terseness: "I have been talking to the white man many years about the land in question. It is strange that they cannot understand me. The country which they claim belonged to my father. Before he died he gave it to me and my people. I will not leave it until I am compelled to do so" (Chalmers, 37).

This statement was addressed to Isaac Stevens, "an impatient, politically ambitious military man" (Josephy, 284). Stevens was territorial governor of Washington, the federal government's superintendent of Indian affairs for the territory, and, at the same time, the major lobbyist for a northern transcontinental railroad that would terminate at Puget Sound, a line that, when it was eventually built, established Seattle as a major urban center combining a seaport with the terminus of a transcontinental railroad line. Stevens was young (thirty-five) and supremely confident of himself and his vision of the Pacific Northwest's Anglo-American future.

By the mid-1870s, Stevens' treaty negotiations had divided the Nez Perces' several bands. Roughly two-thirds of the bands had agreed to accept restriction to reservations and adoption of the immigrants' way of life as farmers and wage laborers. The remaining one-third sided with Joseph and his allies in refusing to sign with Stevens.

Under unrelenting pressure from the United States, Joseph and his band finally agreed to move to Lapwai, but they did so without pleasure, complaining that thirty days, the amount of time allowed them by Howard, was not enough to round up their horses and put the rest of their affairs in order. While the logistics of the move were being worked out, Anglo immigrants stole hundreds of the Nez Perces' horses. A renegade band of young Nez Perces led by young Wahlitis, whose father had been murdered by whites two years earlier, retaliated by killing eighteen settlers. The army was brought in to arrest the "hostiles." Instead of surrendering, the entire band of about 500 men, women, and children quickly decamped and marched into the mountains.

During the next several months, the vastly outnumbered Nez Perces led troops on a 1,500-mile trek through some of the most rugged country on the continent, north and east almost to Canada. Joseph, with at most 250 warriors, fought over a dozen engagements with four army columns totalling 2,000 men and evaded capture several times. On one occasion, in a night raid, the Nez Perces made off with the pursuing army's pack animals.

At other times, the Nez Perces so skillfully evaded army pincer movements that two army columns ran into each other without capturing a single Indian. The army did inflict casualties on the Nez Perces at other times. Eighty-nine were killed in one battle, 50 of them women and children. Despite the deaths, the Nez Perces continued to fight.

Chief Joseph instructed his warriors not to take scalps, because the Nez Perces had earned praise for their military acumen from General William Tecumseh Sherman, who said that the Nez Perces went to great lengths to avoid killing noncombatants. General Nelson A. Miles, whose troops brought the Nez Perces' Long March to an end, echoed Sherman's opinion, saying that the Nez Perces had spared hundreds of lives and thousands of dollars worth of property that they could have destroyed (Brandon, 300). Joseph later said that he forbade the killing of white people so that his people would be allowed (he assumed) to return to their homeland after the Long March. "I wanted to leave a clean trail," he said (Chalmers, 207).

Through the Bitterroot Mountains to the present-day Yellowstone National Park, then to the headwaters of the Missouri River, and to the Bear Paw Mountains, Joseph's band fought a rearguard action with unquestioned brilliance. Joseph's band traveled through parts of four present-day states (Washington, Oregon, Idaho, and Montana) and crossed the Continental Divide twice. Near the end of the march, the survivors suffered immensely, according to army accounts:

> October 4 was cold and blustery. That morning a cannon shell made a direct hit on a shelter pit, burying four women, a little boy, and a girl of about twelve. The Indians dug frantically to get them out. The girl and her grandmother were found dead. The other people were rescued. Those two casualties were the first Nez Perces killed since the initial day of the siege, a reflection of the effectiveness of the shelter pits. (Josephy, 605)

In direct engagements with troops, the Nez Perces' deadliest weapon was their sharpshooting, which was described by an army report:

> At one point of the line, one man, raising his head too high, was shot through the brain; another soldier, lying on his back and trying to get the last few drops of warm water from his canteen, was robbed of the water by a bullet taking off the canteen's neck while it was at his lips. (Brown, 191)

What economy remained to the Nez Perces during the Long March became suited, by necessity, entirely to evasion of pursuit. When the Nez Perces needed supplies, they bought them from merchants and townspeople, often paying with gold dust or paper money saved from earlier days. "Even stories of thefts by the Indians proved groundless," wrote Alvin

Josephy, Jr. "Charges that horses and camping equipment were taken from some homes evaporated when it was revealed that the property had belonged, in the first place, to buffalo-hunting Indians who had left their animals and possessions in the care of white friends earlier in the year" (Josephy, 561).

Joseph found that his ardor for battle declined as he ranged further from home. Fighting to protect a homeland was one thing; running from home to escape arrest by the U.S. Army was another. Joseph's compatriot Yellow Wolf recalled:

> While we were fighting for our land there was reason to fight. But while we are here I have no words to say in favor of fighting for this is not my country. Since we have left our country it matters little where we go. (Chalmers, 111)

Yellow Wolf also provided this description of the Nez Perce camp three days into the Battle of the Bear Paw, shortly before Joseph and his people surrendered to General Miles:

> Morning came, bringing the battle anew. Bullets from everywhere! A big gun throwing bursting shells. From rifle pits, warriors returned shot for shot. Wild and stormy, the cold wind was thick with snow. Air filled with smoke of powder. Flash of guns through it all. As the hidden sun traveled upward, the war did not weaken. . . . Cooking facilities in the besieged camp were piteously meager. The dead brush along the creek—a species of undersized willow—afforded scant kindling. Buffalo chips, though abundant, became buried the first night of the siege beneath a blanket of snow and were available only under cover of darkness. . . . A young warrior, wounded, lay on a buffalo robe dying without complaint. Children crying with cold. No fire. There could be no light. Everywhere the crying, the death wail. . . . All night we remained in those pits. The wind was filled with snow. Only a little sleep. There might be a charge by the soldiers. The warriors watched by turns. A long night. . . . I felt the coming end. All for which we had suffered lost! (Beal, 218)

Exhausted, the Nez Perces surrendered on October 5, 1877, at Eagle Creek, roughly thirty miles south of the Canadian border. Many of the Nez Perces were starving. Several also had been maimed and blinded. Joseph handed his rifle to General Miles and said:

> Tell General Howard I know what is in his heart. What he told me before, I have in my heart. I am tired of fighting. Our chiefs are killed. Looking Glass is dead. Tuhulkutsut is dead. The old men are all dead. It is the young men who say yes or no. He [Alokut] who led the young men is dead. It is cold and we have no blankets. The little children are freezing to death. My people, some of them, have run away to the hills, and have no blankets, no food; no one knows where they are, perhaps freezing to death. I want to have time to look for my children and see how many of them I can find. Maybe I shall find them among the dead. Hear me, my chiefs. My people ask me for food, and I have none to give. It is cold, and we have no

> blankets, no wood. My people are starving to death. Where is my little daughter? I do not know. Perhaps, even now, she is freezing to death. Hear me, my chiefs. I am tired; my heart is sick and sad. From where the sun now stands, Joseph will fight no more forever. (Chalmers, 220)

Chief Joseph then drew his blanket over his face and walked into the army camp a prisoner.

During the afternoon after Joseph's surrender speech, the other Nez Perces filed out of the hollow in which they had endured the troops' siege. A few of the warriors buried their weapons on the hollow, but most turned them in to the soldiers and raised their arms toward the sky to signify that the conflict had ended. The troops were relieved, as well. They spoke with the Indians through interpreters, expressing their respect for the courage of the Nez Perces. The soldiers built large fires and distributed blankets to warm the shivering Indians and served hot food to alleviate their hunger. A few Nez Perces, led by White Bird, refused to surrender; after dusk, they stole away in silence toward Sitting Bull's camp north of the Canadian border.

The Nez Perces emerged from their last battle with 87 warriors (40 of them wounded), 184 women, and 147 children, a total of about 400 people, "sick, freezing, and half-starved, with 1,100 gaunt horses" (Waters, 176–177).

Most of Joseph's family, closest friends, and advisors—his brother Alokut, Looking Glass, Tuhulsutkut, Pile of Clouds, and others—had been killed. Joseph's own mount had been shot from under him and his clothes riddled with bullet holes. About 250 Nez Perces had died during the Long March, roughly equal to the number of U.S. Army soldiers who lost their lives in the campaign. The *New York Times*, commented in an August 11, 1877, editorial that the whole Nez Perce campaign was "a blunder":

> So ends the Nez Perce war—a war gallantly fought, but a costly and sanguinary blunder. A peaceful, non-treaty chief, who, after being wronged in other ways, had been peremptorily ordered to go upon a reservation where he did not belong, was thus goaded to the war-path. (Hayes, 108–109)

After his surrender, much of Chief Joseph's life was spent in attempting to prevail upon his white captors to allow his people to return to their homeland in the Wallowa Valley. This consuming passion to return home runs like a thread through the histories of Native Americans being evicted from their lands across the continent. The Cherokees left their homelands under protest, as did the Navajos, the Poncas, and many others. Joseph complained bitterly that promises made by General Miles at the surrender were forgotten by other officials in different agencies of government:

> General Miles said to me in plain words, "If you will come out and give up your arms, I will spare your lives and send you back to the reservation." General Miles had promised we might return to our country with what stock we had left. . . . I believed General Miles, or I never would have surrendered. (Armstrong, 115)

In 1879, Joseph appealed to Congress, speaking to a full chamber. "It has always been the pride of the Nez Perces that they were the friends of the white men," Chief Joseph told Congress, recounting how the Indians had helped support the first few immigrants. "There was room enough for all to live in peace, and they [Joseph's ancestors] were learning many things from the white men that appeared to be good. . . . Soon [we] found that the white men were growing rich very fast, and were greedy to possess everything the Indian had." Joseph recalled how his father had refused to sign a treaty with Washington territorial governor Isaac Stevens: "I will not sign your paper. . . . You go where you please, so do I; you are not a child; I am no child; I can think for myself. . . . Take away your paper. I will not sign it" (Nabokov, 130, 131). Joseph said that the Nez Perces had given too much, and that they had only gone to war when the whites forced them to abandon their cherished homeland.

Despite Chief Joseph's appeal to Congress, the decision was left to the War Department, which refused his request. Joseph and the other Nez Perces who had survived their Long March were imprisoned at Fort Leavenworth, Kansas, then taken to Indian Territory, to Washington, D.C. (twice), and back to Indian Territory again between 1877 and 1885. At Fort Leavenworth, a third of those who had survived the Long March died of malaria.

On September 6, 1881, Indian Agent Thomas Jordan reported that the death rate among the Nez Perces was so high that "the tribe, unless something is done for them, will soon be extinct" (Beal, 291). Jordan rejected speculation in the Indian bureau that the Nez Perces were dying because they did not look after their own health: "They keep their stock in good order, and are hard working, painstaking people" (Beal, 291). In 1885, 268 surviving Nez Perces were moved to Indian Territory again, where even more of them died.

Later the same year, roughly 140 survivors were finally allowed to return to the Northwest—some to Lapwai, Idaho, and others to the Colville Reservation in eastern Washington. The Nez Perces were provided no supplies when they arrived at the onset of winter. They experienced profound suffering yet again.

Chief Joseph was permitted to visit his old homeland only once, in the year 1900. Four years later, he passed to the spirit world. Joseph's thoughts during his final years often were bitter. To the last, Joseph maintained a yearning affection for the homeland from which his people had been driven in a war that seemed to have been without reason:

I have heard talk and talk, but nothing is done. Good words do not last long unless they amount to something. Words do not pay for my dead people. They do not pay for my country, now overrun by white men. . . . Good words will not give my people good health and stop them from dying. Good words will not get my people a home where they can live in peace and take care of themselves. I am tired of talk that comes to nothing. It makes my heart sick when I remember all the good words and broken promises. . . .

You might as well expect the rivers to run backward as that any man who was born a free man should be contented when penned up and denied liberty to go where he pleases. . . .

Let me be a free man—free to travel, free to stop, free to work, free to trade where I choose, free to choose my own teachers, free to follow the religion of my fathers, free to talk and think and act for myself—and I will obey every law, or submit to the penalty. (Armstrong, 116)

Several years after Joseph's surrender in 1877, General Howard crossed paths with him at Carlisle Indian School. In his children's book *Famous Indian Chiefs I Have Known* (1908), Howard called Joseph "the greatest Indian warrior I ever fought with." At a speech by Joseph, both men posed for photographs together and joked. "For a long time, I did want to kill General Howard," Howard recalled Joseph as having said, "but now I am glad to meet him and we are friends" (Howard, 198).

Joseph died at Colville in 1904, still yearning to go home to the land where he had buried his father. A Lieutenant Wood, who had witnessed Chief Joseph's surrender speech and later wrote a narrative of the Nez Perces' Long March, said, "I think that, in his long career, Joseph cannot accuse the Government of the United States of one single act of justice" (Brandon, 302).

Sitting Bull (c. 1830–1890) and George Armstrong Custer (1839–1876)

The Hunkpapa Sioux Sitting Bull, whose Lakota name Tatanka Yotanka is more accurately translated as portraying a large bull buffalo at rest, was known among the Lakotas as an outstanding warrior as a young man; in later years, he was best known as a spiritual leader—a visionary and a dreamer. Before the Battle of the Little Bighorn in 1876, Sitting Bull had a vision that portended a Native American victory. The vision did a fairly good job of outlining the character flaws of George Armstrong Custer, under whose command a party of the Seventh Cavalry would die at the hands of Sitting Bull's people and their allies.

Sitting Bull, chief of the Hunkpapa division of the Teton Sioux (Lakotas), was one of the principal war chiefs who negotiated the Fort Laramie Treaty of 1868, which forced the United States to abandon several forts and to respect the Lakotas' claim to their sacred Paha Sapa, or Black Hills, "the heart of everything that is." Sitting Bull was probably better known in white America than any other Native American of his time. He was celebrated as one of the last and most influential Native American leaders to evade surrender to reservation life at the hands of the U.S. Army. Sitting Bull's band took refuge in Canada until 1881.

Sitting Bull; George Armstrong Custer. Nebraska State Historical Society

According to Stanley Vestal, Sitting Bull was born in March 1831, during the "Winter-when-Yellow-Eyes-Played-in-the-Snow" (Vestal, 3), on the south bank of the Ree River (now called the Grand River) a few miles downstream from the present town of Bullhead, South Dakota, at a place his people called Many Caches" because of its storage pits. Vestal based his account on the memories of Sitting Bull's compatriots during the 1920s. Robert M. Utley, who used documentary history to profile Sitting Bull's life, says that he could have been born in 1831, 1832, 1834, or even 1837 (Utley, *Lance*, 3); accounts exist to indicate each of these dates. Similarly, Sitting Bull's birthplace also could have been on Willow Creek, a tributary of the Teton River, a few miles west of Fort Pierre, a hundred miles southeast of Many Caches (Utley, *Lance*, 3).

As a child, Sitting Bull was called "Slow," not because of a lack of intelligence, but because his actions were unusually deliberate for a child. At ten, he killed a buffalo, a notable feat for such a young boy. At age fourteen, he counted coup on an enemy (that is, he touched an enemy without injury in battle and escaped unharmed, a measure of skill that brought prestige). On this occasion he was ritually accepted as a man, with his adult name.

Sitting Bull was conscious of his leadership role from early in his life and sought to be first in battle and first in the buffalo hunt. Sitting Bull's enemies held his name in such awe that Hunkpapa warriors could intimidate enemies by shouting, "Tatanka-Iyotanka tahoksila," meaning "We are Sitting Bull's Boys." Sitting Bull grew to be both a great warrior and a *wichasha wakan*—a man of spiritual force, a "medicine man" to European-Americans.

From his young manhood, Sitting Bull was known for his "high, resonant, melodious voice" (Vestal, 21). He also was known for his talents as a composer of songs and found himself much in demand at festivals and ceremonies. Some of Sitting Bull's songs were sung several generations after his death, a high tribute. Sitting Bull's talents as a singer and composer also served him as a political and military leader.

Sitting Bull became known among his own people, as well as the whites, as a man of quality and dignity. Utley wrote that

> Sitting Bull's manners matched his dress, with none of the arrogance or insolence that some chiefs assumed. In relations with fellow tribesmen, he behaved like a common Hunkpapa without rank or status and affected no superior airs. He talked freely at times, but not often. When he spoke, it was slowly and quietly, with great conviction and authority. He also listened intently, never interrupting a speaker. He possessed a keen sense of humor and occasionally laughed heartily. (Utley, *Lance*, 35)

Sitting Bull was known as a good husband and a good provider. Vestal said that women liked him because he "was kind to the family" and often used his influence and wealth to patch up domestic quarrels. Vestal wrote that Sitting Bull's companions said he was like a bull elk, amorous and brave, always helping the women.

The Northern Cheyenne Wooden Leg, who joined Sitting Bull and his people before the Battle of the Little Bighorn, characterized Sitting Bull as a man who "had come into admiration by all Indians as a man whose medicine was good," that is, as a man having a kind heart and good judgment as to the best course of conduct. "He was considered as being altogether brave, but peaceable," said Wooden Leg. "He was strong in religion—the Indian religion. He made medicine many times" (Marquis, 178–179).

In contrast to the many other testimonials describing Sitting Bull's character, Indian Agent James McLaughlin justified his treatment of Sitting Bull, up to and including ordering the arrest that resulted in his death, by imagining the chief as a coward in battle and as "crafty, avaricious, mendacious, and ambitious . . . possessed [of] all the faults of an Indian and none of the nobler attributes which have gone far to redeem some of his people from their deeds of guilt" (McLaughlin, 48). Having never known, in his own mind, a reason to admire or respect Sitting Bull, McLaughlin nevertheless admitted that he was "by far the most influential man of his nation for many years" (McLaughlin, 48).

McLaughlin's views of Native American character were a genteel version of George Armstrong Custer's. Custer, whose inability to take advice would cost him and the rest of his troop their scalps at the Little Bighorn, was born on December 5, 1839, in the rural town of New Rumley, Ohio, one of several children in a large family that combined earlier offspring of a widow and a widower. Custer's father Emanuel was a rough-hewn Jacksonian Democrat and a devout evangelical Methodist.

Young Custer was known from a young age for his strong opinions. When he enrolled at the West Point Military Academy, Custer nearly earned enough demerits to be kicked out. He had no taste for military formalism, especially slavish devotion to piddling regulations. The academy allowed a student 100 demerits in six months before dismissal, and Custer's "skins" (as demerits were called) approached that total regularly. In four years, he accumulated 726 skins (Utley, *Cavalier*, 15). Young Custer also seemed to have accumulated a set of fantasies about military life, judging by the books he checked out of the West Point library, which "featured dashing cavaliers, flashing swords, and beautiful women" (Utley, *Cavalier*, 15).

Custer did satisfy some of West Point's requirements quite well. He was a better soldier physically than most of his classmates, especially on horseback. Academically, however, he very nearly flunked out. Custer survived, however, and graduated in 1861, just in time to go to work as an officer in the Union Army during the Civil War. Custer blazed a trail of legendary heroics through several Civil War battles and earned a temporary posting at the rank of general as he became famous for surviving daring, potentially fatal charges into enemy ranks. These feats of daring presaged his biggest gamble of all, the suicidal attack at the Little Bighorn.

Among the Hunkpapas, not long after Custer graduated from West Point, Sitting Bull became a leading member of the elite warrior society Midnight Strong Hearts. Under his leadership, the society expanded to more than 200 men, who went to war as a unit. Sitting Bull assumed leadership in the society during 1856 after he killed a Crow in combat and sustained a bullet wound that forced him to limp for the rest of his life. Bellowing their cry, "We are Sitting Bull's Boys," they are said to have "struck terror to the enemy" (Vestal, 86). Some of these enemies were Crows and Flatheads whose horse herds were frequently raided by Sitting Bull's "boys." Sitting Bull himself could recount sixty-three coups by 1870, when he was thirty-nine years of age (Vestal, 116).

From the membership of the Midnight Strong Hearts, Sitting Bull picked an inner council of about twenty men whose job was to advise him on leadership of the Teton Sioux. They met over the evening meal and forbade themselves jokes, storytelling, singing, or dancing. The group's serious demeanor caused its members to be called "the Silent Eaters" (Vestal, 96).

No small measure of Sitting Bull's contemporary fame as a warrior developed from his reputation as the "mastermind" (Vestal, xiii) of George Armstrong Custer's defeat at the Little Bighorn in 1876. Despite this reputation, Sitting Bull was not warlike by nature. He was reluctant to engage the U.S. Army in battle until the Hunkpapas' own land was invaded. After that happened, he allied with other Sioux bands, as well as Cheyennes, to try and stem the flood. Sitting Bull and his allies closely watched the invasion of the Black Hills by Custer during 1874 and played a key role in rallying the Lakotas and Cheyennes to defeat Custer in 1876. Just as the visions of Plenty Coups had played a key role in the Crows' decision to accommodate the whites, Sitting Bull's dreams foreshadowed the defeat of Custer. In June 1876, a great sun dance was held on the west bank of the Rosebud. Sitting Bull performed the dance for thirty-six hours straight, after which he had a vision of U.S. Army soldiers without ears falling into a Sioux village, upside down. The soldiers in Sitting Bull's vision had no ears to signify ignorance of the truth. Their upside-down position indicated to Sitting Bull that they would die. After the battle, Sitting Bull accepted the victory that had fulfilled his vision of soldiers falling into camp with resignation. "I feel sorry that so many were killed on each side," he said later, "but when Indians must fight, they must" (Utley, *Lance*, 161).

At the Little Bighorn, the Indian warriors were prepared to fight if they had to, but, according to Stanley Vestal, "[T]hey danced no war dances, they sent no young men against the white men. Their preparations were purely defensive. As Sitting Bull said: 'Even a bird will defend its nest' "

(Vestal, 155). After the battle ended, Sitting Bull stopped young warriors who were chasing escaping cavalry, "not with victory." Sitting Bull told his "Boys" to " 'let them go! Let them live to tell the truth about this battle.' He wanted the white man to know that this fight had been begun by the soldiers, not the Sioux" (Vestal, 165).

The allied camp of the Sioux, Cheyennes, and others, as many as 5,000 people, including as many as 2,000 warriors, followed the Little Bighorn River for about three miles. Even after his Crow scouts told him that the camp was much larger than he had expected, Custer decided to attack the Indians on their home ground. That decision resulted in the deaths of Custer and his entire force of about 225 men. The news of Custer's defeat reached the East Coast in July in time to spoil the centennial celebrations of the United States.

In the debate that weighed extermination against assimilation for Native Americans, Custer himself certainly was no plastic medicine man (contemporary Indian slang for a non-Indian who poses as an Indian healer). He imagined Indians as subhuman beasts and favored extermination with a frankness that made most army officers blush. Custer did not have to think twice about sliding a bayonet through the children of the beasts he imagined Indians to be. A dehumanizing tone was evident when Custer wrote:

> Stripped of the beautiful romance with which we have been so long willing to envelope him, transferred from the inviting pages of the novelist to the localities where we are compelled to meet with him . . . the Indian forfeits his claim to the appellation of "*noble* red man." We see him as he is, and, so far as all knowledge goes, as he ever has been, a savage in every sense of the word . . . whose cruel and ferocious nature far exceeds that of any wild beast in the desert. (Vogel, 167)

Custer's autobiography runs to more than 630 pages, even though he was not available to write the final chapter. The grand stage on which the Boy General makes himself the main actor provides some clues as to why Custer would ride through the night with 225 bone-tired men on exhausted mounts, violating his written orders, ignoring the reports of his Crow scouts indicating the size of the Sioux-Cheyenne camp at the Little Bighorn, and deluding himself into thinking that his tired troops were a match for ten times as many Native American warriors defending their families.

In Custer's version of reality, the Indians are nearly always the attackers. The book is full of Indian raids and depredations—"killed the white men . . . disemboweled and burned them" (Custer, 96), "murdering many of the men and children, burning houses" (Custer, 401). Custer's Indians are forever "dipping their hands in the white man's blood" (Custer, 403), behavior that Custer believes is caused by an Indian hostility to "civilization . . . deep-seated and inbred with the Indian character" (Custer, 24). There is no whisper in Custer's account that a continent was changing hands, and that many of the raids were in retaliation for illegal incursions by Anglo-Americans.

While the crudity with which Custer stereotyped Native Americans was unusual even in his time, his point of view was not unpopular. Regarding the future of Native Americans, Francis Parkman, the noted historian, made a case similar to Custer's, in slightly more elegant language: "Their intractable, unchanging character leaves no alternative than their gradual extinction, or the abandonment of the western world to eternal barbarism" (Vogel, 285).

When Custer led a charge that turned the Southern Cheyennes' Washita camp into a killing field, he called the result a "battle," although a line drawing in his autobiography depicts the mounted Seventh Cavalry shooting its way into an Indian camp (Custer, 323). Custer himself said as much: "The bugles sounded the charge and the entire command dashed rapidly into the village. The Indians were caught napping" (Custer, 335). By Custer's definition, lacking any reference to just cause or provocation, any encounter with Native American peoples was deemed a just war. The fact that the surprised Indians shot back seemed enough to qualify the attack as a "battle." Somehow, in the "battle" of the Washita, Custer convinced himself, contrary to the reality under which most historians labor, that the Seventh Cavalry's bullets hit only battle-worthy warriors, leaving all of the women and children in the village unharmed. The warriors' deaths were justified, to Custer, by the Southern Cheyennes' "unprovoked attacks upon the white man" (Custer, 359). The provocation involved with the taking of Native American homelands again totally escaped Custer.

Into the midst of his battle narrative, Custer slid a third-person word portrait of himself as a self-assured commander at ease, perhaps in the evening, in a fashion that might wrinkle some eyebrows at the officers' clubs of the late twentieth century, where such a display of sartorial vanity would be very unusual:

> General Custer on this occasion appeared in a beautiful crimson robe (red flannel *robe de nuit*), very becoming to his complexion. His hair was worn *au naturel*, and permitted to fall carelessly over his shoulders. In his hand he carried gracefully a handsome Spencer rifle. It is unnecessary to add that he became the observed of all observers. (Custer, 136)

Custer was, more than anything else, a player to the audience. He was looking for a dramatic victory to impress a national audience during the U.S. centennial year of 1876. Rumors also were heard that he even wanted to run for president in the mold of Andrew Jackson. The Battle of the Little Bighorn also took place as Dakota country was filling with European-American immigrants. In 1870, fewer than 5,000 whites had lived in the Dakota Territory. By 1880, the non-Indian population had grown to

134,000, 17,000 of whom were digging gold in the Black Hills. In 1890, the national census reported that whites outnumbered Native Americans in South Dakota seventeen to one, a number that had been generously padded by advocates of statehood (Vestal, 270).

Several times during the 1870s, Sitting Bull and his people refused to give up their traditional style of life and land use as the U.S. Army repeatedly summoned them to reservation life. One account of the time described how

> Sitting Bull then got up and made a long speech. . . . He said he would not sell his land. He said he had never been to an agency and was not going in. He was no agency Indian. He told me to go out and tell the white men at Red Cloud [Agency] that he declared open war and would fight them wherever he met them from that time on. (Utley, *Lance*, 125)

When a government commission under General George Crook attempted to persuade the Sioux to sign away more of their land, Sitting Bull turned him down flat. The government commissioners then persuaded a number of other Sioux leaders, Gall and John Grass among them, to sign against Sitting Bull's desires. Sitting Bull and the Silent Eaters were excluded from the negotiations.

After the government agents failed to bring Sitting Bull's people to reservation life, his band, numbering about 200 people, decided that they could best preserve their buffalo-based way of life by taking up residence in Canada. In Canada, Sitting Bull was afforded the deference due a visiting head of state. He received visitors from around the world. During the hungry winter of 1876–1877, Sitting Bull explained to a trader why he and his people did not wish to surrender to life on a reservation in the United States:

> Because I am a red man. If the Great Spirit had desired me to be a white man he would have made me so in the first place. He put in your heart certain wishes and plans; in my heart he put other and different desires. Each man is good in his sight. It is not necessary for eagles to be crows. Now we are poor but we are free. No white man controls our footsteps. If we must die, we die defending our rights. (Armstrong, 112)

Interviewed in Canada during 1877, Sitting Bull explained why he and his people had gone into exile. The basic issue was land-based self-determination:

> I was driven in force from my land. I never made war on the United States Government. I never stood in the white man's country. I never committed any depredations in the white man's country. I never made the white man's heart bleed. The white man came on my land and followed me. The white man made me fight for my hunting grounds. (Hamilton, 205)

Sitting Bull truly loved the land. Sometimes he sang to the earth:

> Behold, my brothers, the spring has come; the earth has received the embraces of the sun and we shall soon see the results of that love! Every seed has awakened and so has all animal life. It is through this mysterious power that we too have our being and we therefore yield to our neighbors, even our animal neighbors, the same right as ourselves, to inhabit this land. (Stone, 115)

In another account, Sitting Bull expressed his affection for nature's variations on the Great Plains at a time when he and his people still had a homeland, before they were forced to live on the run:

> I wish all to know that I do not propose to sell any part of my country, nor will I have the whites cutting our timber along the rivers, especially the oak. I am particularly fond of the little groves of oak trees. I love to look at them, because they endure the wintry storm and the summer's heat, and—not unlike ourselves—seem to flourish by them. (Stone, 64)

Sitting Bull said that he would never become a farmer. "I will remain what I am until I die, a hunter, and when there are no buffalo or other game I will send my children to hunt and live on prairie mice, for where an Indian is shut up in one place his body becomes weak" (Utley, *Lance*, 206).

Cold, hunger, and disease tightened its grip on Sitting Bull and his people. In 1881, they returned to the United States and surrendered at Fort Buford in North Dakota. As he was being told that he was now a military prisoner, Sitting Bull said, regarding the land, "I do not love war. I was never the aggressor. I fought only to defend my women and children. Now all my people want to return to their native land. Therefore, I submit" (Armstrong, 126). "A cold wind blew across the prairie when the last buffalo fell—a death-wind for my people" (Weaver, 37). During the last years of his life, Sitting Bull looked with muted terror at the life that was being prepared for his children:

> I do not wish to be shut up in a corral. It is bad for young men to be fed by an agent. It makes them lazy and drunken. All agency Indians I have seen are worthless. They are neither red warriors nor white farmers. They are neither wolf nor dog. But my followers are weary of cold and hunger. They wish to see their brothers and their old home, therefore I bow my head. (Armstrong, 126)

At the time of his surrender in 1881, Sitting Bull's band had dwindled to 44 men and 143 women and children. Sitting Bull was taken to the Standing Rock Agency, where he ridiculed efforts to sell Indian land. He told the white men to get a scale and sell it by the pound. Sitting Bull staunchly opposed any form of allotment, and although he adopted farming and sent his children to reservation schools, he maintained until his death that he would rather die as an Indian than live as a white man.

The whites' use of land was nonsensical to Sitting Bull. "The life of white men is slavery," he said on one occasion. "They are prisoners on towns or farms. The life my people want is a life of freedom. I have seen nothing that a white man has, houses or railways or clothing or food, that is as good as the right to move in open country, and live in our own fashion" (Calloway, 183).

Philosophy aside, within two years of his surrender, beginning in 1883 and 1884, Sitting Bull was a star attraction in Buffalo Bill's Wild West Show, posing for photographers side by side, as friends, with William Cody (Buffalo Bill) himself. Sitting Bull made some money from performing with Buffalo Bill's show, but he gave most of it away. He could not pass poor, ragged white children without giving them money. Annie Oakley observed that Sitting Bull never could understand how "so much wealth could go rushing by, unmindful of the poor" (Vestal, 250–251). According to Vestal, "He formed the opinion that the white men would not do much for the Indians when they let their own flesh and blood go hungry" (Vestal, 251). In 1887, Sitting Bull refused to join Buffalo Bill's troupe in England, protesting, "It is bad for our cause for me to parade around, awakening the hatred of white men everywhere. Besides, I am needed here; there is more talk of taking our lands" (Vestal, 255).

In September 1886, Sitting Bull joined a hundred other Lakotas in a journey to Crow territory. Within sight of the monument erected to George Armstrong Custer at the Little Bighorn, the longtime Native American enemies "buried the hatchet." In the meantime, Indian Agent Major James ("White Hair") McLaughlin tried to break Sitting Bull's influence. He appointed Indian police to spy on him and named Gall and Grass as "recognized" chiefs at Standing Rock Agency in an attempt to diminish Sitting Bull's authority. By 1890, the remaining Lakotas were corralled into concentration-camp-like conditions on the plains.

The Ghost Dance religion arrived under these conditions. Spawned by the prophet Wovoka, a Paiute, the Ghost Dance spread among the destitute Native American peoples of the West, from Oregon to Nebraska and into the Dakotas, where Sitting Bull endorsed its vision of Native American restoration. The Sioux took to the Ghost Dance with a frenzy that Wovoka had not anticipated; Sioux medicine men also said that special "Ghost Shirts" would shield the Sioux from soldiers' bullets. Driven by hunger, desperation, and a determined desire to escape from their new, brutal reality, many Sioux ghost dancers worked themselves into a frenzy during which they said that they had seen the return of the buffalo and had spoken with dead relatives.

Sitting Bull's attention never strayed far from the land and the continued appeals of the white men to give them more of it. During 1889, Sitting Bull spoke, with labored patience, of "the Great Father's representatives . . . [who] want us to give up another chunk of our tribal land."

> This is not the first time or the last time. They will try to gain possession of the last piece of ground we possess. They are again telling us what they intend to do if we agree with their wishes. Have we ever set a price on our land and received such a value? No, we never did. What we got under the former treaties were promises of all sorts. They promised how we were going to live peaceably on the land we still own and how they are going to show us the new ways of living—even told us how we can go to heaven when we die, but all we realized out of the agreements with the Great Father was, we are dying off. (Rosenstiel, 148)

Representatives of the Great White Father arrived again and again with papers to sign. Sitting Bull said that they "contain just what they want but ignor[e] our wishes in the matter. . . . The Great Father has proved himself an *unkomiti* [trickster] in our past dealings" (Rosenstiel, 148). Sitting Bull raised the issue of the Black Hills, where the Fort Laramie Treaty of 1868 had been blindly disregarded after an expedition led by George Armstrong Custer found gold there. Figuring that it would be broken anyway, Sitting Bull refused to sign yet another treaty, concluding, "If I agree to dispose of any part of our land to the white people, I would feel guilty of taking food away from our children's mouths" (Rosenstiel, 148).

As Sitting Bull aged, he scoffed at the whites' professed sincerity when treaty signatures were solicited:

> What treaty that the whites have kept has the red man broken? Not one. What treaty that the whites ever made with us red men have they kept? Not one. When I was a boy, the Sioux owned the world. The sun rose and set in their lands. They sent 10,000 horsemen to battle. Where are the warriors today? Who slew them? Where are our lands? Who owns them? What white man can ever say that I stole his lands or a penny of his money? Yet they say I am a thief. What white woman, however lonely, was ever a captive insulted by me? Yet they say I am a bad Indian. What white man has ever seen me drunk? Who has ever come to me hungry and gone unfed? Who has ever seen me beat my wives or abuse my children? What law have I broken? Is it wrong for me to love my own? Is it wicked for me because my skin is red; because I am a Sioux; because I was born where my fathers lived; because I would die for my people and my country? (Hamilton, 194)

By late 1890, an estimated 3,500 Indians were gathered against their wills in the hills near Wounded Knee Creek, which bisects the Pine Ridge Indian Reservation. Many of them demanded the right to practice the Ghost Dance religion. The rules of the reservation laid down by the Bureau of Indian Affairs forbade practice of the religion. Settlers demanded protection from what they regarded as a revolutionary movement. Several thousand troops converged on the reservation from surrounding forts in anticipation of renewed conflict. Troops with itchy trigger fingers were spurred by settlers eager to extinguish the Indian "threat."

Tension intensified between McLaughlin, who was pressuring the Sioux to sign new treaties ceding more of their territory, and Sitting Bull, who had campaigned all his life against signing away Native American homelands. At one point, Sitting Bull's old friend "Buffalo Bill" Cody tried to intercede to negotiate, but failed. Cody had been one of Sitting Bull's very few white friends. A publicity poster for the Wild West Show had shown Sitting Bull and Cody clasping hands over the caption "Foes in '76, Friends in '85."

Sitting Bull was killed on December 15, 1890, a few days before the massacre at Wounded Knee, when forty-three tribal police tried to arrest him. Accounts of Sitting Bull's assassination vary, but it appears that Bullhead, a police officer employed by the Indian agency, served a warrant on Sitting Bull, who protested. Bullhead then shot him in the thigh as his partner, Sgt. Red Tomahawk, shot Sitting Bull in the head. A riot ensued during which six policemen and eight of Sitting Bull's followers, including his son Crow Foot, also were killed.

Red Cloud (c. 1820–1909)

Sitting Bull and Red Cloud led different parts of the sprawling Great Sioux Nation at roughly the same time. Both men were well known as warriors; Red Cloud counted eighty coups during his fighting life; Sitting Bull counted at least sixty-three. Beyond these similarities, the two men were very different.

Red Cloud, whose Lakota name Makhpiya-luta literally means "scarlet cloud" (after an unusual formation of crimson clouds that hovered over the western horizon at sunset when as he was born), was a major leader of the Oglala Lakotas during the late phases of the Plains Indian wars. He led the Oglala Sioux (also called Lakota or Teton Sioux) who later took up residence on the Pine Ridge Reservation, the largest single political unit of the Great Sioux Nation.

As a young man, Red Cloud learned to fight and hunt like most other Sioux boys. Very quickly, he proved himself adept at both. Red Cloud was especially known as a fierce warrior who was always ready to personally take an enemy's scalp. Red Cloud also had at least five children and possibly as many as six wives.

In 1865, Red Cloud and his allies refused to sign a treaty permitting Anglo-American passage across their lands from Fort Laramie along the Powder River to the gold fields of Montana. Red Cloud was angered by

---

Red Cloud. Nebraska State Historical Society

the rapid and ruthless encroachment of European-Americans on the lands of his people; in about 1820, when he was born at the forks of the Platte, only a few whites had lived on the plains and prairies of North America. When he died, in 1909, his people had been pushed onto a tiny fraction of their former land, imprisoned in concentration-camp conditions, famished, and impoverished. Born into the heyday of the Plains horse culture, Red Cloud died in the era of the "vanishing race."

At one point, by the late 1860s, Red Cloud and his allies forced the United States to concede considerable territory in and around the Black Hills, the borders of which were outlined in the Fort Laramie Treaty of 1868. By 1868, forces under Red Cloud's leadership had evicted the U.S. Army from the Bozeman Trail, after which he promised to retire from the warpath and live at peace with the immigrant European-Americans under the terms of the Fort Laramie Treaty that he signed on November 6, 1868.

Red Cloud advised trading with whites, but otherwise avoiding them. His valor as a warrior was legendary. Red Cloud once returned from battle against a contingent of Crows with an arrow through his body. In the late 1860s, when Red Cloud was about forty-five years old, the Sioux dominated the northern plains. When U.S. Army troops built forts without the permission of the Sioux, war parties cut off food supplies to Fort Phil Kearney in northern Wyoming and laid siege to the outpost for two years. In 1868, with the wagon road still closed, the government signed the Fort Laramie Treaty that caused the forts to be dismantled. The Powder River country and the Black Hills were reserved for the Lakotas forever, or so the treaty said.

When the Plains Indian wars were ending, Red Cloud counselled peace and was accused of "selling out" by some younger Oglalas. He later was moved to the Great Sioux Reservation, where, in 1881, Indian Agent V. T. McGillycuddy stripped Red Cloud of his chieftainship.

Red Cloud took up residency at an Indian agency named after him, and for this, Sitting Bull hurled at him the worst insult he could imagine for a fellow Sioux, calling him an "agency Indian." Red Cloud thought that Sitting Bull was posturing for the East Coast liberals, defending a dying way of life based on the buffalo, which were nearly extinct by 1880. Red Cloud took no part in the Battle of the Little Bighorn, although some reports indicate that he aided those who did by secret means. Red Cloud also signed a treaty of cession for the Black Hills in 1876, a move that Sitting Bull viewed as tantamount to treason.

During the 1870s and 1880s, Red Cloud provided aid to Yale professor Othniel C. March, who was searching the area for dinosaur bones. In exchange, March said that he would take Sioux allegations of mistreatment to the highest levels of government. March and his crew dug two tons of bones while he investigated Red Cloud's complaints of rotten food and unmet promises. The Yale professor uncovered massive profiteering by "Indian Rings" in the Grant administration, sparking a congressional investigation and several newspaper exposés. At one point, March confronted President U. S. Grant personally. March and Red Cloud became friends for the rest of their lives, a relationship that continued into the early twentieth century. Red Cloud said that he appreciated the fact that March did not forget his promise after he got his two tons of dinosaur bones.

A white man who could keep a promise was regarded as a rare find by many Native American leaders. Another common concern was that Anglo-American plows would disturb the bones of ancestors. This common thread weaves through Native American discourse regarding the land from Tecumseh to Chief Sea'thl, Chief Joseph, and his associate Tuhulkutsut. Red Cloud expressed thoughts about the keeping of promises and the integrity of the land at the Fort Laramie Treaty of 1868. He was concerned about the enduring validity of government pledges that the Bozeman Trail would be used only for transportation, not to establish a European-American presence in Sioux country:

> Hear ye, Dakotas! When the Great Father at Washington sent us his chief soldier [General William S. Harney] to ask for a path through our hunting grounds, a way for his iron road to the mountains and the western sea, we were told that they wished merely to pass through our country, not to stay among us, but to seek for gold in the far west. Our old chiefs thought to show their friendship and good will, when they allowed this dangerous snake in our midst. . . .
>
> Yet before the ashes of the council fire are cold, the Great Father is building his forts among us. You have heard the sound of the white man's ax upon the Little Piney. His presence here is an insult and a threat. It is an insult to the spirits of our ancestors. Are we then to give up their sacred graves to be plowed for corn? Dakotas, I am for war! (Jones, 102)

Despite their differences, Red Cloud, like Sitting Bull, knew that he was being made an exile in his own land. He told a large audience in New York City's Cooper Union on June 14, 1870:

> When you first came, we were many and you were few. . . . You hear of us only as murderers and thieves. We are not so. If we had more lands to give you, we would give them, but we have no more. We are driven into a very little island. (Rosenstiel, 136)

At the Cooper Union, Red Cloud appealed to the common humanity of his audience, linking the alienation of land with the destruction of the family life that forms the human infrastructure of any culture:

> [H]ave you, or any of your friends here, got children? Do you want to raise them? Look at me; I come here with all these young men. All of them have children and want to raise them. The white children have surrounded me and have left me noth-

ing but an island. When we first had this land we were strong. Now we are melting like snow on the hillside, while you are grown like spring grass. (Calloway, 154)

A *New York Times* correspondent reported that the Cooper Union meeting hall in which Red Cloud spoke resembled a large cellar with a low ceiling, packed densely with people, in heat that reached intolerable levels. The *Times* account said that Red Cloud magnetized the audience, even though his words lost some of their power as they were channeled through an interpreter. Red Cloud threw his hands upward to greet the Great Spirit and spoke with a power that the enraptured *Times* writer said was better classical oratory than one would hear most days on the floor of the U.S. Senate (Hayes, 101–102).

"When the white man comes to my country," said Red Cloud, "he leaves a trail of blood behind him" (Calloway, 154). Red Cloud's eyes beheld the blood of slaughtered buffalo rotting on what had once been Sioux hunting range, the blood of Sioux dying of warfare and disease, and the blood of white men killing each other, as well as the blood of a few last wars between dwindling bands of Native Americans. The Crows and some Sioux bands were still confronting each other as the Anglo-American tide grew around them. Long-lived antipathies sometimes outlasted a common threat that brought an entirely new system of land relations and use from which there seemed, by the late nineteenth century, no escape for the survivors of the last great surge of Indian wars.

Red Cloud's biographer George E. Hyde characterized him in old age as "wrinkled, stooped, and almost blind" (Hyde, 336). Red Cloud was sometimes given to ironic bitterness over what had become of him and his people: "I, who used to control 5,000 warriors, must tell Washington when I am hungry. I must beg for that which I own" (Hyde, 336). Red Cloud spent his final years in retirement, having little to do with his people's affairs. He died on December 10, 1909.

Standing Bear (Ponca) (c. 1830–1908)

The Ponca Standing Bear gained national notoriety in the late 1870s, during a time of forced removal for the Poncas and other Native American peoples on the Great Plains. He led some of the Poncas on two 500-mile marches from Indian Territory (now Oklahoma) back to Nebraska. When the group reached Omaha, Standing Bear became engaged in the first court case to result in a declaration that American Indians should be treated as human beings under the law of habeas corpus. Thus, under U.S. law, the army could not relocate Standing Bear's party by force without cause.

The landmark legal case *Standing Bear v. Crook* never would have occurred if Standing Bear had not possessed an overriding drive that dominated the rest of his life: he sought, against all U.S. government directives, to bury his deceased son in the ancestral earth of the Poncas' traditional homeland. This need compelled him to walk until hunger forced him and his companions to eat their moccasins and to continue walking as their bare feet bled in the snow.

By every Anglo-American measure, the Poncas were "good Indians" before they were sent packing on their own trail of tears. They did what the Great White Father thought was good for them. Before their forced removal from the Niobrara country by the U.S. Army in 1877, the Poncas had begun the transition to farming in the Jefferson yeoman image that "re-

Standing Bear, the Ponca leader. Nebraska State Historical Society

formers" insisted was, with education and Christianity, the Indian's key to the future. The Poncas also had gone to great lengths to maintain friendly relationships with the United States. In 1858, they ceded part of their homeland along the Niobrara in exchange for land in the same area that was then said to be theirs forever.

The Poncas' adaptation to "civilization" was rudely interrupted by a bureaucratic mistake in Washington, D.C. When the United States signed the Treaty of Fort Laramie in 1868, an error by sloppy cartographers ceded the Poncas' homeland to their enemies, the Great Sioux Nation. The U.S. Army was thus compelled to enforce the treaty against the Poncas at the behest of the Sioux. During late January 1877, Indian Inspector Edward C. Kemble told the Poncas that they had to leave home for Indian Territory.

Standing Bear's comment when he was told that his people would be moved to Indian Territory from their homeland evoked a sense of place that was used by native peoples across the continent when they faced dispossession:

> This land is ours; we have never sold it. We have our houses . . . here. Our fathers and some of our children are buried here. Here we wish to live and die. We have harmed no man. We have kept our treaty. We have learned to work. We can make a good living here. We do not wish to sell our land, and we think no man has a right to take it from us. Here we will live, and here we will die. (Tibbles, 6)

Standing Bear and nine other Ponca chiefs were then compelled, against their wishes, to join Kemble on a trip to inspect the new lands to which the government proposed that the Poncas be assigned. Dissatisfied with the new land, the chiefs who were young enough to walk home decided to do so; the rest stayed with Kemble's party.

Standing Bear's group walked for fifty days in the dead of winter with no money, eating raw corn until it gave out and sleeping in haystacks under thin, tattered blankets. "When their moccasins ran out, they walked barefoot in the snow. Barely able to stand on their bloodied feet, they struggled into the Otoe agency in southern Nebraska" (Mathes, 45). Later, Standing Bear recalled that was winter. "We started for home on foot. We barely lived 'til morning, it was so cold. We had nothing but our blankets. We took the ears of corn that had dried in the fields; we ate it raw. The soles of our moccasins wore out. We went barefoot in the snow" (Massey, n.p.).

The Otoes' agent contravened his orders and gave Standing Bear's people food and horses. Five days later, Standing Bear and his small party of Poncas arrived at the Omaha agency, roughly 500 miles from their starting point.

After resting among the Omahas, Standing Bear and the other chiefs traveled to Sioux City to telegraph President Rutherford B. Hayes about their opposition to removal. On his return to Ponca Agency in northern

Nebraska, Standing Bear was arrested for leaving the reservation without permission and was sent to Yankton for a military trial. A sympathetic commander freed Standing Bear, but Secretary of the Interior Carl Schurz demanded that the Poncas, as a group, be compelled to move to Indian Territory.

During 1877, almost a decade after the original error that caused the United States to seek their removal, federal troops forced 723 Poncas from three villages along the Niobrara River. The Poncas were moved at bayonet point. Standing Bear later described the scene as federal troops arrived to escort the Poncas southward:

> They took our reapers, mowers, hand-rakes, spades, ploughs, bedsteads, stoves, cupboards, everything we had on our farms, and put them in one large building. Then they put into the wagons such things as they could carry. We told them that we would rather die than leave our lands; but we could not help ourselves. They took us down. Many died on the road. Two of my children died. After we reached the new land, all my horses died. The water was very bad. All our cattle died. Not one was left. I stayed until one hundred fifty eight of my people had died. Then I ran away with thirty of my people, men, women, and children. Some of the children were orphans. We were three months on the road. We were weak and sick and starved. . . . Half of us were sick. (Jackson, 203–204)

During a cold, stormy April 1877, the first group of Poncas endured a fifty-nine-day march southward under the direction of Indian Agent James Lawrence. The second group departed in May under Agent E. A. Howard. This march, sixty-five days in length, was dogged by heavy rain, a tornado, and several deaths. Once both groups reached Indian Territory, malaria began to weaken and kill many of the Poncas.

Agent Howard left behind a taciturn diary, preserved in the archives of the Bureau of Indian Affairs, that provides an outline of the daily sufferings of the people who were being forced to march southward. Nearly every day brought news of death (usually of children), illness, bad roads, and an unusually large number of severe thunderstorms, especially during May and June of 1877. Once the Poncas arrived in Indian Territory, their most immediate problem became intense humid heat and swarms of biting insects. Suddenly, they also realized that no one had appropriated a single dollar or expended an hour of effort providing them with shelter from the cruelties of the elements in this new land.

Excerpts from Howard's diary sketched the cruelties of the Poncas' forced removal as it was experienced by Standing Bear and others:

> **May 21st.** Broke camp at seven o'clock and marched to Crayton, a distance of thirteen miles. . . . The child that died yesterday was here buried by the Indians. . . . **May 24.** Buried [another] child that died yesterday in the cemetery at Neligh, giving it a Christian burial. . . . **May 27.** . . . Several of the Indians were found to be quite

sick, and, having no physician . . . they gave us much anxiety and no trouble. The daughter of Standing Bear . . . was very low of consumption, and moving her with any degree of comfort was almost impossible. . . . **June 5.** Daughter of Standing Bear . . . died at two o'clock. . . . **June 6.** Prairie Flower, wife of Shine White and daughter of Standing Bear . . . was here given a Christian burial . . . at Milford, Nebraska. (Jackson, 207–213)

An unusually volatile spring on the prairie compounded the rigors of the journey.

June 7. . . . A storm, such as I never before experienced . . . blew a fearful tornado, demolishing every tent in camp, and rending many of them into shreds, overturning wagons, and hurling wagon-boxes . . . through the air in every direction like straws. Some of the people were taken up by the wind and carried as much as three hundred yards. Several of the Indians were quite seriously hurt, and one child died the next day. (Jackson, 214)

Howard's daily journal of the Poncas' march continues:

June 16. . . . During the march a wagon tipped over, injuring a woman quite severely. Indians out of rations, and feeling hostile. . . . **June 18.** . . . Had coffin made for dead Indian. . . . A fearful thunder-storm during the night flooded the camp-equipage. **July 2.** . . . During the last few days of the journey, the weather was exceedingly hot, and the teams [of horses] terribly annoyed and bitten by green-head flies, which attacked them in great numbers. . . . The people are all nearly worn out from the fatigue of the march. (Jackson, 216)

During the fall of 1877, Standing Bear and other Ponca leaders met with President Hayes and Secretary Schurz in Washington, D.C., to request that the Poncas be allowed to leave Indian Territory. They would have found either of two options acceptable: repatriation along the Niobrara on the land from which they had been forced to move, or a home on the Omaha Reservation. The Omahas and Poncas are related by family ties. The appeal was rejected because it conflicted with Interior Department policy to concentrate native peoples on larger reservations (which were said to be easier to administer) in the Indian Territory. In the meantime, nearly half the Poncas who had made the journey south had died, including Standing Bear's only remaining son, who died of malaria. In Indian Territory, the Poncas found illness and death dogging their every step. Standing Bear commented:

It was now in the fall, and the sickness was worse than ever. Families had settled on separate tracts of land, and were scattered around. The whole family would be sick and no one would know it. In some of the families persons would die and the others would not be able to bury them. They would drag them with a pony out on the prairie and leave them there. Men would take sick while at work and die in

> less than a day. . . . There were dead in every family. . . . I lost all my children but one little girl. I was in an awful place, and I was a prisoner there. (Tibbles, 14–15)

The last request of Standing Bear's son was to be buried in the land of his father. Grief-stricken, Standing Bear gathered a group of about thirty tribal members and slipped away from the Poncas' assigned reservation on January 2, 1879. Their accounts, later given to the press in Omaha and distributed nationally by wire, indicated that friendly whites often helped them during their winter trek northward. After ten weeks of hard travel, the Poncas arrived at the Omaha agency, where they were offered food, lodging, and seed for use if they wished to stay.

During March, troops under General George Crook from Fort Omaha arrested Standing Bear and his party and conveyed them to Fort Omaha, just north of the growing frontier city of the same name. Once he had arrived at the fort, which was serving as his headquarters, Crook took the initiative and called Thomas Henry Tibbles, assistant editor of the *Omaha Herald*. Tibbles' stories were wired to larger newspapers on the East Coast, causing a storm of protest letters to Congress on the Poncas' behalf.

Crook already had announced his disgust at how Standing Bear's party was being treated: "An Irishman, German, Chinaman, Turk, or Tartar will be protected in life and property" under the laws of the United States, "but the Indian can command respect for his rights only so long as he inspires terror for his rifle" (Mathes, 46).

Omaha citizens obtained a writ of habeas corpus and brought the army into the federal court of Judge Elmer Dundy, who ruled that an Indian was a person within the meaning of the law, and no law gave the army authority to forcibly remove the Indians from their lands. Further, Dundy ruled that the right of expatriation was "a natural and inherent right of all people, indispensable to the enjoyment of the rights of life, liberty, and the pursuit of happiness" (Armstrong, 164).

Tibbles, who was thirty-nine years of age at the time, described himself as the "ebullient, volatile assistant editor of the Omaha *Daily Herald*" when he first met Standing Bear (Tibbles, xii). Before taking a job at the *Omaha Herald*, Tibbles had been an outspoken abolitionist, a scout in the Civil War, and a circuit-riding preacher.

Tibbles was filling in for the editor of the *Herald*, so he put the Sunday newspaper to bed at 4:30 A.M., slept for two and a half hours, then rose at 7 A.M. and walked four miles north from the newspaper's downtown offices to Fort Omaha. After he interviewed members of Standing Bear's group, Tibbles then made his way south again, running part of the way, stopping at every church he could find, asking pastors if he could address their congregations about the travail of the Poncas. At a Congregational church, the pastor, Rev. Mr. Sherill, allowed him to speak "between the opening hymns" (Tibbles, 27). After hearing Tibbles' account, two churches passed resolutions to the Interior Department and Secretary Carl Schurz on the Poncas' behalf. By the next day, Tibbles was preparing wire dispatches for newspapers in Chicago, New York, and other cities as he searched for attorneys who would represent Standing Bear and his people in Omaha federal district court.

When the case went to court in May 1879, Standing Bear and the rest of the Poncas drew a large audience to Judge Dundy's courtroom, many of whom ignored Judge Dundy's instructions not to applaud the chief's remarks:

> [Standing Bear] claimed that, although his skin was of a different hue, yet he was a man, and that God made him. He said he was not a savage, and related how he had saved the life of a soldier whom he had found on the Plains, starved, and almost frozen to death, and of a man who had lost his way on the trackless prairie, whom he had fed and guided to his destination. In spite of the orders of the court and the efforts of the bailiffs, he was greeted with continual rounds of applause. (Tibbles, 93)

Dundy's legal reasoning was as follows:

> [I]t must be borne in mind that the *habeas corpus* act describes applicants for the writ as "persons" or "parties," who may be entitled thereto. It nowhere describes them as citizens, nor is citizenship in any way or place made a qualification for suing out the writ. . . . I must hold, then, that Indians, and consequently the relators, are persons, such as are described by and included within the laws before quoted. (Armstrong, 169)

Within a few months of Judge Dundy's ruling, the Standing Bear case became famous in the press across the United States as an instance of how even the most cooperative of small native nations could be grievously wronged by U.S. Indian policy. Everyone except the most obtuse Indian haters was convinced that the Poncas had been wronged legally and morally. General Crook, whose name appears as respondent in the court case, was convinced that the Poncas should be able to go home. Even Secretary of the Interior Carl Schurz admitted in 1879 that "the Poncas were grievously wronged by . . . a mistake in making the Sioux treaty" (Armstrong, 119).

Senator Henry Dawes, who later would become known to history as the primary author of the Allotment Act, which broke up Indians' common land holdings, is said to have become a "warm advocate of their cause" (Jackson, 207). The Ponca chief White Eagle, who had lost his wife and four children to removal, and who himself was dying of malaria contracted in Indian Territory, came to Washington and testified eloquently, after which Congress restored the Poncas' homeland.

The *New York Times* joined the popular newspaper crusades for restoration of Ponca lands after the trial of Standing Bear in Judge Dundy's Omaha federal court. An editorial on February 21, 1880, provided a short summary of the Poncas' troubles over their picturesque homeland along the Niobrara in northernmost Nebraska, beginning with the U.S. government's blunder of ceding to the Sioux land already guaranteed the Poncas by a previous treaty. "To this robbery of the tribe was added the destruction of their houses, movable property, and farms," the *Times* editorialized. "A citizen of the United States would have redress in the courts for such outrage as this" (Hayes, 37–38). The Poncas had done their best to become farmers as the Great Father had instructed them, and they had been wronged at every turn. The *Times* described Helen Hunt Jackson's advocacy of the Poncas' case along the East Coast as she took *A Century of Dishonor* to press. Jackson herself compared Judge Dundy's ruling to Abraham Lincoln's signing of the Emancipation Proclamation (Jackson, 203). The *Times* was a consistent supporter of both Jackson and the Poncas:

> In the history of the blunders and wrongs characterizing the so-called Indian policy of the United States (which is no policy), we find no darker page than that on which is recorded the wrongs of the Ponca Indians. . . . They ought to have their lands again at any cost to the Government under whose authority they have been so tyrannically despoiled. (Hayes, 221, 223)

The Standing Bear trial led to some interesting adventures in interracial acculturation in and around the frontier city of Omaha: The Anglo-American Tibbles befriended the Ponca Standing Bear while Susette LaFlesche, an Omaha Indian, and Tibbles fell in love and married. "Armed with news clippings on the Ponca story and endorsements from General [George] Crook, the mayor of Omaha, and leading Nebraska clergymen" (Tibbles, 129), in June Tibbles and LaFlesche traveled the East Coast with Standing Bear raising support for restoration of Ponca lands. In Boston, where support for Standing Bear's Poncas was very strong, a citizens' committee formed that included Henry Wadsworth Longfellow. While Susette LaFlesche was visiting Boston with Standing Bear, Longfellow said of her, "*This* is Minnehaha" (Tibbles, 130).

In Boston, Tibbles, LaFlesche, and Standing Bear first met Helen Hunt Jackson. Meeting them and hearing the Poncas' story inflamed Jackson's conscience and changed her life. Heretofore known as a poet, Jackson set out to write *A Century of Dishonor*, a best-selling book that described the angst of an America debating the future of the native peoples who had survived the last of the Indian wars. She became a major figure in the Anglo-American debate over the future of Native Americans that will be described in Chapter 7. Unlike Chief Joseph, Standing Bear and his people were allowed to return home to the Niobrara River after Congress investigated the conditions under which they had been evicted. He died there in 1908.

REFERENCES

Armstrong, Virginia Irving. *I Have Spoken: American History through the Voices of the Indians*. Athens, OH: Swallow Press, 1984.

Beal, Merrill D. *"I Will Fight No More Forever."* Seattle: University of Washington Press, 1963.

Brandon, William. *The American Heritage Book of Indians*. New York: Dell, 1964.

Brown, Mark H. *The Flight of the Nez Perce*. Lincoln: University of Nebraska Press, 1982.

Calloway, Colin, ed. *Our Hearts Fell to the Ground: Plains Indian Views of How the West Was Lost*. Boston: Bedford Books/St. Martin's Press, 1996.

Chalmers, Harvey. *The Last Stand of the Nez Perce*. New York: Twayne, 1962.

Custer, George A. *My Life on the Plains*. Ed. Milo Milton Quaife. Lincoln: University of Nebraska Press, 1952.

Hamilton, Charles, ed. *Cry of the Thunderbird*. Norman: University of Oklahoma Press, 1972.

Hayes, Robert G. *A Race at Bay: New York Times Editorials on "the Indian Problem," 1860–1900*. Carbondale: Southern Illinois University Press, 1997.

Howard, Oliver Otis. *Famous Indian Chiefs I Have Known*. 1908. Lincoln: University of Nebraska Press, 1989.

Hyde, George E. *Red Cloud's Folk: A History of the Oglala Sioux Indians*. Norman: University of Oklahoma Press, 1967.

Jackson, Helen Hunt. *A Century of Dishonor: A Sketch of the United States Government's Dealings with Some of the Indian Tribes*. Boston: Roberts Bros., 1888. Reprint. St. Clair Shores, MI: Scholarly Press, 1972.

Jones, Louis Thomas. *Aboriginal American Oratory: The Tradition of Eloquence among the Indians of the United States*. Los Angeles: Southwest Museum, 1965.

Josephy, Alvin M., Jr. *The Nez Perce Indians and the Opening of the Northwest*. 1965. Lincoln: University of Nebraska Press, 1979.

Marquis, Thomas B. *A Warrior Who Fought Custer*. Minneapolis: Midwest Co., 1931.

Massey, Rosemary, and the Omaha Indian Center. *Footprints in Blood: Standing Bear's Struggle for Freedom and Human Dignity*. Omaha: American Indian Center of Omaha, 1979.

Mathes, Valerie Sherer. "Helen Hunt Jackson and the Ponca Controversy." *Montana: The Magazine of Western History* 39:1 (Winter 1989): 42–53.

McLaughlin, James. *My Friend the Indian*. 1910. Seattle: Superior Publishing Co., 1970.

Moquin, Wayne, ed. *Great Documents in American Indian History*. New York: Praeger, 1973.

Nabokov, Peter, ed. *Native American Testimony*. New York: Viking, 1991.

Rosenstiel, Annette. *Red and White: Indian Views of the White Man, 1492–1982*. New York: Universe Books, 1983.

Stone, Jana, ed. *Every Part of This Earth Is Sacred: Native American Voices in Praise of Nature.* San Francisco: HarperCollins, 1993.

Tibbles, Thomas Henry. *The Ponca Chiefs: An Account of the Trial of Standing Bear.* Ed. Kay Graber. 1880. Lincoln: University of Nebraska Press, 1972.

Utley, Robert M. *Cavalier in Buckskin: George Armstrong Custer and the Western Military Frontier.* Norman: University of Oklahoma Press, 1988.

———. *The Lance and the Shield: The Life and Times of Sitting Bull.* New York: Henry Holt, 1993.

Vestal, Stanley. *Sitting Bull: Champion of the Sioux.* 1932. Norman: University of Oklahoma Press, 1957.

Vogel, Virgil J. *This Land Was Ours: A Documentary History of the American Indian.* New York: Harper & Row, 1972.

Waters, Frank. *Brave Are My People: Indian Heroes Not Forgotten.* Santa Fe, NM: Clear Light, 1993.

Weaver, Jace, ed. *Defending Mother Earth: Native American Perspectives on Environmental Justice.* Maryknoll, NY: Orbis Books, 1996.

Mother Earth. Courtesy of the artist,
John Kahionhes Fadden

6

MOTHER EARTH OR MOTHER LODE?

Chief Sea'thl, Black Elk, and Luther Standing Bear

Native American philosophy often combines spiritual and environmental themes in ways that appeal to many non-Indian environmental activists today. The words of Chief Sea'thl, Black Elk, and Luther Standing Bear therefore resound to much larger audiences in our time than during the time in which they lived, thought, and spoke a century or more ago. A lively scholarly debate has flared regarding how Native Americans generally conceived of the earth, especially whether the image of earth as mother is actually indigenous or has been forced into Indians' mouths by non-Indians looking to justify their own ways of thinking. The historiography of Sea'thl's "farewell speech" will be examined here, along with conceptions of earth as mother in the spirituality of Black Elk and characterizations of the natural world in the works of Luther Standing Bear.

Sea'thl (c. 1788–1866)

Sea'thl was a Duwamish and Suquamish who probably was born on Blake Island in Puget Sound. In his twenties, Sea'thl became the principal chief of the Duwamish, whose homeland in 1850 today comprises an industrial area immediately south of downtown Seattle, a city founded during the early 1850s and bearing an anglicized version of the chief's name. Pronounced in the original Duwamish, the name ends with an intricate twist of the tongue that is unknown in English and is most accurately transcribed as "Sealth" or "Sea'thl."

Henry A. Smith, a young medical doctor who met Sea'thl in the early 1850s, related in the *Seattle Star* of October 29, 1887:

> Old Chief Seattle was the largest Indian I ever saw, and by far the noblest looking. He stood six feet full in his moccasins, was broad-shouldered, deep-chested, and finely proportioned. His eyes were large, intelligent, expressive, and friendly when in repose. . . . He was usually solemn, silent, and dignified, but on great occasions moved among assembled multitudes like a Titan among Liliputians, and his lightest word was law. (Smith, n.p.)

An early Puget Sound resident, a Dr. Tolmie, said during the early 1830s that Sea'thl was "the finest physical specimen of Indian manhood that he . . . had seen" (Bagley, 245).

Chief Sea'thl (Seattle). Washington State Historical Society, Tacoma

Son of the Duwamish chief Schweabe, Sea'thl was about seven years of age when George Vancouver sailed the *Discovery* into Puget Sound and met briefly with the Duwamish and their allies the Suquamish. Sea'thl later aided his father and other Duwamish in the construction of the Old Man House, a community longhouse one thousand feet long that housed forty families. The Duwamish and the Suquamish maintained an alliance that ringed Puget Sound. Sea'thl took his first wife, La-da-ila, and became chief of the Duwamish-Suquamish alliance at the age of twenty-two. La-da-ila had died by 1833.

Sea'thl is said to have had two wives and several mistresses during his life, almost a half century of which was spent as the principal chief of the Suquamish, Duwamish, and, in varying numbers over time, as many as forty other native bands that lived the length of Puget Sound. Sea'thl was not the titular head of all these peoples, but at any place where members of several groups congregated, he was usually the acknowledged leader.

Several years before a city named Seattle existed, several Puget Sound tribes heard that Indians from inland were planning to make them the target of slave raids. Sea'thl, who was perhaps twenty to twenty-five years of age at the time, emerged as a regional leader after he conceived a "water ambush" against the invaders. Sea'thl led a party of warriors to a stream that he figured the invaders would use to transport them down the slopes of the Cascades and felled a large tree across it, around a bend so it was difficult to see from a distance. The invaders, as expected, rode their chances down the river, rounded the bend, hit the felled tree, and fell into the water, where Sea'thl's party attacked them and ended the threat.

Sea'thl was an agent of change among his people. By the early 1830s, for example, he had broken with tradition and freed his slaves. The holding of slaves by prominent people in other Northwest coast cultures continued through much of the century. Slaves could be put to death on special occasions, such as the dedication of a new family longhouse. After his slaves had been freed, Sea'thl then played a leading role in stopping human sacrifices among the Suquamish and Duwamish.

During 1841, the first "Bostons," as the Duwamish called whites (it was said that they had come from Boston), sailed into central Puget Sound, Duwamish and Suquamish territory, landing at Alki Point in what is now West Seattle. Ten years later, the schooner *Exact* delivered the first settlers on the site that later became downtown Seattle. From the beginning, Sea'thl resolved to cooperate with the settlers, but when they proposed naming their city after him, he protested.

It is possible (although, as with many purported facts attending Sea'thl's life, hardly sustainable beyond a reasonable doubt) that Sea'thl was unhappy that the city had been named after him because, in his culture, a soul could not reach its proper resting place if anyone mentioned the deceased person's name after his death. If this was the case, Sea'thl may have reacted with cold comfort to the undebatable fact that the European-Americans who adopted the name had trouble pronouncing the original and so changed it to "Seattle." Sea'thl seems, from accounts of the time, to have been very upset at the fact that the urban area had been named for him, upset enough to order his canoe paddled to Olympia, the territorial capital, about sixty miles, to protest the naming before Governor Isaac Stevens. Stevens, in whose culture notoriety after death could be a high honor, seemed unable to fathom Sea'thl's strenuous objections. The governor, who had a pronounced streak of vanity in his personality, may have been wondering, with a notable degree of envy, why the citizens of Seattle had not named their city after him.

Sea'thl's daughter Angeline is said to have told her contemporaries in the city of Seattle that the chief was not at all happy that the city had been named for him, that he was "very much displeased and remonstrated with the whites. He said that when he died he would have no rest, for he would be turning over [in his grave] all the time." Sea'thl's remonstrations were in vain, as city residents insisted on paying him the "honor." Clarence Bagley, in whose scholarly care this story has been passed down, says that he doubts its veracity, but does not say why (Bagley, 271).

Accounts of early Seattle's earliest immigrants tell of native gatherings of several thousand people congregating on the sandy beaches that once lined Elliott Bay, "standing around, or talking in groups . . . listening to the deliberations of the council of about twenty of the oldest Indians seated around a circle on the ground" (Bagley, 246). All who spoke at the council addressed themselves to "a venerable looking old native, who was apparently acting as a judge." This man was Chief Sea'thl.

These meetings sometimes assembled close to the aborning town of Seattle, along the waterfront near an area now called Pioneer Square. Sea'thl usually arrived at such gatherings in a canoe paddled by four to six younger men.

> Usually he wore a white shirt and a blanket draped around him from his middle downward . . . but occasionally he appeared clad in white men's array, coat, vest, pantaloons, each of a different color and texture, and considerably worse for wear. These were topped by a high black hat of the kind then known as "stovepipe." (Bagley, 260)

The Indians usually camped near the New England Hotel at "the Point," on the waterfront near present-day First Avenue and Marion Street in downtown Seattle. "When these heard Chief Seattle's voice, they would turn their heads in a listening attitude and evidently understood what he was saying, although he was nearly half a mile away, such was the resonance and carrying power of his voice" (Bagley, 264).

Sea'thl was well known along the Seattle waterfront until the mid-1850s, when his band moved westward across Puget Sound after signing the Treaty of Point Elliott with Governor Stevens. Sea'thl's most notable speech, to be examined later, was given in the context of arrangements for that move. In the mid-1850s, when the Yakima War spilled over the Cascades into Seattle under Chief Leschi, Sea'thl and his people looked on from their retreat on the western shores of Puget Sound.

Sea'thl's health failed during 1866. He grew physically weaker month by month, but his mind remained alert until his death at his people's retreat on June 7 of a fever. One of Sea'thl's sons, in a funeral oration, said, "We are all glad that the great chief's hands were never stained with a white man's blood" (Bagley, 267). Several hundred people, white and Indian, attended his funeral, performed with a combination of Catholic and native rites, at the Old Man House, the traditional meeting place that Sea'thl had helped build in his youth. Mourners at his funeral could look across Puget Sound at the growing city of Seattle. Business ceased in the area the day Sea'thl was put to rest. Even the sawmill at Point Madison was shut down.

In the development of an environmental philosophy, Chief Sea'thl's words often are cited in the late twentieth century as evidence that many Native Americans practiced a stewardship ethic toward the earth long before such attitudes became popular in non-Indian society. The debate ranges from acceptance of several versions of Sea'thl's speech (some of them embellished) to a belief that the original translator, Dr. Henry Smith, as well as many people who followed him, put ecological concepts into the chief's mouth.

Sea'thl's "farewell speech" is one of the more intriguing historical enigmas to confront historians of Indian-white relations in North America, in part because of its scanty written history, but also because of how often, and to what extent, the first written version of the speech has been edited in modern times to make it sound more like a contemporary environmental theme statement. The origins of the speech are historically murky enough to raise some questions about its authenticity. At the same time, the speech contains enough references to reality to make of it a fascinating case study in the making of history. The themes of this speech, authentic or not, again raise basic questions that underlie the entire course of Native American relations with immigrant Europeans in North America: who owns the land, and what are the implications and responsibilities of ownership or possession?

The exact date of Chief Sea'thl's speech is not known with certainty, one of many debates surrounding it. The most likely date appears to be January 12, 1854, although several others during the first half of that year have been advanced (Furtwangler, 48–49). The speech is not mentioned in records kept by Stevens, who is said to have crossed paths with the chief on the Seattle waterfront at some time, most likely during the first half of 1854, only a year or two after the city had first taken the chief's name as its own. This meeting between Stevens and Sea'thl was not a formal treaty council, and thus no governmental record exists, although the prospect of a treaty is mentioned by Sea'thl in the only written record of the speech, which was published as a newspaper account three decades later.

No written record of the "farewell speech" existed until 1887, when Dr. Smith published a version of it in the *Seattle Star*. Smith, by his own account, was present and taking notes in his diary as the chief spoke. What Smith heard was Sea'thl's native tongue translated into English by an interpreter of unknown competence. It is possible that one interpreter converted Sea'thl's words into Chinook, a trade jargon, while a second rendered this version into English (Furtwangler, 43).

No written recollections of the speech exist other than Smith's (Furtwangler, 5). The quality of anyone's recollections after a third of a century (even with notes available) may be debated, but one who has read Smith's version of what he maintains is the text of Sea'thl's speech cannot help but remark at evident differences in style compared to the rest of Smith's writing. The grand tone and sweeping philosophical range of the words attributed to Sea'thl are missing from the rest of Smith's written record, which includes some of the most strained and tortured small-town poetic boosterism in the written history of the American West. The tone of the speech seems simply too elegant to have been woven out of whole cloth by Smith's meager literary talents. For purposes of comparison, one may consider a verse of poetry penned by Smith to describe Chief Sea'thl:

> *And the chieftain from whom it* [Seattle] *descended*
> *Was portly, massive, and tall,*
> *And many a white man befriended,*
> *When the hand-writing showed on the wall.*
> (Furtwangler, 40)

Because the speech has spread to so many audiences and has been partially rewritten so many times, anyone who is concerned over whether he or she is being taken for a rhetorical ride should trace sources back to Smith's 1887 account, which has been reprinted several times in journals and books that are more enduring than the one tattered copy of the original 1887 newspaper account that survives in an archive at the University of Washington.

Albert Furtwangler argues cogently that the chief did not speak the language of the modern-day environmental movement that has embraced the speech. So far, so good. With an academic rationalist's penchant for neatly placing everything in its own little intellectual box, however, Furtwangler argues that Sea'thl's speech employed spiritual images, which also is very true. He seems not to have entertained the thought that Sea'thl's environmentalism (like that of Black Elk, discussed later) was anchored in his sense of the sacred. If we are to believe Dr. Smith's account, our only available source, Sea'thl did speak elegantly of his people's relationship with the earth in terms that have warmed the hearts of many an environmental advocate during the late twentieth century. For example:

> The son of the white chief says his father sends us greetings of friendship and goodwill. This is kind, for we know that he has little need of our friendship in return, because his people are many. They are like the grass that covers the vast prairies, while my people are few, and resemble the scattered trees of a storm-swept plain. (Smith, n.p.)

> Our dead never forget the beautiful world that gave them being. They still love its verdant valleys, its murmuring rivers, its magnificent mountains, sequestered vales and verdant-lined lakes and bays. . . . Every part of this soil is sacred in the estimation of my people. Every hillside, every valley, every plain and grove has been hallowed by some sad or happy event in days long vanished. Even the rocks, which seem to be dumb and dead as they swelter in the sun along the silent shore, thrill with memories of stirring events connected with the lives of my people. (Vanderwerth, 120–121)

Sea'thl's conception of the earth seems definitely rooted in his conception of greater power, a common element in many other Native American orations during the nineteenth century. A reader will find in Sea'thl's words echoes or premonitions of Black Elk, Standing Bear, Tecumseh, Sitting Bull, and many others:

> The white man's god cannot love his red children[,] or he would protect them. . . . Your God seems to us to be partial. He came to the white man. We never saw Him; we never even heard His voice. . . . No, we are two distinct races and must ever remain so. There is little in common between us. The ashes of our ancestors are sacred and their final resting place is hallowed ground, while you wander away from the tombs of your fathers seemingly without regret.
>
> Your religion was written on tables of stone by the iron fingers of an angry God lest you forget it. The Red Man could not remember nor comprehend it. Our religion is the traditions of our ancestors, the dreams of our old men, given to them by the Great Spirit, and the visions of our sachems; and it is written in the hearts of our people.
>
> Your dead cease to love you and the homes of their nativity as soon as they pass the portals of the tomb. They wander far off among the stars, are soon forgotten, and never return. Our dead never forget the world that gave them being. They still love its winding rivers, its great mountains, and its sequestered vales, and they ever yearn in tenderest affection over the lonely hearted living and often return to visit and comfort them. (Furtwangler, 14–15)

> It matters but little where we pass the remnants of our days. . . . A few more moons, a few more winters, and not one of all the mighty hosts that once filled this broad

land . . . will remain to weep over the tombs of a people once as powerful and hopeful as your own. (Smith, n.p.)

The most evocative and most often-quoted part of Chief Sea'thl's speech precedes its conclusion. In this part of the speech, Chief Sea'thl reflects on the course of empire:

> But why should we repine? Why should I murmur at the fate of my people? Tribes are made up of individuals and are no better than they. Men come and go like the waves of the sea. A tear, a *tahmanawis* [mourning ceremony], a dirge, and they are gone from our longing eyes forever. Even the white men, whose God walked and talked with him, as friend to friend, is not exempt from the common destiny. We *may* be brothers after all. We shall see. (Smith, n.p.; emphasis in original)

Sea'thl ended his oration, according to Smith's version, by expressing general agreement with Stevens' request that his people move to an assigned reservation as long as their right to visit the graves of their ancestors was respected. Sea'thl then closed by telling the whites that the ashes stirred by their boots were those of his Native American ancestors: "The soil is rich with the life of our kindred. . . . The dead are not altogether powerless" (Smith, n.p.).

While Sea'thl never says that "The earth is our mother" in so many words (as he has been often quoted in edited versions of the speech), he does return time and again to his people's relationship with the land, the philosophical basis of most environmental analysis. This fundamental point is entirely missed by Albert Furtwangler in *Answering Chief Seattle*. It is difficult to believe that Dr. Smith, in 1854 or 1887, would have consciously fabricated an environmental theme for an English-speaking audience to which environmental conservation was not an issue, for which new homes most often represented a "mother lode" of land and resources rather than a conception of earth as mother. No one, at least, has provided any motive for such a fabrication. Smith was not an environmentalist by nature. He was, it should be noted, an avid civic booster who welcomed white development along Puget Sound.

Embellishment of Sea'thl's most famous speech did occur shortly after the modern advent of Earth Day in 1972 by Ted Perry, a scriptwriter, who put several phrases in the chief's mouth in the script of his 1972 film *Home*. Two examples: Sea'thl never said, "The earth is our mother" in those words. Nor did he discourse on the whites' slaughter of the buffalo. His people's culture was based on salmon, not buffalo. Nevertheless, Perry's paraphrased version of Sea'thl's speech enjoyed wide circulation from the 1970s through the 1990s.

Furtwangler's apparent belief that modern-day environmental advocates have put the "mother-earth" concept into the mouths of Sea'thl is not original with him. A decade before publication of *Answering Chief Seattle*, Sam Gill devoted an entire book, *Mother Earth: An American Story* (1987) to that singular idea. Gill maintains that "Mother Earth has come to be a major goddess to the Indians within this century and . . . her development has been necessarily dependent not only upon the crisis caused by Americans of European ancestry but also upon European-American interpretations and expectations of Indians and their religions" (Gill, *Mother Earth*, 150).

Some ethnohistorians maintain that Native Americans possessed little or no environmental philosophy, and that any attempt to assemble evidence to sustain a Native American ecological paradigm is doomed to failure because the entire argument is an exercise in wishful thinking by environmental activists seeking sentimental support for their own views. William A. Starna, professor of anthropology at the State University of New York (College at Oneonta), calls the argument that Native Americans had an environmental ethic "pan-Indian mythology" (Starna, 468). As he does in the face of evidence that the Iroquois helped inspire democracy, Starna asserts that modern Indian activists created the idea of Native American environmentalism.

One wishes to be intellectually charitable and not to unfairly alienate Furtwangler, Gill, Starna, and others who share their beliefs about the recent, non-Indian genesis of the mother-earth image. However, their assertions that Native Americans had no concept of mother earth before immigrant peoples fantasized it in their name during the twentieth-century environmental movement miss an astonishing amount of the historical record, not to mention Native American oral histories. References to "mother earth" in Native American cosmology are not scarce. They are abundant, according to George Cornell:

> Native peoples almost universally view the earth as a feminine figure. The Mother provides for the sustenance and well-being of her children: it is from her that all subsistence is drawn. The relationship of native peoples to the earth, their Mother, is a sacred bond with the creation. (Cornell, 3)

Many native cosmologies conceive of the sky (including the sun) as a masculine counterpart to mother earth; sky and earth are a loving couple who are sometimes prone to many of the failings of human relationships between men and women. While the Christian Bible commands subordination of the earth, many native cosmologies place human beings in a web of interdependent relationships with all facets of the Creation. In this web, all things are animate, even objects, such as the pebbles under one's feet, that European languages characterize as lifeless. In the web of Native American experience, the landscape of life envelops all of reality.

Gill is a professor of religious studies at the University of Colorado at Denver. He also has authored a textbook on Native American religions

(Gill, *Native American Religions*). By any measure, Professor Gill has the credentials of an expert in Native American theology. Yet for all his credentials, Gill looks straight into a rich record of Native American associations of earth with feminine images and finds almost nothing. His is a case study of how exclusive devotion to Western European assumptions can blind a scholar to even the most obvious tenets of thought in many Native American cultures.

Reacting to Gill's *Mother Earth*, Vine Deloria, Jr., suggests that scholars who contend that European-Americans have "invented" the image of the Indian as ecologist may be showing their own ignorance of history.

> As a by-product of researching Indian treaties, I have come up with numerous references to Mother Earth. Of course I did not find these references in ethnographic materials—I found them in minutes of councils and treaty negotiations. . . . Indians were not sitting around in seminar rooms articulating a nature philosophy for the benefit of non-Indian students, after all. They were trying to save their lands from exploitation and expropriation. (Deloria, 406)

Deloria documents the natural metaphor of earth as mother as far back as 1776. On June 21, at a conference in Pittsburgh during the Revolutionary War, Cornstalk, who was trying to convince the Mingos (Ohio Valley Iroquois) to ally with the Americans, said:

> You have heard the good Talks which our Brother [George Morgan] Weepemachukthe [The White Deer] has delivered to us from the Great Council at Philadelphia representing all our white brethren who have grown out of this same ground with ourselves[,] for this Big [Turtle] Island being our common Mother, we and they are like one Flesh and Blood. (Deloria, 406)

European-Americans have been hearing Native Americans characterize the earth as mother since shortly after the *Mayflower* landed. Massasoit, who invited the Pilgrims to the first Pilgrim Thanksgiving dinner, faced European ideas of land tenure with a few questions of his own:

> What is this you call property? It cannot be the earth, for the land is our mother, nourishing all her children, beasts, birds, fish, and all men. The woods, the streams, everything on it belongs to everybody and is for the use of all. How can one man say it belongs only to him? (Weaver, 10)

Gill, in denying that Native Americans had an earth-centered religious ethos, seems to be implying that non-Indians made up the whole idea and put it into Indians' mouths for various ulterior motives, one of which is (to Gill) a slavish devotion to the stereotype of the Noble Savage. Gill also repeatedly refers to the idea of "mother earth" as a "goddess," but actual belief systems do not restrict the idea to a single person in human form, which is a European conception of deity. Similarly, characterizations of "mother earth" are usually metaphorical rather than human centered in Native American religions. Native American cosmology may be characterized as a "church" of the earth, even though the very idea of a "church" is a European concept. Ethnohistorian Harold Hickerson calls Native American spiritual expression "the religion of nature" (Vecsey and Venables, 2).

The concept of earth as mother is evoked in a Pawnee chant:

The signs of the dawn are seen in the east
And the breath of the new life is here . . .
Mother Earth is the first to be called to awake . . .
She moves, she awakes, she rises,
he feels the breath of the new-born Dawn.
The leaves and the grass stir;
All things move with the breath of the new day;
Everywhere life is renewed.

This is very mysterious;
We are speaking of something very sacred,
Although it happens every day.
(Hughes, vi)

The image of earth as mother is evoked in a Winnebago proverb: "Holy Mother Earth, the trees, and all nature, are witnesses of your thoughts and deeds" (McLuhan, 5). Sitting Bull, who has been quoted extensively on his affection for the land in Chapter 5, characterized his beloved territory as "mother" during a council at Powder River in 1877:

Yet, hear me, people, we have now to deal with another race, small and feeble when our fathers first met them, but now great and overbearing. Strangely enough, they have a mind to till the soil and the love of possession is a disease with them. These people have made many rules that the rich may break but the poor may not. They take tithes from the poor and weak to support the rich who rule. They claim this mother of ours, the earth, for their own and fence their neighbors away; they deface her with their buildings and their refuse. That nation is like a spring freshet that overruns its bank and destroys all who are in its path. (McLuhan, 90)

Robert M. Utley's biography of Sitting Bull, which begins with an account of how the White Buffalo Woman gave the Lakotas the Sacred Calf Pipe, includes a reference to earth as mother: " 'With this sacred pipe,' she said, 'you will walk upon the Earth; for the Earth is your grandmother and mother and she is sacred' " (Jahner, 52, cited in Utley, 2).

Ecological metaphors also have been woven into the languages of many Native American cultures. "Who cuts the trees as he pleases cuts short his own life," said the Maya, long before pan-Indianism or arguments about it. The Maya word for "tree sap" is the same as the word for "blood" (Stuart, 95).

About the year 1900, Bedagi (Big Thunder), a leader whose ancestry may have been drawn from one or more of several New England native nations (Passamaquoddy, MicMac, and Maliseet), is reported to have offered the following gendered ecological metaphor:

> The Great Spirit is our father, but the earth is our mother. She nourishes us; that which we put in the ground she returns to us, and healing plants she gives us likewise. If we are wounded, we go to our mother and seek to lay the wounded part against her, to be healed. Animals, too, do thus, and lay their wounds to the earth. (Curtis, 11)

In the Navajo worldview, "This beautiful land . . . is our mother" (Gorman, 19), "the sacred resting place of the ancestors . . . not something to be owned privately" (Hughes, 61). The image of mother earth, paired with father sky, appears in Navajo sacred sandpaintings. One such sandpainting is described by Trudy Griffin-Pierce:

> At the center of Mother Earth is the lake that filled the Place of Emergence. The four sacred plants—corn, beans, squashes, and tobacco—emerge from this lake; the roots of these plants firmly connect them to the lake and to the Earth. The constellations fill the body of Father Sky, whose arms and legs lie over those of Mother Earth, just as the sky lies above the Earth. (Griffin-Pierce, Plate 4)

The pronoun "she" reflects the feminine nature of the earth in Navajo cosmology. Changing Woman, a Navajo deity, "represents the powers of renewal inherent in the earth" (Griffin-Pierce, 30). The image of earth as mother is prominent in the creation legend of the Zuñis:

> With his substance of flesh outdrawn from the surface of his person, the Sun-father formed the seed-stuff of twain worlds, impregnating therewith the great waters, and lo! in the heat of his light these waters of the sea grew green and scums rose upon them, waxing wide and weighty until, behold! they became Awitelin Tsita, the "Four-fold Containing Mother-earth, and Apoyan Tä´chu the "All-covering Father-sky." (Moquin, 7)

Carl Sweezy, an Arapaho, described his people's traditional environmental theology in terms shared by his contemporary Black Elk:

> We believed in a power that was higher than all people and all the created world, and we called this power the Man Above. We believed in some power in the world that governed everything that grew, and we called this power Mother-Earth. We believed in the power of the sun, of the Night-Sun or Moon, of the Morning Star,

of the Four Old Men who direct the winds and the rains and the seasons, and give us the breath of life. We believed that everything created is holy and has some part in the power that is over all. (Weaver, frontispiece)

When they separate religion from ecology, Furtwangler, Starna, Gill, and those who agree with them display a rather profound ignorance of ways in which Native American peoples construct their realities. They are miscasting Native American ways of thinking to fit academic categories. Such distinctions are lost on many Native Americans, including the late Tadadaho (speaker) of the Haudenosaunee (Iroquois) Confederacy, Leon Shenandoah, who has been quoted as saying, "Nature, that's our religion, our way of life" (Vecsey and Venables, 2).

Those who dismiss a native ecological ethic as the invention of modern-day hippies and pan-Indianists are missing something much deeper than mere mentions of "mother earth" in nineteenth-century primary sources. They are missing the fundamental nature of many Native American traditions, the terms in which native thought conceptualizes the land and the life it nurtures. To Roger Dunsmore, Western thought creates hierarchies and categories that do not exist in Native American thoughtways. The very cognitive map for conceptualizing life is different, as illustrated in recent time by the example of "a Wasco Indian logger (a faller), who quit logging (Warm Springs Camp A) and sold his chainsaw because he couldn't stand hearing the trees scream as he cut into them" (Dunsmore, 7). This is a worldview in which "the whole world is perceived and valued. Even the flies" (Dunsmore, 15). A sense of a web of life connecting all things framed the cognitive map of Chief Joseph when he said, "The Earth and I are of one mind" (Dunsmore, 39).

In the Haudenosaunee creation epic, the earth mother provides the people with "the three sisters"—corn, squashes, and beans. Women till the fields, maintain the hearth, and caucus in clans to choose the nation's political leaders. Informed of Professor Starna's assumptions about the mother-earth image, Mohawk artist and culture bearer John Kahionhes Fadden replied, "Does he think that the Haudenosaunee Thanksgiving Prayer was somehow dreamed up by the hippies of the 1960s?" (Fadden, personal correspondence). The Thanksgiving Prayer specifically invokes the image of earth as mother, thanking her for sustenance. The image of mother earth also emerges from an Iroquois thanksgiving offering that was first made available to a non-Indian audience in Lewis Henry Morgan's *League of the Haudenosunee, or Iroquois*, first published during 1851:

We return thanks to our mother, the earth, which sustains us. We return thanks to the rivers and streams, which supply us with water. We return thanks to all herbs, which furnish medicines for the cure of our diseases. We return thanks to the corn, and to her sisters, the beans and squashes, which give us life. (Morgan, I:194)

The image of mother earth is mentioned in Henry David Thoreau's Indian notebooks, which are held in the Pierpont Morgan Library in eleven manuscript volumes and are his notes and abstracts from reading more than two hundred books. One such reference, to Tecumseh, seems to have been borrowed from the work of Henry Rowe Schoolcraft described in Chapter 3: "The Indians consider the earth as their universal mother" (Fleck, 22). At other points in his Indian notebooks, Thoreau describes a concept of "common mother" as a reference to the earth in Mohawk legends (Fleck, 27).

The use of the earth-mother image is not restricted to Native American peoples of North America. The primary spirit of Peruvian Aguaruna women is Nugkui, who has been interpreted as "earth mother [or mothers]" (Barner, 70). Early Spanish records indicate that the Incas of both sexes have worshipped a deity of the earth mother for at least 4,000 years:

> It is a common thing among the Indians to adore the fertile earth . . . which they call *Pachamama* [earth mother], offering her chicha [corn bear] by spilling it on the ground, as well as cocoa and other things. (Murúa, *Historian*, in Silverblatt, 24)

Sometimes a belief in the earth as mother is reflected in Native American languages. In the Algonquian Ojibwe language, for example, "The words for Earth and the vagina, respectively *aki* and *akitun*, share the same root" (Paper, 14). Each native people in the Americas has its own origin story, but many share common elements. The characterization of the earth in the feminine, using kin terminology, is one of these.

Native American perspectives on the environment often were virtually opposite those of many early settlers, who sought to "tame" the "wilderness." Many Native American peoples endowed all living things with spirit, even items that Europeans regarded as nonliving, such as rocks. Most Native Americans saw themselves as enmeshed in a web of mutually complementary life. As Black Elk said, "With all beings and all things, we shall be as relatives" (Black Elk, *Sacred Pipe*, 105).

The building of a case that Native Americans often thought in terms of "mother earth" does not imply that Europeans, Asians, and Africans did not have similar ideas in their histories—"Mother Russia" or "Mother Nature," for example. That said, the metaphor of earth as sustainer (most often "mother") laces many of the statements of Native American leaders recorded by European-American observers in many areas of North America, many of them long before Chief Sea'thl's speech. Tecumseh, rallying Native American allies in an appeal for alliance about 1805, said, "Let us unite as brothers, as sons of one Mother Earth. . . . Sell our land? Why not sell the air. . . . Land cannot be sold" (Waters, 62–63). Black Hawk, exiled to a reservation near Fort Madison, Iowa, after the three-month war that bears his name, opened a Fourth of July address to a mainly non-Indian audience in the late 1830s by observing, "The Earth is our mother; we are on it, with the Great Spirit above us" (Waters, 76).

Black Elk (1863–1950)

Black Elk was eleven years old during the summer of 1874 when, by his account, published in *Black Elk Speaks*, an expedition under Gen. George Armstrong Custer invaded the Paha Sapa ("hills that are black"), the holy land of the Lakotas. The Black Hills had been guaranteed to the Lakotas "in perpetuity" by the Fort Laramie Treaty of 1868. Custer's expedition was on a geological mission, not a military one. Custer was looking for gold. He found it, and in his wake, several thousand gold seekers poured into the Black Hills, ignoring the treaty.

Black Elk came of age during the late nineteenth century as European settlement closed in around his homeland. Raised as a shaman, Black Elk was a witness to important events in Sioux history, from General Custer's invasion of the Black Hills in 1874 and the Battle of the Little Bighorn in 1876 to the massacre at Wounded Knee in 1890. In 1886, when he was twenty-three years of age, Black Elk joined Buffalo Bill's Wild West Show. After a tour of large cities on the eastern seaboard, the troupe traveled to England. A contemporary photograph shows a young Black Elk dressed to dance in buckskins and mirrors.

Black Elk near the end of his life, in the 1940s. National Anthropological Archives, Smithsonian Institution

Black Elk later recalled what he witnessed at Wounded Knee following the massacre during late December 1890:

> We followed down the dry gulch, and what we saw was terrible. Dead and wounded women and children and little babies were scattered all along where they had been trying to run away. The soldiers had followed along the gulch, as they ran, and murdered them in there. Sometimes they were in heaps because they had huddled together, and some were scattered all along. Sometimes bunches of them had been killed and torn to pieces where the wagon [Hotchkiss] guns had hit them.

Black Elk (left) as a young man, dressed to dance in England. National Anthropological Archives, Smithsonian Institution

> I saw a little baby trying to suck its mother, but she was bloody and dead. (Black Elk, *Black Elk Speaks*, 259)

The *New York Times* editorialized trenchantly on December 31, 1890, fundamentally agreeing with Black Elk: "It would be an abuse of language to describe as a battle the encounter that took place on Monday between United States troops and hostile Indians" (Hayes, 227). After the Wounded Knee massacre, Black Elk watched his people, once the mounted lords of the plains, become hungry, impoverished prisoners, pent up on fragmented government reservations.

In the words of Black Elk, the Lakotas and Cheyennes "painted their faces black"—went to war—to regain the Black Hills. The result was the Battle of the Little Bighorn (1876). In *Black Elk Speaks*, Black Elk told John Neihardt that he had been a young warrior at the battle of the Little Bighorn, and that he had witnessed the battle. Young Black Elk tried to take his first scalp at that battle. The soldier under Black Elk's hatchet proved to have an unusually tough scalp, so Black Elk shot him.

The Seventh Cavalry initiated a battle that the Lakota chief Kill Eagle likened to a hurricane or bees swarming out of a hive. Completely surrounded and cut off from reinforcements stationed only nine miles away, Custer's force was cut to ribbons during one furious, bloody hour on a battleground that nearly disappeared under a huge cloud of dust. Black Elk was heartened by the outcome. He was not sorry at all, believing that the *Wasi'chus* had come to kill their families in their own homes. The battle provoked momentary joy among the Sioux and Cheyennes, who for decades had watched their hunting ranges curtailed by what Black Elk called the gnawing flood of the *Wasi'chu*.

European-American immigrants stamped their land-use patterns on the hills in many ways after Custer led the expedition that found gold there in 1874, two years before the Sioux and allied Cheyennes avenged that invasion by annihilating Custer's small army at the Little Bighorn. In more modern times, the Black Hills have yielded billions of dollars worth of minerals, from gold to uranium. Other areas have become tourist traps crowned by the images of four U.S. presidents carved from Mount Rushmore. The four presidential visages stare out with no apparent irony regarding the fact that the Sioux have never legally ceded the land and have never accepted a land-claims settlement that by the 1990s passed $400 million, with accumulated interest. As he described why the Lakotas have declined offers to sell the Black Hills, Black Elk returned to the same theme:

> The *Wasi'chus* [whites] went to some of the chiefs alone and got them to put their marks on the treaty. Maybe some of them did this when they were crazy from drinking the *minne wakan* [whiskey] the *Wasi'chus* gave them. But only crazy or very foolish men would sell their Mother Earth. (Black Elk, *Black Elk Speaks*, 135)

The Black Hills—Paha Sapa, "hills that are black," in Black Elk's language—became sacred to the Sioux as the rugged, craggy, haunting heart of the natural world. The hills were rich with small game, a "meat pack," as Sitting Bull called them (Utley, 115), insurance against hard times elsewhere. The hills also included sheltered valleys with abundant firewood, as well as stands of lodgepole pine (favored as tipi poles), all of which made the area a superior winter camp.

Black Elk gave voice to his ecological theology as he observed the Black Hills' invasion by Anglo gold miners when he was a young man. In John Neihardt's telling of this event, Black Elk expresses a fundamental sense of wonder at why so many people would move so far and expend so much energy trespassing on Lakota holy land seeking a metal that in his economic system had no practical use or monetary value. He called gold "the yellow metal they worship that makes them [*Wasi'chus*] crazy" (Black Elk, *Black Elk Speaks*, 30).

One wonders how Sam Gill, a professor of Native American religion, could have constructed a book on the earth-as-mother image in Native American cosmology without having considered the gendered ecological metaphors in records left us by Black Elk, as told to John Neihardt and other scholars. If he has read Black Elk, did Professor Gill notice the way in which he describes humankind's relationship with the natural world? Is the logical extension of Gill's argument an assertion that John Neihardt invented it all? Long before "pan-Indian mythology," and long before environmental contamination became a widespread problem, Black Elk couched an environmental metaphor in a theological context: "Every step that we take upon You [the earth] should be done in a sacred manner; every step should be taken as a prayer" (Black Elk, *The Sacred Pipe*, 13–14).

Michael Steltenkamp's *Black Elk: Holy Man of the Oglala* (1993) describes Black Elk's years as a Roman Catholic missionary. Steltenkamp, who is a Jesuit himself as well as an anthropologist, said that he learned of Black Elk's conversion from Lucy Looks Twice, Black Elk's only surviving child, who died in 1978. Looks Twice recalled that the Jesuits had sponsored travel by Black Elk among other Indians—Arapahoes, Winnebagos, Omahas, and others—where he instructed potential converts in Catholicism through an interpreter. The church also sent Black Elk on fund-raising trips to cities such as New York, Boston, Chicago, Washington, D.C., and Omaha. In 1934, shortly after publication of *Black Elk Speaks*, he complained that Neihardt had not said enough about his life as a Catholic. Black Elk added that everyone in his family had been baptized.

In his later years, Black Elk combined Catholic missionary work with occasional showmanship at South Dakota tourist attractions that capitalized on his image as a Lakota holy man. Steltenkamp says that Black Elk sensed no contradictions in mixing the two interpretations of the "great mystery." Black Elk's life has always been remembered with an air of mystery. It is said that on the night he died, in 1950, an intense meteor shower created natural fireworks in the sky over Pine Ridge.

Black Elk was about seventy years of age when he first met the poet John Neihardt, whose *Black Elk Speaks* popularized Black Elk's views later in the twentieth century. *Black Elk Speaks* is usually read as a religious text, as indeed it is. It is a religious text, however, that is laced with ecological metaphors. As with Dr. Henry Smith's account of Sea'thl's "farewell speech," Black Elk's story was told to a non-Indian through an interpreter a considerable time after the history it narrates. Black Elk described to Neihardt events that occurred mainly between 1863, the year of his birth, and 1890, during and after the Wounded Knee massacre. The telling itself took place roughly three decades into the twentieth century.

At the beginning of Neihardt's account, Black Elk twice calls upon the image of mother earth in so many words:

> Is not the sky a father and the earth a mother, and are not all living things with feet or wings or roots their children? And this hide upon the mouthpiece here, which should be bison hide, is for the earth, from whence we came, and at whose breast we suck as babies all our lives, along with all the animals and birds and trees and grasses. And because it means all this, and more than any man can understand, the pipe is holy. . . . Behold! And you, Mother Earth, the only Mother, you who have shown mercy to your children! (Black Elk, *Black Elk Speaks*, 3, 6)

Elsewhere in Neihardt's account, Black Elk speaks of "Mother Earth" again (Black Elk, *Black Elk Speaks*, 10) and "the spirit of the earth" (Black Elk, *Black Elk Speaks*, 30), a phrase that clearly presents his assumed unity of spirituality in an earth-centered context. In Black Elk's *Sacred Pipe*, an account of the Lakotas' most important religious rituals, as told to Joseph Epes Brown in the late 1940s, just before Black Elk died in 1950, references to mother earth are something more than incidental. This idea is referenced no less than thirty-seven times in *The Sacred Pipe*, with sometimes as many as four different references on a single page (Black Elk, *Sacred Pipe*, 8–9, 13, 14, 15, 24, 25, 27, 34, 38, 47, 61, 72, 77, 78, 79, 80, 104, 105, 108, 109, 113, 119, 121, 123, 125, 126, 133, 137).

A *wakan* (mysterious, awesome, or holy) woman introduces the Sacred Pipe to the Lakotas with a description of the earth mother:

> He who keeps the soul of a person must be a good and pure man, and he should use the pipe so that all the people with the soul, will together send their voices to *Wakan-Tanka*. The fruit of your Mother the Earth and the fruit of all that bears will be blessed in this manner, and your people will then walk the path of life in a sacred manner. (Black Elk, *Sacred Pipe*, 8–9)

High Hollow Horn, an associate of Black Elk, wove themes that Western scholars might categorize in three "boxes" feminism (recognizing women's role in creation), environmental consciousness, and spirituality, in ways similar to Chief Sea'thl's farewell speech half a continent away. Here he echoes Black Elk's sentiments:

> My relatives, this pipe is *wakan*. We all know that it cannot lie. . . . My relatives, Grandmother and Mother Earth, we are of earth, and we belong to you. O Mother Earth from whom we receive our food, you care for our own growth as do our own mothers. Every step that we take upon you should be taken in a sacred manner; each step should be as a prayer. (Black Elk, *Sacred Pipe*, 13)

Dale A. Stover, a colleague who is a student of Black Elk, reminds me that Joseph Epes Brown probably did not take notes while he was interviewing Black Elk during the 1940s. Even with no notes, the pervasive nature of the mother-earth image in the resulting testimony is very difficult to dismiss as the interviewer's invention, especially when the same image appears in John Neihardt's *Black Elk Speaks* as well as in a book published by Neihardt's daughter Hilda, who was often with him during the interviews. Joseph Epes Brown's account is laced with too many references for him to have put them all in Black Elk's mouth. Trying to read *The Sacred Pipe* without reference to mother earth would be about as difficult as reading the New Testament without reference to the Virgin Mary. (A student of comparative cultures might remark that most of the Bible also was not written until many years after the events it describes.)

References to the image of earth as mother also occur with regularity in the teachings of Black Elk as presented in Raymond J. DeMallie's *The Sixth Grandfather*, which examines John Neihardt's interviews with the Lakota holy man during 1931 and 1944. DeMallie himself believes that John Neihardt

> was an extraordinarily faithful spokesman for Black Elk. What he wrote was an interpretation of Black Elk's life, but not one that was embellished in any way. Instead, he tried to write what he thought that the old man himself would have expressed. The book [*Black Elk Speaks*] is Black Elk's story as he gave it to Neihardt, but the literary quality and the tone of the work are Neihardt's. (DeMallie, 51)

The notes on which John Neihardt based *Black Elk Speaks* (as well as additional interviewing during 1944), as presented by DeMallie, contain at least fourteen references to the earth as mother, most of them in association with rituals related to the sacred pipe, when the pipe is presented to the four directions, the Great Spirit, and to mother earth (DeMallie, 117, 224, 233, 236, 238, 286, 288, 290, 313, 340, 392).

> The spirit horses had been dancing around the circle of the tipi. When we went in there we all sat there and Black Road, the medicine man who helped me perform

this ceremony, lit the peace pipe and offered it to the four quarters, above, and to mother earth, and we smoked for the good of the people. (DeMallie, 224)

The theological pipe ritual and the ecological image of mother earth are intimately intertwined: "Through the offering of my pipe to all the quarters, above, and to mother earth, may you all hear me" (DeMallie, 238); "You should smoke this pipe every morning, offering it to the six grandfathers of the west, asking them to guide you, and also to the north, south, and east, and to the Great Spirit above and to mother earth" (DeMallie, 288).

The image of mother earth also is invoked in connection with the origin story of the Lakotas: "The second grandfather represented the north. He said: 'Behold the mother earth, for you shall create a nation' " (DeMallie, 117). The same image is raised several times during both the 1931 and 1944 interviews as a way of describing the earth in a more generally ecological manner, apart from the rituals specifically describing Lakota origins and handling of the sacred pipe, for example: "All over the earth, faces of living things are alike. Mother Earth has turned these faces out of the earth with tenderness" (DeMallie, 288); "The four-leggeds and the wings of the air and the mother earth were supposed to be relative-like and all three of us lived together on mother earth" (DeMallie, 288); "Always remember, your grandmother is underneath your feet always. You are always on her, and your father is above" (DeMallie, 313).

In Hilda Neihardt's account, Black Elk returned to the metaphor of mother earth when he described handling of the sacred pipe:

"Then, standing in the center of the circle, we raise the pipe and offer it to the sky, sending forth a voice. 'You in the depths of the heavens, an eagle of power, behold!'

"And last of all, we offer the sacred pipe to the earth, saying, 'And you, Mother Earth, the only mother, you who have shown mercy to your children.' " (Hilda Neihardt, 60)

Black Elk Speaks has spread around the world and has been republished in several languages. Carl Jung liked the book so much that he arranged to have it published in German, a language that was spoken in the Neihardt family (Hilda Neihardt, 101).

In Descriptions of the Oglala Lakota spiritual leader Black Elk's relation to the land of his birth, one encounters some of the same problems as with Sea'thl's "farewell speech." How much of the speech is Sea'thl, and how much of it was Dr. Henry A. Smith's conception of him thirty-three years later? Black Elk's conceptions of nature and land, like those of Sea'thl, use the language of religion and so are usually studied in a theological and not an ecological context in North American mainstream academia. Like Sea'thl, however, the urge to place Black Elk neatly in any one curricular box ignores at least some of what he was saying.

How much of Black Elk's story is his own, and how much of it is really the conception of John Neihardt, poet laureate of Nebraska? It is granted that every writer brings part of himself to the story he or she tells, and Neihardt is no exception. He has, however, been occasionally targeted by students of history who think that the poet took ahistorical license with Black Elk's memoirs. Criticism ranges from noting the usual problems with transcription and translation to a rather scathing indictment by William S. Penn, who seems to assume, from the distance of six and a half decades, a certainty about Neihardt's psychological motives that might surprise any thoughtful psychologist or police detective because he assumes so much without evident factual support:

> [In] the most famous fake of all, *Black Elk Speaks* . . . John Neihardt *freely* augmented, embellished, and altered the notes his niece recorded in her own invented stenographic shorthand as Black Elk's nephew translated what his uncle was saying—*without regard* for the multiple difficulties of translation, transmission, and recording. (Pann, 2; emphasis added)

Julian Rice, in the *Handbook of Native American Literature*, laments Neihardt's Christian biases while also mentioning that by the time Black Elk told his story to Neihardt, he had been a professing Catholic himself for thirty years (Rice, 211–213). Whatever his Eurocentric biases, Neihardt was careful to reproduce Black Elk's own words as accurately as the ambiguities of translation allowed. Black Elk spoke in Lakota that was interpreted in English by Ben Black Elk. Neihardt would then recast Ben's rendition into standard English, sometimes asking Ben to request clarification from Black Elk. The result of this process was copied in shorthand by members of Neihardt's family. These notes became Neihardt's source material for the text of *Black Elk Speaks*, which must be appreciated as epic poetry as much as it is regarded as narrative biography.

Penn and other scholars may wish that they had sources with less "static" in the "communication channel." What happens, however, after one totally dismisses the accounts of Black Elk prepared by Neihardt and Epes Brown and all the secondary scholarship based on them on the basis that the original sources are fundamentally flawed? Black Elk then becomes largely a historical nonperson, yet another Native American life ground into obliterated memory by the conquest's imposition of an alien language and ways of making history on the land he once called home.

Black Elk speaks in the context of a Lakota worldview that includes as one of its four most important figures the figure of Maka (also Maka-akan, Maka Ina, or Makakan), the feminine creator of the universe, "Earth . . . the grandmother of all things" (Walker, 10) or "Mother Earth" (Powers, 35). Maka is very influential in Lakota cosmology, to the point where some Lakotas, told by the federal government to farm, "believed that 'scratching the bowels' of *Maka Ina*, Mother Earth, with a plow [was] a heinous act" and refused to take up the plow (Powers, 107).

> In the cosmology it is woman whose social transgression leads to the creation of time and space. It is woman, who, bored with the natural universe, conspires with the culture hero to coax humans, her own people called the Buffalo Nation, from their subterranean world to the earth. It is she who in concert with the trickster teaches the people about culture, and it is she who suddenly then leaves them to face the vicissitudes of nature alone. (Powers, 35)

Black Elk looked at the future with foreboding as one regime of land tenure on the Great Plains rolled over and engulfed another. By the time he was interviewed by John Neihardt around 1930, his people lived mainly in "square gray houses, scattered here and there across this hungry land." Around them, said Black Elk, "the Wasichus [white men] had drawn a line to keep them in." This denial of freedom had broken the nation's sacred hoop, leaving the people in despair.

> They seemed heavy to me, heavy and dark; so heavy that it seemed they could not be lifted; so dark that they could not be made to see any more. Hunger was among us often now, for much of what the Great Father in Washington sent us must have been stolen by Wasichus who were crazy to get money. (Calloway, 150, 152)

Black Elk was horrified by the wanton destruction of buffalo. During the fall of 1883, he witnessed the slaughter of the last great buffalo herds by white hunters who often took nothing but the animal's hide or tongue.

> I can remember when the bison were so many that they could not be counted, but more and more Wasichus came to kill them until there were only heaps of bones scattered where they used to be. The Wasichus did not kill them to eat; they killed them for the metal that makes them crazy, and they took only the hides to sell. Sometimes they did not even take the hides, only the tongues; and I have heard that fireboats came down the Missouri loaded with dried bison tongues. You can see that the men who did this were crazy. (Forbes, 65–66)

Black Elk's sense of foreboding at the new culture, economy, and society flooding the Great Plains is palpable:

And now when I look upon my people in despair, I feel like crying and I wish my vision could have been given to a man more worthy. I wonder why it came to me, a pitiful old man who can do nothing. Men and women and children I have cured of sickness with the power the vision gave me; but my nation I could not help. (Dunsmore, 69)

Luther Standing Bear (1868–1939)

Earth-as-mother imagery also was a strong element in the writings of Luther Standing Bear, one of the founders of a remarkable Sioux literary tradition that includes Charles Eastman, Gertrude Bonnin (Zitkala-Sa) and Vine Deloria, Jr. Recognition of Standing Bear's works, which range from social commentary to autobiography, grew during the twentieth century, when he was often seen as voicing concerns salient to a pan-Indian sense of identity as well as concern about abuses of the environment.

Standing Bear's father, who also was called Standing Bear, participated in the Battle of the Little Bighorn and later represented his people at a conference in Washington, D.C. Standing Bear's father returned from that conference dressed in a Prince Albert coat and other formal Anglo-American trappings, including a silk top hat that was later used to carry water. Standing Bear was at first called Ota Kre (Plenty Kill) because of his father's reputation as a warrior. The young Standing Bear was trained traditionally to become a hunter and warrior just as increasing European-American presence was making the old ways impossible.

Standing Bear was one of the first students at the Carlisle Indian Industrial School and a personal favorite of the school's founder, Richard Henry Pratt. He was one of about 150 Indian young people, mainly Sioux, recruited by Pratt in 1879 for Carlisle's initial class. Later, Standing Bear

---

Luther Standing Bear. Nebraska State Historical Society

recounted how the young students were lined up in front of a blackboard with symbols on it that they did not understand. Each was told to choose a "white man's name." Standing Bear choose Luther. On recommendation of Pratt, Standing Bear secured his first professional job as a schoolteacher on the Rosebud Reservation at a salary of $300 a year (Standing Bear, *My People*, xiii).

During his life, Standing Bear was not as well known as Eastman or Bonnin. He often was compelled to take odd jobs to support his family. Standing Bear was an unabashed Native American traditionalist during a time when the dominant ideology in non-Indian society was "Kill the Indian, Save the Man," a slogan invented by General Pratt.

As a young man on leave from Carlisle, Standing Bear in 1884 attended a speech in Philadelphia given by the legendary Hunkpapa Sioux chief Sitting Bull. Sitting Bull's speech stressed the need for education and detailed how he was about to talk peace with the Great Father in Washington.

Later, Standing Bear joined Buffalo Bill Cody's traveling road show and traveled to the big cities of the eastern seaboard, as well as London, England. Standing Bear was not usually a performer in the show; he managed the payroll and the complicated logistics of conveying horses, tipis, tents, and a large group of people from place to place.

Standing Bear turned to writing late in his life. He produced four books intended to describe his people. The first was *My People, The Sioux* (1928), a memoir that described the debate over allotment among the Lakotas. In 1931, Standing Bear published an autobiographical work, *My Indian Boyhood*, followed in 1933 by *Land of the Spotted Eagle* and in 1934 by *Stories of the Sioux*. Standing Bear also played leading roles in several motion pictures, beginning with *White Oak* (1921) and including *Santa Fe Trail* (1930). Standing Bear died while he was working on the film *Union Pacific* during 1939. His books did not reach larger audiences until after his death.

References to indigenous affection for nature permeated the thoughts of Standing Bear, who wrote:

> The Lakota was a true naturalist—a lover of Nature. He loved the earth and all things of the earth, the attachment growing with age. The old people came literally to love the soil and they sat or reclined on the ground with a feeling of being close to a mothering power. . . . In talking to children, the old Lakota would place a hand on the ground and explain: "We sit in the lap of our mother. From her, we, and all other living things, come. We shall soon pass, but the place where we now rest will last forever. . . . Our altars were built on the ground and were altars of thankfulness and gratefulness. They were made of sacred earth and placed upon the holiest of all places—the lap of Mother Earth. (Standing Bear, *Land*, 192, 194, 200)

Standing Bear defined his people's relationship to everything else on earth, writing that in the native view everything is animate—"possessed of personality," he said. He compared the world to a library, with "the stones, leaves, grass, brooks . . . birds, and animals" as its books" (Hughes, 80). Many times, wrote Standing Bear, the Indian is embarrassed and baffled by the white man's alienation from nature, as reflected in allusions to nature in such terms as "crude, primitive, wild, rude, untamed, and savage" (Standing Bear, *Land*, 196). To Standing Bear, many whites imagined Native Americans as savages to "salve . . . [their] sore and troubled conscience[s] now hardened through the habitual practice of injustice" (Standing Bear, *Land*, 251).

Standing Bear, who watched large-scale Anglo-American immigration change the face of the Great Plains, contrasted European-American and Native American conceptions of the natural world of North America:

> We did not think of the great open plains, the beautiful rolling hills, and winding streams with tangled brush, as "wild." Only to the white man was nature "a wilderness" and only to him was the land "infested" with "wild" animals and "savage" people. To us it was tame. Earth was bountiful, and we are surrounded with the blessings of the Great Mystery. Not until the hairy man from the east came and with brutal frenzy heaped injustices upon us and the families we loved was it "wild" for us. When the very animals of the forest began fleeing from his approach, then it was for us that the "Wild West" began. (Standing Bear, *Land*, 38)

Luther Standing Bear's view of nature included the painful as well as the pleasant, with an awareness that the land into which he had been born was being changed beyond recognition of earlier generations within his lifetime. He realized that "we cannot have back the days of the buffalo and beaver . . . and we can never again expect the beautiful rapport we once had with Nature." The plow, wrote Standing Bear, "has changed the face of the world" (Stone, 73).

Standing Bear was a severe critic of the whites' attitudes toward nature. He said that he knew of no species of plant, bird, or animal that had been exterminated in America until the coming of the white man. For some years after the buffalo disappeared, there still remained huge herds of antelope, but the hunter's work was no sooner done in the destruction of the buffalo than his attention was attracted toward the deer. "The white man considered natural animal life just as he did natural [Native American] life upon this continent, as 'pests,' " wrote Standing Bear. "Plants which the Indian found beneficial were also 'pests.' There is no word in the Lakota vocabulary with the English meaning of this word" (Standing Bear, *Land*, 165).

Like Black Elk, Tecumseh, Black Hawk, and others, Luther Standing Bear invoked the image of mother earth in his writing. Luther Standing Bear's use of the earth-mother image is particularly striking when it is placed next to similar language used by Black Elk that has been passed to us through accounts by Neihardt, Epes Brown, and others. Unlike accounts attributed to Black Elk, Tecumseh, and Sea'thl, however, the use of the image by Standing Bear raises no questions of interpretation because he wrote in English acquired at the Carlisle Indian School.

> There is a great difference in the attitude taken by the Indian and the Caucasian toward nature, and this difference made of one a conservationist and the other a non-conservationist of life. The Indian, as well as other creatures that were given birth, were sustained by the common mother—earth. He was therefore kin to all living things and he gave to all creatures equal rights with himself. . . . The . . . Caucasian . . . bestowing upon himself the position and title of a superior creature, others in the scheme were, in the natural order of things, of inferior position and title; and this attitude dominated his actions toward all things. The worth and right to live were his, thus he heartlessly destroyed. Forests were mowed down, the buffalo exterminated, the beaver driven to extinction and his wonderfully constructed dams dynamited. . . . [T]he white man has come to be the symbol of extinction for all things natural to this continent. (Standing Bear, *Land*, 166)

Standing Bear also was a critic of European-American society generally, in words appreciating nature and his forefathers and foremothers that recall those of Sea'thl three-quarters of a century earlier. He also evoked the same sacred tree of life that was familiar to Black Elk:

> The white man does not understand the Indian for the reason that he does not understand America. He is too far removed from its formative processes. The roots of the tree of his life have not yet grasped the rock and soil. The white man is still troubled with primitive fears; he still has in his consciousness the perils of this frontier continent. . . . He shudders still with the memory of the loss of his forefathers upon its scorching deserts and forbidding mountain-tops. The man from Europe is still a foreigner and an alien. And he still hates the man who questioned his path across the continent. (Armstrong, xi–xii)

Standing Bear, in *My People the Sioux* (67), recalled with revulsion his first sight, as a boy, of massive buffalo kills by white immigrants on the Great Plains. The sight of buffalo left dead to rot revolted Standing Bear, who knew that the traditional life of the Sioux died with the buffalo.

A wide variety of immigrants made targets of the buffalo. Some, enticed by railroad advertising of big-game hunting in comfort, shot the animals from inside, or close to, railroad club cars. The vast majority, however, were battling degrading poverty, living in sod huts, and going without bathing for lengthy periods of time as they harvested hides to be packed and sold to middlemen. These were the first white people Standing Bear had ever seen, and their sight revolted him. "Now we began to see white people living in dugouts, just like wild bears," he wrote. "These people were dirty . . . and very repulsive to us" (Standing Bear, *My People*, 67).

That such people could be forcing their ways of life on the native peoples of the Great Plains seemed very strange to Standing Bear. While most of non-Indian society was predicting that Native Americans would lose their racial identity and culture to the American "melting pot," Standing Bear believed the opposite:

> Maybe they are kind and altruistic motives that prompt the white brother to seek to remake the red man in his own likeness, and even some red men themselves hope they are "progressive," having donned the white collar for breechclout and outrageous boots for their comfortable and beautiful moccasins; nevertheless, Mother Nature and *Wakan Tanka* rule, and the last drop of Indian blood will disappear in white veins before man can remake his brother man. (Standing Bear, *Land*, 67–68)

To Standing Bear, the arrival of the white people represented a wrenching change in the way his people lived, including ways their land was being used—whom it would support and the style of life that Native American survivors of this holocaust would live.

Within two generations, the population of buffalo on the Great Plains fell from about 30 million to a few thousand. The hunters who lived in the mud huts were taking Standing Bear's people's sustenance, debilitating their economic livelihood, "taking away the source of the clothing and lodges that had been provided for us by our Creator" (Standing Bear, *My People*, 67–68).

In 1933, six years before he died, Standing Bear wrote to President Franklin Roosevelt suggesting that a bill be drawn up to require the teaching of American Indian history and culture in non-Indian schools, a prescient idea that foreshadowed the establishment of Native American studies programs around the United States after 1970. The same year, he critiqued the smugness of the "reformers" who had tried to obliterate Native American culture and land base as a solution to "the Indian problem." The "Indian problem" had more to do with the "white man's cast of mind" than native peoples themselves, Standing Bear wrote (Rosenstiel, 162). The white man had brought change, he said, but much of it, for the Indian, "was sickening and deadening. And if it be the part of civilization to maim, rob, and thwart, then what is progress?" (Rosenstiel, 162).

Only a few non-Indians at the time doubted their own definition of progress, a point of view that was left largely to literate Native Americans such as Luther Standing Bear. The two major poles of non-Indian debate on the future of North America's surviving native peoples were described in Richard Henry Pratt's educational slogan "Kill the Indian, Save the Man." Assimilation was being sold to Indians as a survival strategy, as will be described in the next chapter.

REFERENCES

Armstrong, Virginia Irving. *I Have Spoken: American History through the Voices of the Indians*. Athens, OH: Swallow Press, 1984.

Bagley, Clarence B. "Chief Seattle and Angeline." *Washington Historical Quarterly* 22 (1931): 243–275.

Black Elk. *Black Elk Speaks: Being the Life Story of a Holy Man of the Oglala Sioux/as Told through John G. Neihardt (Flaming Rainbow)*. 1932. Lincoln: University of Nebraska Press, 1979.

———. *The Sacred Pipe: Black Elk's Account of the Seven Rites of the Oglala Sioux, Recorded and Edited by Joseph Epes Brown*. 1953. Norman: University of Oklahoma Press, 1967.

Calloway, Colin, ed. *Our Hearts Fell to the Ground: Plains Indian Views of How the West Was Lost*. Boston: Bedford Books/St. Martin's Press, 1996.

Churchill, Ward. "A Little Matter of Genocide: Sam Gill's Mother Earth, Colonialism, and the Appropriation of Indigenous Spiritual Tradition in Academia." In *Fantasies of the Master Race: Literature, Cinema, and the Colonization of American Indians*, ed. M. Annette Jaimes, 187–213. Monroe, ME: Common Courage Press, 1992.

Cornell, George. "Native American Perceptions of the Environment." *Northeast Indian Quarterly* 7:2 (Summer 1990): 3–13.

Curtis, Natalie. *The Indian's Book*. New York: Harper & Brothers, 1907.

Deloria, Vine, Jr. "Comfortable Fictions and the Struggle for Turf: An Essay Review of James Clifton," *The Invented Indian: Cultural Fictions and Government Policies. American Indian Quarterly* 16:3 (1992): 397–410.

DeMallie, Raymond J., ed. *The Sixth Grandfather: Black Elk's Teachings Given to John G. Neihardt*. Lincoln: University of Nebraska Press, 1984.

Dunsmore, Roger. *Earth's Mind*. Albuquerque: University of New Mexico Press, 1997.

Fadden, John Kahionhes. Personal correspondence with author, March 31, 1998, in author's files.

Fleck, Richard F., ed. *The Indians of Thoreau: Selections from the Indian Notebooks*. Albuquerque: Hummingbird Press, 1974.

Forbes, Jack D., ed. *The Indian in America's Past*. Englewood Cliffs, NJ: Prentice-Hall, 1964.

Furtwangler, Albert. *Answering Chief Seattle*. Seattle: University of Washington Press, 1997.

Gill, Sam. *Mother Earth: An American Story*. Chicago: University of Chicago Press, 1987.

Gorman, Carl N. "Navajo Vision of Earth and Man." *Indian Historian* 6 (Fall 1973): 19–22.

Griffin-Pierce, Trudy. *Earth Is My Mother, Sky Is My Father: Space, Time, and Astronomy in Navajo Sandpainting*. Albuquerque: University of New Mexico Press, 1992.

Harner, Michael J. *The Jivaro: People of the Sacred Waterfalls*. New York: Natural History Press, 1972.

Hayes, Robert G. *A Race at Bay: New York Times Editorials on "the Indian Problem," 1860–1900*. Carbondale: Southern Illinois University Press, 1997.

Hughes, J. Donald. *American Indian Ecology*. El Paso: Texas Western Press, 1983.

Jahner, Elaine A. "Lakota Genesis: The Oral Tradition." In *Sioux Indian Religion: Tradition and Innovation*, ed. Raymond J. DeMallie and Douglas R. Parks. Norman: University of Oklahoma Press, 1987.

McLuhan, T. C., ed. *Touch the Earth: A Self-Portrait of Indian Existence*. New York: Outerbridge & Dienstfrey, 1971.

Moquin, Wayne, ed. *Great Documents in American Indian History*. New York: Praeger, 1973.

Morgan, Lewis H. *League of the Ho-de-no-saunee or Iroquois*. Ed. Herbert M. Lloyd. New York: Burt Franklin, 1901. 2 vols.

Murúa, Martín de. *Historia de origen y genealogía real de los reyes Incas del Perú*. 1590. Cited in Irene Silverblatt. *Moon, Sun, and Witches: Gender Ideologies and Class in Inca and Colonial Peru*. Princeton, NJ: Princeton University Press, 1987.

Neihardt, Hilda. *Black Elk and Flaming Rainbow: Personal Memories of the Lakota Holy Man and John Neihardt*. Lincoln: University of Nebraska Press, 1995.

Paper, Jordan. "Through the Earth Darkly: The Female Spirit in Native American Religions." In *Religion in Native North America*, ed. Christopher Vecsey, 3–19. Moscow: University of Idaho Press, 1990.

Penn, William S., ed. *As We Are Now: Mixblood Essays on Race and Identity*. Berkeley: University of California Press, 1997.

Powers, Marla N. *Oglala Women: Myth, Ritual, and Reality*. Chicago: University of Chicago Press, 1986.

Rice, Julian. "Black Elk." In *Handbook of Native American Literature*, ed. Andrew Wiget, 211–216. New York: Garland Publishing, 1996.

———. *Black Elk's Story: Distinguishing Its Lakota Purpose*. Albuquerque: University of New Mexico Press, 1991.

Rosenstiel, Annette. *Red and White: Indian Views of the White Man, 1492–1982*. New York: Universe Books, 1983.

Smith, Dr. Henry A. "Early Reminiscences. Number Ten. Scraps from a Diary. Chief Seattle—a Gentleman by Instinct—His Native Eloquence, etc., etc." *Seattle Star*, October 29, 1887, n.p.

Standing Bear, Luther. *Land of the Spotted Eagle*. 1928. Lincoln: University of Nebraska Press, 1978.

———. *My People, the Sioux*. Boston: Houghton Mifflin, 1928.

———. *My People, the Sioux*. 1933. Lincoln: University of Nebraska Press, 1975.

Starna, William A. [Review of Vecsey and Venables, *American Indian Environments*.] *American Anthropologist* 84 (1982): 468.

Steltenkamp, Michael F. *Black Elk, Holy Man of the Oglala*. Norman: University of Oklahoma Press, 1993.

Stone, Jana, ed. *Every Part of This Earth Is Sacred: Native American Voices in Praise of Nature*. San Francisco: HarperCollins, 1993.

Stuart, George E. "Maya Heartland under Siege." *National Geographic*, November 1992, 94–107.

Utley, Robert M. *The Lance and the Shield: The Life and Times of Sitting Bull.* New York: Henry Holt, 1993.

Vanderwerth, W. C., ed. *Indian Oratory: Famous Speeches by Noted Indian Chieftains.* Norman: University of Oklahoma Press, 1971.

Vecsey, Christopher, and Robert W. Venables, eds. *American Indian Environments: Ecological Issues in Native American History.* Syracuse, NY: Syracuse University Press, 1980.

Walker, James R. *Lakota Myth.* Ed. Elaine A. Jahner. Lincoln: University of Nebraska Press, 1983.

Waters, Frank. *Brave Are My People: Indian Heroes Not Forgotten.* Santa Fe, NM: Clear Light, 1993.

Weaver, Jace, ed. *Defending Mother Earth: Native American Perspectives on Environmental Justice.* Maryknoll, NY: Orbis Books, 1996.

White, Richard. "American Indians and the Environment." *Environmental Review* 9 (1985): 101–103.

7

"KILL THE INDIAN, SAVE THE MAN"

Helen Hunt Jackson, L. Frank Baum, Richard Henry Pratt, and Other Participants in the Anglo-American Debate Regarding Native Americans' Future

With Sitting Bull's surrender in 1881, the Plains Indian wars ended. Once Native Americans had been removed from their lands or restricted to dwindling fractions of their prior holdings, a debate arose in the United States regarding how to deal with the survivors of almost three centuries of warfare and disease. One position in this debate held that Indians could only be divorced from the land by extermination, the rawest form of genocide, a point of view that was advocated by such prominent Anglo-Americans as L. Frank Baum, who later authored the *Oz* books, and Horace Greeley, the newspaper editor and abolition advocate.

The opposite position in this debate sought to "reform" Indians, not exterminate them. During 1879, with Chief Joseph's surrender two years in the past and Sitting Bull's two years in the future, Standing Bear's Poncas had toured the East Coast raising support for efforts to regain their homeland in northern Nebraska. At a meeting of Ponca supporters in Boston, Helen Hunt Jackson, known at the time as one of America's best poets, was enraptured by the Poncas' story of manifest injustice. On the spot, Jackson decided to devote the rest of her life to advocating the rights of Native Americans, especially the Poncas. Out of this dedication, which lasted six years until her death in 1885, Jackson wrote two best-selling books, *A Century of Dishonor* and *Ramona*, that kindled a pitched debate among non-Indians over Native Americans' future in a postconquest world.

Also during 1879, General Richard Henry Pratt had enrolled the first class at Carlisle Indian Industrial School. Jackson and Pratt were two prominent examples of "Indian reformers," who believed (contrary to a minority of extermination advocates) that "the Indians" could be salvaged from the ruins of conquest only if they assimilated into majority society as individual landowning farmers and urban workers. Jackson and Pratt's sense of mission was shared by a number of Bureau of Indian Affairs superintendents whose memoirs found sizable audiences. All advocated remaking Native Americans (especially children) in the white man's image through instruction in farming on allotted land, education, and organized religion. Both sides in this debate were preparing dwindling numbers of Indians for eventual extinguishment of their now-fragmented land bases.

While extermination and assimilation were the two major poles of popular debate, a wide variety of opinions were expressed on the "Indian problem" by non-Indians. In contrast to the hunt-them-down mentality shared by George Armstrong Custer, Greeley, and Baum, a minority of whites expressed beliefs that Indian societies would model some aspects of America's future. Opinions of this kind were expressed by the poet Walt Whitman, as well as feminist pioneers Matilda Joslyn Gage and Elizabeth Cady Stanton.

Indians—especially "bad Indians" who chafed at reservation life—were only very rarely consulted on the subject of their own futures during the late nineteenth century. For people attached to their homelands in a collective fashion, removal to unknown lands and allotment of land as individual parcels were recommended; for peoples so devoted to family that they often called the sky "father" and the earth "mother," education on a U.S. Army model was proposed, taking children far from their homes. Pratt coined the assimilationist slogan "Kill the Indian, Save the Man" as a public-opinion counterweight to the exterminationists.

The predominant axis of opinion in this debate was sketched by the *New York Times* in an editorial published on April 15, 1875. The editorial demarcated two main attitudes toward Native Americans in non-Indian America, "the Manifest Destiny policy," which "hardly is willing, in any division of the spoils of this continent, to give the red man the buzzard. . . . [I]t looks to no future for him but extermination" (Hayes, 69). The extermination advocates, said the *Times*, "remorsely appropriate his hunting grounds, wantonly kill the game upon which he subsists, civilizes him enough to appreciate whiskey, and then gets him drunk and swindles him out of every valuable he possesses. . . . It then declares him a savage, [and] declares him incapable of civilization" (Hayes, 69–70). "The other policy," wrote the *Times* editorialist, "is that of humanity." The *Times* favored this policy, which, it said, "treats the Indian as a human being having rights . . . as an original inhabitant of this continent." The humanitarians offered, according to the *Times*, "a chance at the real civilization of this century." The humanitarians were said to believe that "the Indian's savagery . . . is not incurable" (Hayes, 70). The *Times* noted that government policy seemed to have been an amalgamation of these two poles of belief, molded by the pressures of special interests, whether they were Indian-baiting frontier squatters, the army's high brass, various religious orders, or various other "friends of the Indian."

The *Times* could become nearly euphoric in its endorsement of the assimilationist policy. For example, an editorial titled "A Modern Indian" (August 19, 1886) began:

> Day by day, new and touching illustrations of the progress of civilization are made known, and each succeeding edition of the census shows a wider spread of sweetness and light among the people. Western theorists have declared that the only good Indian is a dead Indian, but they must sink into silence before the overwhelming evidences that the untutored savage is adopting the habits of his wiser white brother. (Hayes, 198)

Helen Hunt Jackson (1830–1885) and Other "Friends of the Indian"

Helen Maria Fiske, who would become known later in life as Helen Hunt Jackson, was born on October 15, 1830, in Amherst, Massachusetts, daughter of Nathan Welby Fiske, a professor of languages at Amherst College. She was described as "a child of dangerous versatility and vivacity" (Mathes, *Helen Hunt Jackson*, 21). Variously described as brilliant and something of a pest, the young Helen Fiske became literate earlier than most children, drawing from collegiate surroundings and developing into a young woman "with candid beaming eyes, in which kindness contended with penetration," a "soul of fire," with the ability to "strongly love, to frankly hate" (Mathes, *Helen Hunt Jackson*, 22).

As a girl, Helen became close friends with Emily Dickinson, who also was growing up in Amherst and was also the daughter of an Amherst faculty member. These two and Emily Fowler, who was briefly well known as an author in her later life, came to be known as the "Amherst girls," a group of talented women born to Amherst faculty members. In her own time, Helen was better known as a poet than Dickinson, who spent much of her own life as a writer in obscurity.

At the age of eleven, Helen Fiske was sent to the first of several boarding

---

Helen Hunt Jackson. Special Collections, Tutt Library, Colorado College, Colorado Springs, Colorado

schools where she spent her teenage years. By age nineteen, she had been orphaned—both of her parents died of tuberculosis. Early in her life, Helen determined to support herself as an independent woman, not an easy role in a society in which women were defined as men's property. She decided to make her living as a writer.

Jackson first became known as a romantic poet. Later she expanded her scope to travel articles, short stories, novels, and books for children. Before Jackson became famous for her Indian-reform work late in her life, she had been "an Army wife, mother, and woman of society . . . a literary person, a poet and essayist, writer of travel sketches and short stories" (Banning, xix). She was, according to her biographer Evelyn Banning, a woman of contradictions. While some of her writings laughed at fashion, she dressed elegantly, often beyond the station of the junior army officer, Edward B. Hunt, whom she married at the age of twenty-two. Before the treatment of the Poncas tripped her sense of indignity, Helen Hunt Jackson had been a nearly apolitical person, having taken no published position even on women's suffrage or slavery while she "burst the bounds . . . [of] the separate sphere assigned to women during the Victorian era" (Mathes, *Helen Hunt Jackson*, ix).

Within fifteen years after she married Edward Hunt, Helen gave birth to two sons and lost both, one at the age of one year, the other at age nine. Her husband also died, leaving Helen Fiske Hunt nearly alone in the world. She assuaged her loneliness by writing poetry and became one of the best-regarded poets of nineteenth-century America. Ralph Waldo Emerson often carried her poetry in his pocket to show to friends (Banning, xx). She married again, to William S. Jackson of Colorado Springs, whose name she carried when her Indian-reform work became well known. At the age of forty-nine, she took up the cause of "the Indian" with a fervor that consumed her attention and energies for the last few remaining years of her short life.

Jackson's attention was turned toward the condition of Native Americans during October 1879, shortly after Judge Elmer Dundy had ruled in *Standing Bear v. Crook*. In Boston, Jackson heard a speech describing the travail of Standing Bear and his band of Poncas who, forced off their land in northern Nebraska, had escaped reservation life in Indian Territory. They had trekked 500 miles northward during the worst of a midcontinental winter to take shelter with the U'mahas (Omahas) near the city of Omaha, where, in 1879, the year Jackson heard the speech, Judge Dundy ruled that Standing Bear must be regarded as a human being under the law of habeas corpus.

Jackson was visiting some of her publishers in Boston when, on October 29, she attended a meeting of the Omaha Indian Committee and found Boston "highly aroused over the story of their cruel eviction . . . people spoke of little else" (Banning, 144–145). The Ponca tour that Jackson joined in mid-November also had visited or would visit Chicago, New York

City, Philadelphia, and Baltimore, as well as Boston. It was in Boston, however, that support was greatest; $3,000 of the $4,000 the Poncas thought that they would need to pursue their land claim was raised there (Mathes, "Ponca Controversy," 46). Henry Wadsworth Longfellow played a crucial role in the success of the Poncas' efforts in Boston. The Poncas stayed in Boston several weeks from late October into December and were presented at numerous fundraisers. In early December, more than a thousand Bostonians gathered at Faneuil Hall to hear Standing Bear speak. After the speeches, more than half the audience crowded the stage to shake hands with him (Mathes, "Ponca Controversy," 47).

Reading accounts of Bostonians rallying around Standing Bear, I recall an eastern editor who asked me with unbelief in his voice how a frontier town (Omaha) could possibly provide the gist of an Indian-rights movement among Anglo-Americans during the heyday of Manifest Destiny. Society, especially high society, in the United States accommodated both extremes in a range of opinion that will startle any reader who is not familiar with the time. Eastern cities had Indian support groups of substantial size, as Standing Bear's reception in Boston literary circles demonstrates. One will recall (see Chapter 5) that Thomas Tibbles rarely forgot to send his dispatches on Standing Bear to newspaper editors in large eastern cities, who published many of them.

After hearing the story of the Poncas, Jackson collected funds for the Poncas, encouraged others to take an active part, and appealed to all who would listen. The mayor of Boston joined a fund-raising committee for the Poncas' legal campaign to win back their homeland. Jackson herself joined Standing Bear, Thomas Henry Tibbles, and Susette ("Bright Eyes") La-Flesche, his Omaha wife, on tour throughout New England. Tibbles credited Jackson's support as being one of the major factors in the Poncas' ultimate victory (Banning, 150).

Jackson's acquaintance with the Poncas started her down the literary road that produced *A Century of Dishonor* and *Ramona*. Within two years of first hearing the Poncas' heart-rending story, Jackson had published *A Century of Dishonor*. Three years later, having made a pledge to write a novel that would become the Native American version of *Uncle Tom's Cabin*, she published the best-seller *Ramona*.

A Century of Dishonor is a factual sketch of broken treaties and corruption in the Bureau of Indian Affairs; *Ramona* is a fictional account of the abuses suffered by the Mission Indians of California, based on Jackson's travels in that area shortly after *A Century of Dishonor* was published. Both books were very popular, among the best-sellers of their time, one more indication of just how many non-Indians sympathized with the Native American victims of westward expansion.

Ramona was reprinted 300 times after Jackson's death and was adapted for stage and screen several times. "Every incident in *Ramona* . . . is true,"

Jackson wrote. "A Cahuilla Indian was shot two years ago exactly as Alessandro is—and his wife's name was Ramona, and I never knew this fact until *Ramona* was half written" (Mathes, "Legacy," 43).

Jackson's books may have been so immensely popular during the 1880s because many people in the expanding United States, finding a need to reconcile the taking of a continent with notions of their own civility, sought to deal with "the Indian problem" in what they believed to be a civilized and humane manner. Thus cultural genocide (a late-twentieth-century phrase) was advanced in the modulated tones of civility, of doing what was believed to be best for "the Indian." Jackson's books fueled a national debate over what would become of Native Americans who had survived subjugation by immigrating European-Americans. Most of the books combined condemnation of the government's earlier behavior with advocacy of favored solutions to "the Indian problem," such as religious instruction, boarding schools, and allotment.

In addition to her two books, Jackson also authored hundreds of letters, several magazine articles, and a government report on the condition of the California Mission Indians during the six years between her first association with the Poncas and her death in 1885 (Mathes, *Helen Hunt Jackson*, xiv). Jackson's campaign on behalf of Indians consumed her totally and drew her into contact with some of the most prominent politicians of her time. Among them was Interior Secretary Carl Schurz, whom she called "an adroit liar" to his face (Mathes, *Helen Hunt Jackson*, xiv). In 1883, despite her intense criticism of the government, Jackson was appointed by the Interior Department as a "special agent" to the Mission Indians of California. Jackson at first reflected curiously on the change in her life, thinking of herself not as a person with a cause, but as "a woman with a hobby":

> I have done now, I believe, the last of the things I have said I would never do. I have become what I have said a thousand times was the most odious thing in the world, "a woman with a hobby." But I cannot help it. . . . I believe the time is drawing near for a great change in our policy toward the Indians. (Banning, 148)

After *A Century of Dishonor* was published, Jackson sent a copy of it to each member of Congress at her own expense. She then visited each member of Congress personally to emphasize what she thought must be done to remove the stain of the dishonorable century she had described. Jackson had died by the time Congress turned allotment (which she had believed would save Native Americans from extinction) into a real-estate agency for homesteaders and corporations through which two-thirds of Native Americans' remaining land base was taken within half a century.

As a result of allotment, Indian-owned land holdings shrank from 138 million acres in 1887 to about 48 million in 1934. Sixty million acres were lost through the release of "surplus" lands to federal government ownership or sale to homesteaders. Twenty-six million acres were transferred to non-Indians after they were released from trust status by purchase, fraud, mortgage foreclosures, and tax sales. Of the 48 million acres remaining in Indian hands by 1934, 20 million were too arid for productive farming, which had been the goal of allotment. By 1933, 49 percent of Indians on allotted reservations were landless. At that time, 96 percent of all reservation Indians were earning less than $200 a year.

By the middle 1880s, Jackson was suffering recurring bouts of malarial symptoms and other health problems that gradually debilitated her. During 1885, on her deathbed, Jackson wrote of her work, "As I lie here, nothing looks to me of any value except the words I have spoken for the Indians" (Banning, 224). Her last letter, dated August 8, was written to President Grover Cleveland:

> I ask you to read my *Century of Dishonor*. I am dying happier in the belief I have that it is your hand that is destined to strike the first steady blow toward lifting the burden of infamy from our country and righting the wrongs of the Indian race. (Banning, 225)

Jackson died on August 12, 1885. Upon hearing of her death, Susette LaFlesche "shut herself into her room and wept all day long," according to her husband Thomas Henry Tibbles. "For weeks afterward she mourned the loss of this closest of her intimate friends, who had given herself wholeheartedly to save an unhappy race" (Mathes, "Legacy," 44). Emily Dickinson penned a verse in eulogy of Jackson:

> *Helen of Troy will die*
> *but Helen of Colorado, never.*
> *"Dear friend, you can walk"*
> *were the last words I wrote her—*
> *"Dear friend, I can fly"—*
> *her immortal reply.*
> (Banning, frontispiece)

Jackson's text in *A Century of Dishonor* is preceded by two introductions, both advocating Christianity as a major civilizing influence for Indians. "Where once was only heard the medicine-drum and the song of the scalp-dance," enthused H. B. Whipple, bishop of Minnesota, "there is now the bell calling Christians to prayer" (Jackson, ix). The book's second introduction, by Julius H. Seelye, president of Amherst College, sounded the call for killing the "Indian" in the "man" as he expressed the central assumptions of the assimilationist movement:

> It will be admitted now on every hand that the only solution of the Indian problem involves the entire change of these people from a savage to a civilized life. They are

> not likely to be exterminated. . . . When the Indian, through wise and Christian treatment, becomes invested with all the rights and duties of citizenship, his special tribal relations will become extinct. (Jackson, 2)

A Century of Dishonor is introduced with a lament that "the Indian is the only human being within our territory who has no individual right in the soil" (Jackson, vi). The historical irony was not lost on peoples whose collective ownership of traditional homelands was reduced by as much as 90 percent during the allotment that established their individual rights to landownership. A policy pitched to Congress as a favor to the Indians had, in the end, become a revolving real-estate agency that siphoned native estate into the hands of non-Indian immigrants. Allotment wiped out prior Indian claims to the land and presented them with the same rights as the homesteading immigrant: 160 acres for a family, 80 for an individual, along with U.S. citizenship.

Jackson was relentless in her indictment of government policy and, at the same time, just as adamantly (and ironically) convinced that new policies advocated by the same government (including allotment, education, and Christianity) would pull Indians from the embers of the holocaust that attended the conquest of a continent. In *A Century of Dishonor*, Jackson sketched the problem as she saw it:

> The history of the United States government's repeated violations of faith with the Indians thus convicts us, as a nation . . . of having outraged the principles of justice, which are the basis of International Law. . . . A full history of the wrongs they have suffered at the hands of authorities, military and civil, and also of the citizens of this country . . . would take years to write and volumes to hold. (Jackson, 29)

Jackson approached the same government that had defrauded the Indians for a century with a certain degree of naïveté: "What an opportunity for the Congress of 1880 to cover itself with a luster of glory, as the first to cut short our nation's records of cruelties and perjuries! The first to attempt to redeem the name of the United States from the stain of a century of dishonor!" (Jackson, 31).

Some of Jackson's accounts in *A Century of Dishonor*, including a chapter on Standing Bear and the Poncas, were very recent history when she wrote. The book also provides an occasional glimpse into what Jackson assumes will be a better "civilized" future for the allotted and assimilated Indian of the future. Jackson outlines the history of the Delawares, Cheyennes, Nez Perces, Sioux, Poncas, Winnebagos, and Cherokees, then chronicles "massacres of Indians by whites" (Jackson, iii–iv). She quotes approvingly from a report of the same Bureau of Indian Affairs that she has just indicted for decades of malfeasance to the effect that the Sioux are increasingly engaged in "civilized labor," as "there is an almost universal call for lands in severalty."

> That all this should be true of these wild, warlike Sioux, after so many years of hardships and forced wanderings and removals, is incontrovertible proof that there is in them a native strength of character, power of endurance, and indomitable courage, which will make of them ultimately a noble and superior race of people, if civilization will only give them time to become civilized, and Christians will leave them time and peace to learn Christianity. (Jackson, 185)

Allotment was offered Indians as a privilege, as a gate to civilization. An allottee was required to be a U.S. citizen; those who refused citizenship were left with no property. One-half or more Indian blood was required and had to be proved on paper, something not always easy to do. Geographical restrictions also were applied. Cherokees, Creeks, and Choctaws living in Arkansas instead of in Indian Territory were denied recognition and rights to allotments, for example (Churchill, 203). Sometimes allotment and removal were presented to members of Native American nations in one package. In a treaty dated July 4, 1866, provision was made for removal of the Delawares from Kansas (to which they had been moved earlier from the East) to Indian Territory. At the same time, allotment and U.S. citizenship were written into the removal treaty (Kinney, 153).

The General Allotment Act was passed by Congress at a time of growing non-Indian pressure to open remaining Native American lands. At the time, the Sioux Nation, by treaty, still owned most of western South Dakota; the Flatheads and Blackfeet held title to much of western Montana; and a coalition of local native nations, such as the Kiowas, and "removed" Indians, such as the Cheyennes and Apaches, occupied western Oklahoma. The Crows held a large area in southern Montana.

Because allotment was based on the model of the Anglo-American nuclear family, many Indians who were subjected to its provisions were required to do more than change their property-holding customs. Indian extended families were devastated by the allotment system, in which close relatives who had lived together often were given distant parcels of land, forcing them apart. Long-established ties between grandmothers and their children were severed, and long-standing family structures were destroyed. Indian men who were married to more than one wife were told to divest their extra relatives.

Several U.S. political leaders understood that the main purpose of allotment was to break up native land holdings, a point that Jackson and other reformers conceded and accepted. The retention of native traditions that became central to native self-determination politics a century later was not part of the agenda espoused by Jackson and the other reformers. None of the reformers seem to have realized that many native people did not want to adopt Anglo-American property-owning conventions. Helen Hunt Jackson's books may have sold so well because she stood at this consensus point in the debate among non-Indians.

President Theodore Roosevelt, for example, said that allotment was "a mighty pulverizing engine to break up the tribal mass, which acts directly upon the family and the individual" (Johansen, "Taking," 21). Over the ensuing generations, many individual allotments were subdivided into minuscule plots by inheritances, making many of them nearly useless for agriculture. Publications of the Bureau of Indian Affairs acknowledge that the thrust of U.S. Indian policy in the 1870s and 1880s was to "further minimize the functions of tribal leaders and tribal institutions and to continually strengthen the position of the government representative and his subordinates, and to improve the effectiveness of their programs to break down traditional patterns within the Indian communities" (Johansen, "Taking," 21).

Some non-Indian people protested allotment and other forms of assimilation. Ethnologist Lewis Henry Morgan, known as the founder of American anthropology, predicted with a measure of prescience (which Jackson did not share) that the major result of allotment "would unquestionably be, that in a very short time he would divest himself of every foot of land and fall into poverty" (Johansen, "Taking," 21). Morgan was echoing the minority opinion of the Congressional Committee of Indian Affairs on the Allotment Act:

> The real purpose of this bill is to get at the Indian lands and open them up to settlement. The provisions for the apparent benefit of the Indians are but the pretext to get his lands and occupy them. . . . If this were done in the name of greed, it would be bad enough; but to do it in the name of humanity, and under the cloak of an ardent desire to promote the Indian's welfare by making him like ourselves whether he will or not, is infinitely worse. (Johansen, "Taking," 21)

While allotment improverished many Indians, the Bureau of Indian Affairs prospered. By 1934, with Indian estate comprising less than half the area it had before allotment began, the bureau had increased its staff (6,000 people) and its budget ($23 million a year) by roughly 400 percent in half a century.

Helen Hunt Jackson's work is remarkable for its intensity, its self-righteousness, and its total confidence that a new and improved non-Indian establishment would and could atone for the "century of dishonor" that Jackson described so breathlessly. She wrote feel-good history for literate, liberal non-Indians who wanted to believe that their generation would do a better job on "the Indian problem." In retrospect, Jackson's naïveté is as remarkable as her assumption that making Indians over in the white man's image would improve their lives. In reality, some lives were improved, but many others were utterly destroyed as their land bases, cultures, and societal structures were "pulverized."

Jackson was hardly alone in her condemnation of the government's Indian policies. Even the government did this, with remarkably little effect on future atrocities. Native American leaders of the late eighteenth century often remarked at how often the Great White Father would promise one thing and deliver nothing, or something less, or much different, than previously advertised. Treaty making seemed to be an eternal game of bait and switch. The dust had barely settled after the massacre at Sand Creek in 1864 when a Joint Committee on the Conduct of the War compiled a report that gushed with moral indignation:

> It is difficult to believe that beings in the form of men, and disgracing the uniform of the United States soldiers and officers, could commit or countenance the commission of such acts of cruelty and barbarity as are detailed in the testimony. (Vogel, 158)

To a mind informed by debates over "political correctness" in the last years of the twentieth century, the arrogant certitude of late-nineteenth-century "friends of the Indian" can come as something of a temporal culture shock. A book titled *The Indian's Side of the Indian Question*, by William Barrows, a doctor of divinity, has little to do with native views of what has happened to them. It is, rather, a long sermon that does not ask a single Native American how to solve the "Indian question." Barrows presents what purports to be the Indian side of the question with a homily on the Allotment Act: "We are now entering an era of hope for the Indian under the Dawes Bill" (Barrows, 3). Barrows looks for a nice way to tell "the Indian" that a measure of genocide is in order:

> [T]he average sentiment west of the Mississippi concerning "the Indian" is that he is a worthless remnant of his race, and incapable of elevation to the average American grade; and it is no harsh judgement to express that the two-thirds of our domain thus indicated would greatly prefer a civil and moral quarantine between them and an Indian community—the breadth of a State or a Territory. This is the gentler way with some of saying that the best Indian is a dead Indian. (Barrows, 5)

Barrows, like Helen Hunt Jackson, found detailed, basic faults in previous government relations with the Indians, but he, like Jackson and many other reformers, believed that a dose of high morals on the frontier would eradicate greed, avarice, and land hunger and thus would answer "the Indian question" by allowing the polite white people to teach Indians their lifeways. Barrows wove the story of government perfidy in the Trail of Tears with no hint that the allotment policies of which he was so enamored were about to strip away the land and cultural infrastructure that sustained Native American peoples just as effectively as removal.

When Helen Hunt Jackson published *A Century of Dishonor*, she was not engaging in a solitary act. Indictments of past Anglo-American behavior toward North America's first inhabitants were all the rage at the time. Even a former commissioner of Indian affairs could publish a scathing history of white perfidy and then, like Helen Hunt Jackson, assure the reader that the government's present plans (including education and allotment) would fix everything. George W. Manypenny, commissioner of Indian affairs from 1853 to 1857 and chairman of a commission appointed to negotiate with the Sioux in 1876, introduces his book, *Our Indian Wards*, with a straightforward admission:

> It cannot be denied, that from the period when the first infant settlements were made upon the Atlantic sea-board by European colonists, until the present time, there have been constant, persistent, and unceasing efforts on the part of the white man to drive the Indian from his hunting ground and home. When the encroachments of the former became unbearable, they were forcibly resisted by the latter. (Manypenny, vii)

Manypenny is notably unstinting in his criticism of Custer's 1874 expedition into the Black Hills, only six years before his book was published. The expedition was, in Manypenny's words, "unlawful . . . simply a gold hunting invasion" (Manypenny, xvii). Manypenny traces the results of avarice inspired by land hunger on government policy right up to his own time and then instructs "the Indian" in the imperial voice that trust is in order because the government is now under new management.

Manypenny's book includes detailed descriptions of betrayals from his own time to a few years after the Pilgrims disembarked from the *Mayflower;* one needs to be reminded at times that the author was a participant in the juggernaut that swept across the continent. Manypenny calls the Sand Creek massacre "an indiscriminate slaughter. . . . Fleeing women, holding up their hands and praying for mercy . . . brutally shot down; infants . . . killed and scalped in derision" (Manypenny, 165). Describing the Battle of the Little Bighorn, Manypenny reminds newspapermen who wrote screaming headlines about a "massacre" that "the attack was made by Gen. Custer, and not by Sitting Bull. It was in broad daylight" (Manypenny, 311). The army's pursuit and killing of Dull Knife's escaping Northern Cheyennes to Manypenny constituted "remorseless and inhumane butchery . . . [that] can find no justification" (Manypenny, 341).

A capable researcher of documents, Manypenny takes his readers on horseback with General O. O. Howard and Chief Joseph the Younger as Joseph explains that "the earth was his mother. He was made of the earth, and grew up upon her bosom" (Manypenny, 144). Joseph was trying to explain to Howard why his people preferred to retain their traditional ways of life, a point that seemed lost on Howard, as well as Manypenny, who, in his next breath, prescribes for "the Indian" the entire new white world that Joseph rejects. The possibility that Joseph may not desire the future that Manypenny imagines for him seems beyond the borders of his cognitive map.

When Manypenny considers the future of the native people who have survived the conquest, he wholly swallows the popular assumptions of his time. Like most other self-professed "friends of the Indian," Manypenny provides a monologue in which he does nearly all of the talking. There remains no place in his vision of the future for any of his Indian "wards" to define or design even a scrap of their own futures. As he outlines almost three centuries of massacres, land frauds, and forced removals, Manypenny, speaking for "the Indian," portrays him embracing the white man's next purported solution to "the Indian problem":

> [T]here should be no doubt of the willingness of the Indian to accept our civilization, or of his capability to become a useful member of society. Let the red man have what he never has had, appropriate protection and support, and fair opportunity. (Manypenny, xii)

"To begin," writes Manypenny, "let him have a fixed and settled home. This is imperative." Manypenny seems accustomed to defining such imperatives. His assumptions frame the future he imagines: "A fixed and settled home" from which "the Indian" will be "lifted up" to "civilization" (Manypenny, xii). Like Jackson and others, Manypenny supports allotment with a nearly religious fervor, forgetting how laws in the past had been turned to the profit of the land-industry machine that he deplores. To Manypenny, Indians are not a vanishing race. They are, he writes, "destined to be and remain with us for ages to come" (Manypenny, xxi). He believes that Native American human beings will retain a genetic shell; they will be empty vessels to be filled with Anglo-American landholding habits and the Puritan work ethic, as well as the agricultural and industrial skills appropriate for economic survival in a non-Indian society that places no value on indigenous American traditions. Manypenny's Indians seem to be stamped with cookie-cutter identities made to order in the factory of civilization. "It is not uncommon at this day for Indian families, who have advanced civilization more rapidly than their fellows, to sever the tribal relation and become merged with the population in the white settlements" (Manypenny, xxii). Manypenny's cultural makeover of Native America prescribes practically every step that "the Indian" will take, reversing many traditional roles:

> The Indian women must cease to do the outdoor work, and confine themselves to domestic duties and the cares of the house and family. The labor in the garden and

the field must be done by the men and the boys. . . . [W]ith proper prompting and encouragement, accessions will continually be made to the ranks of labor. (Manypenny, xv)

Absent from Manypenny's analysis was any hint that Native American peoples themselves might favor collective landholdings or cultural practices ("the tribal relation") that had sustained them for many thousands of years before Europeans arrived in their midst. Such a design, which sounds very familiar to students of native self-assertion a century later, was thought by Manypenny, Jackson, and other Indian "reformers" to be impossible given the intolerances of the society in which they lived. Thus "the Indian" was being remade in the reformers' image as a favor to them and as a credit to civilization, or so the reformers believed.

L. Frank Baum (1856–1919) and Other Advocates of Genocide

Lyman Frank Baum was born in Chittenango, New York, near Syracuse, to an affluent family. His father had invested in the oil industry in its infancy and had done well financially. By the age of seventeen, young Baum was producing publishable work (a stamp directory, in this case). Baum's family owned a string of theatres that staged Shakespeare's plays, and as a boy, he sometimes toured with the actors' troupes. By his twenties, Baum had worked as a journalist for the *New Era*, in Pennsylvania; he also wrote (at the age of twenty-six) *The Maid of Arran*, a stage play that was performed from the prairies of Canada to Kansas.

In 1882, Baum courted and married Faud Gage, a relative of Matilda Joslyn Gage, the noted feminist. They had two sons. To support his family, Baum abandoned his writing and went to work in the family oil business as a salesman. Within two years, his father had died and the once-flush business had gone bankrupt. In 1888, Baum and his family migrated to Aberdeen, South Dakota, where he at first tried to provide for them by founding a dry-goods store. Baum's Bazaar went out of business within a year.

Some contemporary literary critics see premonitions of a multicultural society in the characters of L. Frank Baum's many *Oz* books, with their wide diversity of characters occupying a fantasy world in a more or less

---

L. Frank Baum. Photo by F. S. & M. V. Fox, Chicago, Ill.
Library of Congress, LC-USZ62-103204

happy symbiosis. Before he wrote the *Oz* books, however, the historical persona of this well-known author was much different. Baum held several jobs briefly before he published the first *Oz* book at the age of forty-four in 1900. Baum was a chicken breeder and traveling dry-goods salesman (or "drummer," as such people were called at the time). He also edited the *Aberdeen Saturday Pioneer* from 1888 to 1891. During this time, he penned two vitriolic editorials that fanned racial hatred in the state before and after the massacre at Wounded Knee in December 1890. On December 20, 1890, days after the assassination of Sitting Bull and slightly more than a week before the Wounded Knee massacre, he wrote:

> The proud spirit of the original owners of these vast prairies . . . lingered last in the bosom of Sitting Bull. With his fall, the nobility of the Redskin is extinguished, and what few are left are a pack of whining curs who lick the hand that smites them. The Whites, by law of conquest, by justice of civilization, are masters of the American continent, and the best safety of the frontier settlers will be secured by the total annihilation of the few remaining Indians. . . . Why not annihilation? Their glory has fled, their spirit broken, their manhood effaced, better that they should die than live the miserable wretches that they are. (Johansen, "Baum," 9)

A week after the massacre, the demand for annihilation was repeated in Baum's newspaper, with one difference. He misspelled "extermination" as "extirmination." When General Nelson A. Miles tried to get the instigators of the massacre court-martialed, Baum called him "weak and vacillating" (Johansen, "Baum," 9). Baum was probably the most notable of several South Dakota newspaper editors who inflamed whites' opinions against the Sioux and the Ghost Dance late in 1890, bringing to the area troops and out-of-state reporters looking for a last, great Indian war and setting the stage for the massacre at Wounded Knee.

Baum's sentiments were not unusual in his time. The 1890 national census, the same document that declared the frontier "closed," considered the subject of genocide:

> Such has been his [the Indian's] life, such the result, that if the entire remaining Indians were instantly and completely wiped from the face of the earth, they would leave no monuments, no buildings, no written language save one, no literature, no inventions, nothing in the arts and sciences, and absolutely nothing for the benefit of mankind. (Cohen, 266)

Francis E. Leupp, who became commissioner of Indian affairs under Theodore Roosevelt during 1901, seemed to regret having to say it, but he also thought that a certain magnitude of genocide was inevitable:

> Perhaps in the course of merging this . . . race into our body politic, many individuals, unable to keep up the pace, may fall by the wayside and be trodden underfoot.

Deeply as we deplore this possibility, we must not let it blind us to our duty to the race as a whole. It is one of the cruel incidents of all civilization in large masses that some, perhaps a multitude, of its subjects will be lost in the process. (Kinney, 238)

The most popular ideological weapon of those who favored extermination of the Indians was a belief that they were childlike beings with no right to the land and no knowledge in ways to adequately "develop" the natural resources of America. In 1859, Horace Greeley (1811–1872), who was famous for his liberalism on other subjects, provided a striking denigration of Native American character: "[T]he Indians are children. Their arts, wars, treaties, alliances, habitations, crafts, properties, commerce, comforts, all belong to the very lowest and crudest ages of human existence." Greeley gave credit to some native leaders who "have a narrow and short-sighted shrewdness."

Very rarely in their history, a really great man, like Pontiac or Tecumseh, has arisen among them; but this does not shake the general truth that they are utterly incompetent to cope in any way with the European or Caucasian race. Any band of schoolboys . . . are quite as capable of ruling their appetites, devising and upholding a public policy, constituting and conducting a state or community, as the average Indian tribe. (Greeley, quoted in Black and Weidman, 129–130)

A liberal on abolition and universal suffrage, Gresley gives no humanistic quarter to American Indians, whom he scarcely recognizes as members of the human family: "[T]he poetic Indian—the Indian of Cooper and Longfellow—is only visible to the poet's eye. To the prosaic observer, the average Indian of the woods and prairies is a being who does little credit to human nature—a slave of appetite and sloth, never emancipated from the tyranny of one animal passion save by the more ravenous demands of another." Having degraded Indian character, Greeley sees genocide nearly as an errand of mercy: "I could not help saying, 'These people must die out—here is no help for them. God has given this earth to those who will subdue and cultivate it, and it is vain to struggle against His righteous decree' " (Black and Weidman, 257, 258).

In words similar to Greeley's, Theodore Roosevelt reflected on the course of empire in *The Strenuous Life* (1901):

Of course our whole national history has been one of expansion . . . that the barbarians receded or be[came] conquered, with the attendant fact that peace follows their retrogression or conquest . . . due solely to the power of the mighty civilized races which have not lost their fighting instinct, and which by their expansion are gradually bringing peace into the red wastes where the barbarian peoples of the world hold sway. (Churchill, 37)

Roosevelt was not taking an extreme position for his time. All across the United States, calls for extermination of remaining native peoples had been common for several decades. The Indian's white-defined shortcomings became the best excuse for taking their land. One example, a poem in an Omaha newspaper during 1873, called for extermination in the rawest and most stereotypical of terms:

Hunt the murderous Modoc down,
Bid, the paltering cease.
Martyred Canby's blood demands,
Righteous vengeance at our hands.
Aye, nor Canby's blood alone.
Death these fiends have broadcast sown.
Let them pay each gory crown.
Hunt them down!

Hunt the savage murderers down.
Red of hand and black of heart.
Lies and treachery all their art.
Cowards, robbers, pawns, and scum,
Of the desert whence they come.
All the human that they bear,
Seems the outward shape they wear.
Reeking with unnumbered crimes,
Faithless unbred a thousand times.
(Reilly, 43–44)

It was against such calls that Richard Henry Pratt mobilized public opinion in favor of education for the children of the Indian wars.

Richard Henry Pratt (1840–1924)

Another self-styled friend of the Indian, Richard Henry Pratt became known as a major advocate of assimilation through education. Pratt, who rose to the rank of general in the U.S. Army, founded the Carlisle Indian Industrial School, the prototype for a nationwide network of such institutions.

Pratt was born on December 6, 1840, in Rushford, New York, the eldest of three sons of Richard and Mary Pratt. In 1846, the family moved to Logansport, Indiana; in 1849, Richard, senior, was lured to California by the gold rush. The senior Pratt made a small fortune in the gold fields, but was robbed and murdered by another gold seeker as he returned home. At the age of thirteen, young Richard left school to earn money to help support his mother and brothers. He worked for five years as a printer's devil, earning less than two dollars a week, and also took a second job splitting rails. At the age of eighteen, Pratt apprenticed himself to a tinsmith, one of the crafts that he would teach in the Carlisle School decades later (Pratt, ix–x).

At the beginning of the Civil War in 1861, Pratt enlisted in the Union Army and fought on several fronts for the next four years. Recruiting for the army in Indiana during 1864, Pratt met his future wife, Anna Laura Mason. A year later, after the war was over, Pratt mustered out of the

---

General Richard Henry Pratt. St. Augustine Historical Society

army. He began a second term of service two years later with a commission as a second lieutenant.

Pratt's first assignment as a commissioned officer in the army was with the Tenth United States Cavalry, a regiment comprised of black soldiers and white officers. He was promoted rapidly and ended his career after forty-one years in the army with the rank of brigadier general. Much of Pratt's career in the army was spent shepherding and educating American Indians, first as a supervisor of prisoners, then as initiator of a system of Indian schools that would span the United States. Pratt also occasionally organized and led parties of Native American scouts for the army.

The man who coined the phrase "Kill the Indian, Save the Man" comes off in his writings as an affable fellow who is hardly as stern as his military rank and sloganeering talents seemed to indicate. His writing bears little of the racist cant of some other Indian "reformers" at the time. He seemed capable of forging genuine friendships with a large number of Indians, all the while maintaining strenuously that they and their children would be better off heeding his prescription for assimilation. Pratt once upbraided the Sioux leader Spotted Tail for signing treaties on behalf of thousands of people that he was unable to read.

Pratt also displayed a talent for negotiation from his initial assignment in charge of "Indian relations" at Fort Arbuckle in southern Indian Territory beginning in 1867. A group of Kiowas took captive a young white boy, after which the commander of the fort proposed that ransom of a mule and goods worth about $300 be paid. That proposal drew a stinging retort from Lt. Gen. William Tecumseh Sherman at the headquarters of the Military Division of the Missouri at Fort Leavenworth, Kansas:

> This paper happens to meet me here. It is now about as good a time as any for us to come to an understanding, and rather than submit to this practice of paying for stolen children it is better the Indian race be obliterated.
>
> I now have power to call out the volunteer forces of the frontier, and the Commanding Officer of Ft. Arbuckle may, in his own way, convey notice to the tribe that this boy must be surrendered or else war to the death will be ordered. There will be no ransom paid. (Pratt, 15)

Within the context of this tense situation, Pratt wrote that thousands of Indians converged on the area around the fort to socialize and feed their horses. "It was a wonderful sight," he recalled in his memoirs (Pratt, 15). Shortly thereafter, Pratt arranged a meeting between chiefs of the assembled bands and the fort's commanding officer, which, he reported later, was "quite friendly" (Pratt, 15). He heard the Indians out. White men made war on them, not sparing their women and children, the Indians told Pratt. "They were only returning the treatment the white men gave to them,"

Pratt wrote; "that the white man in raiding their homes did not stop to make prisoners, but shot and killed their women and children indiscriminately." The Indians believed that they were not as bad as the white man, "because they saved the lives of some who fell into their power and took them back to their camps and treated them kindly, whereas the white man killed all" (Pratt, 16). Both parties agreed that they would be better off without going to war, and after a council among themselves, the chiefs announced that they would return the captive boy without a ransom, along with all other prisoners they were holding.

The real police problem, according to Pratt, was with "white renegades from justice." Theft and murder by these renegades was common, Pratt recalled, with horse theft being their main source of ready cash. Gangs of renegades also stole "large herds of cattle on the frontier of Texas . . . [getting] away with their quarry by driving them through the buffalo range, where their trail was obliterated by thousands of buffalo" (Pratt, 22).

Life on the frontier could be dangerous. Fort Arbuckle's mail carrier was murdered and his load rifled by renegades while Pratt was stationed there. A second mail carrier was recruited with great difficulty, "but one was found brave enough to undertake the service" (Pratt, 23). He too was ambushed and murdered. Another major frontier policing problem for the soldiers at Fort Arbuckle involved the growing number of white liquor dealers who were seeking and finding native customers.

> Frontiersmen sold Indians whiskey, while their behavior under its influence was then taken to indicate their alleged savage qualities. The fact that the same whisky worked the same ruin on the white man, and that, under its influence, the white man was constantly demonstrating no less savage qualities, did not alleviate the indictment against the Indian. (Pratt, 53)

Pratt told neighboring Indians that the dealers could be convicted of crimes in white courts for selling liquor to Indians in their home villages. He asked the chiefs to call on him at any hour of the day or night to arrest the alcohol salesmen. On such occasions, wrote Pratt, "I got a squad of men, went to the camp and captured the men and their stock, made the Indians give me what they had bought, and threw all the bottles on the rocks, put the men in the guardhouse, and reported the case to the nearest United States commissioner" (Pratt, 57). Pratt added proudly that "the men were tried and imprisoned, as the law provided. Thereafter I had no troubles with the Tonkawas about whisky. The chief and I worked together and became the best of friends" (Pratt, 57).

On the frontier, the new white towns often were much more violent than neighboring Native American settlements. Pratt described visiting a town near Fort Leavenworth and being told by the town's leading merchant that the local cemetery was made up of eighty-four graves, "and eighty-three died with their boots on" (Pratt, 53). Most of the dead had been killed in fights over gambling and drunken brawls. Two days after the interview, yet another white immigrant was killed in yet another bar brawl.

Pratt served as "Indian relations" manager at several Indian Territory forts before he began his career in education. When he acted as social director, intercultural socializing was the order of the day. During the fall of 1874, officers at Fort Sill planned a large dance and banquet to celebrate the opening of a new hospital on the base. The officers asked Pratt to bring "some of the big chiefs in their regalia" (Pratt, 102) to add to the evening. Pratt arrived at the Indian camp early and found Kicking Bird's wives "helping to paint and feather him" (Pratt, 102).

> I asked whether they could paint and dress me as one of the chiefs. This pleased Kicking Bird and wives very much, and they agreed to fix me up all right. Borrowing some things they gave me Indian garments, leggings, moccasins, beaded shirt, etc., which I put on over my underwear, and they painted my face most vividly and furnished me with a fine war bonnet. Kicking Bird and his two wives were intensely gratified that they had made me look so completely Indian. (Pratt, 102)

Pratt and Kicking Bird's party drove to Fort Sill and arrived while the celebration was in full swing. Pratt relished the practical joke when many of the officers and their wives failed to recognize him at first. The evening also was enlivened for some of the Indians by their first taste of ice cream. Pratt recalled later that "Lone Wolf asked to have his taken out and warmed" (Pratt, 103).

Pratt's writings reveal a man insistent to a fault that he uphold his oath as an army officer to support and defend the Constitution of the United States against all enemies, foreign and domestic. With the Fourteenth and Fifteenth amendments to the Constitution following the Civil War, Pratt interpreted his oath as active implementation of blacks' and Indians' rights under their wording: "All persons born or naturalized in the United States and subject to its jurisdiction, are citizens thereof" (Pratt, 7). He wrote:

> It seemed plain that under this amendment the Negro could not be relegated in Army service to the Negro units of enlisted men solely, and that the Indian could not be continued imprisoned on separate tribal reservations. The rights of citizenship included fraternity and equal privilege for development. None of our people were held under as severe "jurisdiction" as our Indians. (Pratt, 7)

Pratt's educational experiment began in the 1870s with seventy-two Native American men, most of them Cheyennes, who were imprisoned in an old Spanish fort at Saint Augustine, Florida. In 1878, this group "graduated," and Pratt petitioned Congress for an appropriation to begin an Indian industrial school on an abandoned army post at Carlisle, Pennsylvania.

Like many other Indian "reformers" during the late nineteenth century, Pratt earnestly believed that the Indians' only survivable course in Anglo-American society was education and assimilation, including abandonment not only of Native American economy but also of Indian culture. The alternative, to Jackson, Pratt, and other "reformers," was outright extermination.

To recruit students for his new school, Pratt visited the Sioux of the high plains. Roughly 150 students traveled eastward in 1879 to form Carlisle's first class. Included was Luther Standing Bear, who later became a well-known author. Standing Bear recalled his days at Carlisle in *My Indian Boyhood.* Luther Standing Bear's Sioux name was Plenty Kill when he entered the first class at Carlisle School in 1879 at the age of eleven years. While Standing Bear and his father thought that the school was doing him some good, other parents were not so sure. Spotted Tail, for example, withdrew his three children from Carlisle after a visit.

Carlisle's curriculum included both academic and industrial education; the goal was to teach Native American young people to read, write, and speak English and to acquire trades that would afford them employment. The goal was lofty, but in practice many native young people returned to reservations where the only full-time employment was monopolized by Bureau of Indian Affairs patronage employees. Young men trained in blacksmithing, wagon making, carpentry, tailoring, farming, and other trades rarely found employment at home on the reservations. Young women were taught Anglo-American domestic skills.

The Carlisle School was run on an army model. Students were strictly regimented and were forced to divest themselves of all vestiges of Indian identity. They wore uniforms, their hair was cut, and they were forbidden to speak their own languages. Missionaries also were brought in to teach them Christianity. Runaways were punished severely; many students died of disease or other causes. This system produced a notable amount of alienation among some Native American young people, such as Plenty Horses, a young Sioux. It also produced some notable success stories, such as those of Jim Thorpe and Luther Standing Bear. According to Colin Calloway,

> For many Indian students, the boarding school experience was traumatic and final. The cemetery at Carlisle is filled with the graves of children who died far from home—of tuberculosis, suicide, and heartbreak. The regimen, racism, and culture shock the children experienced left an imprint on impressionable minds and personalities from which some students never recovered. (Calloway, 169)

After five years at Carlisle Indian School, Plenty Horses, one of Pratt's students, returned to the Pine Ridge Indian Reservation angry and alienated, just in time to witness the 1890 massacre at Wounded Knee. A few days after the massacre, on January 7, 1891, he shot army officer Lt. Edward W. Casey in the back, hoping to be hung for his bravery. Plenty Horses' wife, Roan Horse, was killed in the ensuing melee.

After his arrest, Plenty Horses said that he had killed Casey because

> I am an Indian. Five years I attended Carlisle and was educated in the ways of the white man. When I returned to my people, I was an outcast among them. I was no longer an Indian. I was not a white man. I was lonely. I shot the lieutenant so I might make a place for myself among my people. I am now one of them. I shall be hung, and the Indians will bury me as a warrior. They will be proud of me. I am satisfied. (Jensen, Paul, and Carter, 162)

Plenty Horses was jailed at Fort Meade and tried in Sioux Falls, South Dakota. Instead of convicting Plenty Horses of murder and sentencing him to hang, a judge threw the case out because a state of war had existed on the Pine Ridge Reservation—the same state of war that the army was using as a reason not to prosecute the soldiers who had taken part in the massacre. Instead, the army awarded them two dozen Medals of Honor. Young Plenty Horses was sent home to Rosebud, still very confused and alienated. He died at Pine Ridge during the 1930s.

By 1903, Pratt's last year as Carlisle's superintendent, the school enrolled more than 1,200 pupils at a time. During Pratt's twenty-four years as head of the school, it educated 4,903 Indian boys and girls. During the 1880s, congressional appropriations for Indian schools rose from $150,000 to more than $1 million a year (Pratt, xiii). Because of political conflicts, despite a record that seemed exemplary, Pratt was forced to retire as Carlisle's superintendent in 1904. He died at an army hospital in San Francisco on April 23, 1924, at eighty-four years of age.

By the turn of the century, Carlisle was the prototype for twenty-five Indian industrial schools in thirteen states. Within a decade after Pratt died, however, even the government was losing faith in forced assimilation. The boarding schools began to close after enactment of reform legislation under Franklin Delano Roosevelt and his commissioner of Indian Affairs, and John Collier in the 1930s. By that time, inklings of Indian self-determination were surfacing in the making of policies in which Native Americans had at least some voice in plotting their own futures.

REFERENCES

Banning, Evelyn. *Helen Hunt Jackson.* New York: Vanguard Press, 1973.

Barrows, William. *The Indian's Side of the Indian Question.* Boston: D. Lothrop Co., 1887.

Black, Nancy B., and Bette S. Weidman, eds. *White on Red: Images of the American Indian.* Port Washington, NY: Kennikat Press, 1976.

Calloway, Colin, ed. *Our Hearts Fell to the Ground: Plains Indian Views of How the West Was Lost.* Boston: Bedford Books/St. Martin's Press, 1996.

Churchill, Ward. *From a Native Son: Selected Essays in Indigenism, 1985–1995.* Boston: South End Press, 1996.

Cohen, Felix. *The Legal Conscience: Selected Papers of Felix S. Cohen.* Ed. Lucy Kramer Cohen. New Haven: Yale University Press, 1960.

Hayes, Robert G. *A Race at Bay: New York Times Editorials on "the Indian Problem," 1860–1900.* Carbondale: Southern Illinois University Press, 1997.

Jackson, Helen Hunt. *A Century of Dishonor: A Sketch of the United States Government's Dealings with Some of the Indian Tribes.* Boston: Roberts Bros., 1888. Reprint. St. Clair Shores, MI: Scholarly Press, 1972.

Jensen, Richard E., R. Eli Paul, and John E. Carter. *Eyewitness at Wounded Knee.* Lincoln: University of Nebraska Press, 1991.

Johansen, Bruce E. "L. Frank Baum's Call to Genocide." *Native Americas* 14:1 (Spring 1997): 9.

———. "Taking Indians for a Ride: The BIA's Missing $2.4 Billion." *Native Americas* 14:1 (Spring 1997): 14–23.

Kinney, J. P. *A Continent Lost—A Civilization Won: Indian Land Tenure in America.* 1937. New York: Arno Press, 1975.

Manypenny, George W. *Our Indian Wards.* Cincinnati: Robert Clarke & Co., 1880.

Mathes, Valerie Sherer. "Helen Hunt Jackson: A Legacy of Indian Reform." *Essays and Monographs in Colorado History* 4 (1986): 25–58.

———. *Helen Hunt Jackson and Her Indian Reform Legacy.* Austin: University of Texas Press, 1990.

———. "Helen Hunt Jackson and the Ponca Controversy." *Montana: The Magazine of Western History* 39:1 (Winter 1989): 42–53.

Pratt, Richard Henry. *Battlefield and Classroom: Four Decades with the American Indian, 1867–1904.* Ed. Robert M. Utley. 1964. Lincoln: University of Nebraska Press, 1987.

Reilly, Hugh. "Treatment of Native Americans by the Frontier Press: An Omaha, Nebraska, Case Study." M.A. thesis, University of Nebraska at Omaha, 1997.

Vogel, Virgil J. *This Country Was Ours: A Documentary History of the American Indian.* New York: Harper & Row, 1972.

8

LAND BASE AND THE RECLAMATION OF CULTURE, 1934–2000

Felix Cohen, Vine Deloria, Jr., Oren Lyons, and Slade Gorton

Very few non-Indians during the latter half of the nineteenth century dissented from the paradigm of a monocultural future manifest in the debate over extinction versus assimilation. One who did so was the poet Walt Whitman. In a letter to city officials in Santa Fe, New Mexico, during 1883, Whitman touched on themes that resonate richly a century later:

> As to our aboriginal or Indian population . . . I know it seems to be agreed that they must gradually dwindle as time rolls on, and in a few generations more leave only a reminiscence, a blank. But I am not at all clear about that. As America . . . develops, adapts, entwines, faithfully identifies its own—are we to see it cheerfully accepting using all the contributions of foreign lands from the whole outside globe—and then rejecting the only ones distinctively its own? (Moquin, 5–6)

Walt Whitman was a notable member of a small minority in his own time when he characterized the United States as a multicultural mosaic in 1883. He was speaking the language of another century and was one of very few thinking people in his time who entertained any thought that Native American peoples and cultures would not vanish. Instead, Whitman, with his gift of foresight, might appreciate the era of the plastic medicine man, when assimilation sometimes runs opposite to what the "reformers" of the prior century had in mind. There were no plastic medicine men in Whitman's time. There was only an inkling in general society of Indian "self-determination" or sovereignty, two of the cardinal liberating phrases of Native American activism during the late twentieth century.

The late-nineteenth-century debate on extermination versus assimilation ignored one other possible course for Native Americans who survived the conquest: reassertion of land base, language, and other aspects of culture. The late twentieth century has witnessed such a revival, contrary to most expectations of a century ago.

Felix Cohen, as solicitor general in the Interior Department, advanced doctrines promoting reclamation of land base and culture at midcentury; Vine Deloria, Jr., provided an ideological foundation for Native American activism beginning during the 1960s and continuing today. Oren Lyons has addressed many world forums advocating the kind of earth stewardship anticipated by Sea'thl and Black Elk more than a century earlier.

Slade Gorton, U.S. senator from Washington State, provides a contrast to these assertions of sovereignty by maintaining a political position that was popular in the late nineteenth century: that Indian land base should be eradicated and treaty rights annulled for Native Americans' own good. While Gorton does not evidence much knowledge of Native American history, some of his comments evoke the century-and-a-half-old nostrums of Andrew Jackson. The object of such advocacy now, as then, is to provide an ideological and legal basis for the removal from the American body politic of Native Americans as organized peoples sharing identified land, rights, and cultures—"Kill the Indian, Save the Man" adapted to the public-relations requirements of late-twentieth-century spin-doctoring. Gorton's is a minority view in his own time, however, instead of the dominant social and political paradigm, as it was late in the nineteenth century. In the space of a century, many of the assumptions of debate regarding Native Americans have been turned on their heads as doubts arise over the ecological future of Western industrialism, and as native populations and cultures grow and flourish.

Felix Cohen (1907–1953)

Felix Cohen was the author of the *Handbook of Federal Indian Law* (1942), a basic reference book in its field for decades afterwards. Cohen also served as associate solicitor of the Interior Department and chaired the department's Board of Appeals. He played an instrumental part in drafting the legal infrastructure of the Indian Claims Commission, which was founded in 1946. Cohen was especially active in securing for American Indians the right to vote and Social Security benefits.

Cohen's brilliant legal mind never lost a view of how the law affected human beings, especially Native Americans. He fought a political tide that had brought allotment and was bringing termination to American Indians, both of which cost Indians large portions of their surviving land base. Cohen died of cancer at the young age of forty-six at the height of his legal career, the same year termination legislation was passed by Congress.

Cohen also authored a number of books, including *Ethical Systems and Legal Ideals* (1933) and *Combatting Totalitarian Propaganda: A Legal Appraisal* (1944). In his introduction to *The Legal Conscience*, Eugene V. Rostow wrote of Cohen:

> Felix Cohen died at forty-six, but he had already moved mountains as a public servant, as a practitioner, and as a law teacher and philosophical scholar of law. . . .

Felix Cohen. Archives, City College of New York, CUNY

> Both the scholarly and practical aspects of Felix Cohen's work in law represent the same noble thought: the truth is with us . . . and it is something to be done, not said. Man's duty is goodness. And the men of law must forever labor to make the measure of ethics the measure of law. (Cohen, *Legal Conscience*, xv–xvi)

Cohen himself saw law as "a social tool." That is to say, Cohen wrote, that "law must be valued in terms of what it *does* in our social order, in terms of its effects upon human lives. If a given legal rule helps men to lead good lives, it is good; if it helps men to lead bad lives, it is bad" (Cohen, *Legal Conscience*, 30).

Elegant of speech, erudite of pen, with a humane heart, Cohen sailed headlong into the political gauntlet that had once favored allotment and in his time sought termination of Native American nations as collective bodies.

> We have often disposed of them [Indians] spiritually by denying their existence as a people, or by taking refuge in the Myth of the Vanishing Indian, or by blaming our grandfathers for the wrongs we commit. In this way, we have often assured ourselves that our national sins are of purely antiquarian significance. (Cohen, *Legal Conscience*, 264)

Felix Cohen was born in New York City and earned an A.B. degree summa cum laude in 1926 from City College, New York City, where, as a student, he edited a student newspaper, the *Campus*. Cohen earned a Ph.D. from Harvard in 1929 and an LL.B. from Columbia Law School in 1931.

Cohen was the son of Morris Raphael Cohen, who was a legal philosopher, writer, and professor at City College. The younger Cohen became well known in the field of law beyond cases concerning American Indians. In 1951, Cohen coauthored a textbook in law with his father, *Readings in Jurisprudence and Legal Philosophy*. The book contained the usual descriptions of European legal precedents, from Aristotle to the English common law, but also included a chapter titled "Law and Anthropology" that described the legal traditions of tribal peoples in North America, including the Sioux and Cheyennes.

Cohen also was a student of Native American societies and a social critic. On one occasion, Cohen compared Native American influence on immigrants from Europe to the ways in which the Greeks shaped Roman culture:

> When the Roman legions conquered Greece, Roman historians wrote with as little imagination as did the European historians who have written of the white man's conquest of America. What the Roman historians did not see was that captive Greece would take captive conquering Rome [with] Greek science [and] Greek philosophy. (Cohen, "Americanizing," 180)

Cohen wrote that American historians had too often paid attention to military victories and changing land boundaries while failing to see that in agriculture, in government, in sport, in education, and in our views of nature and our fellow men, the first Americans also had helped shape their battlefield conquerors. American historians have seen America mainly as an imitation of Europe, Cohen asserted. In his view, the real epic of America was the yet-unfinished story of the Americanization of the white man.

In 1952, Cohen argued that "it is out of a rich Indian democratic tradition that the distinctive political ideals of American life emerged." These ideals included universal suffrage for women as well as for men, the pattern of states that we call federalism, the habit of treating chiefs as servants of the people instead of their masters, and the insistence that the community must respect the diversity of men and the diversity of their dreams. "All these things were part of the American way of life before Columbus landed" (Cohen, "Americanizing," 179–180).

One may ask how Cohen developed his points of view on American Indian law. It is likely that Cohen honed his definition of these ideas with Mohawk culture bearer Ray Fadden, of Onchiota, New York, in the Adirondacks. For many years in the 1940s, Cohen had a cabin at Buck Pond, within walking distance of the Fadden home. John Kahionhes Fadden, Ray's son, recalled his father and Cohen walking in the woods and having long conversations during John's childhood, when I visited the Faddens' homes in the Adirondacks and walked some of the same paths.

Cohen resigned from government service during 1948 to practice American Indian law in the New York City–Washington, D.C., firm of Riegelman, Stasser, Sohwartz, and Spiegelberg. He often represented the interests of the Montana Blackfest, the Oglala Sioux, the All-Pueblo Council, and the San Carlos Apaches. Cohen also served as a visiting professor of law at Yale University and City College. He also taught at Rutgers Law School and the New School for Social Research.

Cohen died of cancer on October 19, 1953, at his home in New York City. At his funeral, which was held in Washington, D.C., pallbearers included Felix Frankfurter, an associate justice of the U.S. Supreme Court, Senator Hubert H. Humphrey, John Collier, former commissioner of Indian affairs, and Oliver LaFarge, author and president of the Association on American Indian Affairs. Three days after his death, the *New York Times* editorially eulogized Cohen, saying that his death "comes at a time when the American Indian can least afford to lose a stalwart friend." The editorial mentioned efforts to alienate Indian land through termination legislation and efforts to allow state jurisdiction over Native American lands, later expressed as Public Law 280. Rostow evaluated Cohen's career:

> Felix Cohen was a teacher of power and purpose. He talked with his students as equals. He left them with a renewed awareness of the issues in law that spell the

> difference between life and death. . . . [H]is writings have been a force in the world's literature of legal philosophy and jurisprudence. In my judgement, his has been, and will remain, one of the best-balanced and one of the most creative voices in the literature of what is loosely called American legal realism. (Cohen, *Legal Conscience*, xvi)

In Cohen's time, his main political battle was against termination, the last gasp, before the liberating currents of the 1960s, of an ideology that sought to expunge Native Americans' cultures from America's collective memory. It is significant that the termination bill was passed a year after Cohen's death. He had long fought it as one more attempt by special interests to lay their hands on what was left of Native American land in America. As with removal and allotment, the land-tenure implications of termination were largely ignored by its sponsors. Instead, also like removal and allotment, termination was enacted as a purported favor to the Indians, to propel them into the "mainstream."

Passed as House Concurrent Resolution 108 in 1953, termination legislation was aimed at dissolving remaining Indian lands and Indian communal relationships. The act was phrased in terms of equality, an attempt to make Indians subject to the same laws and entitled to the same privileges as other citizens of the United States. The Termination Act was designed to end Indians' status as wards of the United States. Between 1954 and 1966, 109 American Indian nations and bands were dissolved under the provisions of this legislation. Roughly 11,400 people lost their status as Indians belonging to "recognized" Native American governments; 1.5 million acres of land were removed from trust status. Most of the terminated groups were small bands, but two of them, the Menominees of Wisconsin (with 3,270 members at termination) and the Klamaths of Oregon (with 2,133 members) were substantial communities.

The Menominees of Wisconsin shared ownership of property valued at $34 million when their termination bill was enacted in 1953, the year that termination was enacted and also the year Felix Cohen died. By 1961, the federal government was out of Menominee Country, and each of the Menominees' former members had become the owner of 100 shares of stock and a negotiable bond valued at $3,000, issued in the name of Menominee Enterprises, Inc. (MEI), a private enterprise that held the former nation's land and businesses. Governmentally, the Menominee Nation had become Menominee County, the smallest (in terms of population) and poorest (in terms of cash income) in Wisconsin.

As a county, Menominee had to raise taxes to pay for its share of services, including welfare, health services, utilities, and the like. The only taxable property owner in the county was MEI, which was forced to raise the funds to pay its tax bill by restructuring so that stockholders had to buy their homes and the property on which they had been built. Most of the

Menominees had little money saved except their $3,000 bonds, which were then sold to MEI to make the required residential purchases. Many Menominees faced private-sector health costs, property taxes, and other expenses with no more money than they had before termination. Unemployment in Menominee County rose to levels that most of the United States had known only during the Great Depression.

By 1965, health indicators in Menominee County sounded like a reprint of the Meriam Report (an outline of Indian poverty) almost four decades earlier. Tuberculosis afflicted nearly 35 percent of the population, and infant mortality was three times the national average. Termination, like allotment, was an abject failure at anything other than alienating Indian land. The termination of the Menominees was such an abysmal failure that in 1973 their federal trust relationship was reestablished by Congress.

Vine Deloria, Jr. (b. 1933)

Vine Deloria, Jr., is a member of a renowned Sioux family that had an impact on American life and letters before his birth. As a member of the faculty at Columbia University beginning in 1929, Ella Cara Deloria (1889–1971) gained notice as an outstanding anthropologist and linguist. She wrote *Dakota Texts* (1932), which is bilingual in Dakota and English, and *Speaking of Indians* (1944), a description of Native American life before the arrival of Europeans.

Ella Cara Deloria was born in Wakpala, South Dakota; her Dakota name, Anbpetu Wastewin, meant "good woman of the day." She attended Oberlin College and Columbia University, from which she graduated in 1915 with a bachelor's degree. After working as a schoolteacher and an employee of the YMCA (in Indian education), Ella Cara Deloria returned to Columbia as a professor of anthropology, where she worked with Franz Boas on two major studies of Dakota language. Deloria also authored a novel, *Waterlily*, during the 1940s. It was published in 1988, seventeen years after her death.

In her later years, Deloria continued to write, speak, and work with reservation mission schools while she added to her Dakota grammar, fearing that it might join other Native American languages in historical oblivion

---

Vine Deloria, Jr. Courtesy of Vine Deloria, Jr.

before she could finish. Deloria died of pneumonia at the Tripp Nursing Home in Vermillion, South Dakota, on February 12, 1971.

One of the first American Indians to become an Episcopal minister, Philip Deloria (Yankton Sioux, 1854–1931) is one of about ninety historical figures whose statues surround *Christ in Majesty* at the Washington, D.C., National Episcopal Cathedral. As the longtime rector of St. Elizabeth Mission on the Standing Rock Reservation, Deloria was said to have converted thousands of Sioux to Christianity. He was the father of Ella Cara Deloria and grandfather of Vine Deloria, Jr.

Vine Deloria, Jr., rose to prominence as a spokesman for Native self-determination movements during the 1960s and 1970s, becoming a widely respected professor, author, and social critic. He is one of the best-known founders of Native American studies as a field of scholarly inquiry in the late twentieth century. During the early 1990s, Deloria was teaching and writing on the University of Colorado's Boulder campus. By the late 1990s, Deloria was described by Roger Dunsmore in the *Handbook of Native American Literature* as

> the most significant voice in this generation regarding the presentation and analysis of contemporary Indian affairs, their history, present shape, and meaning. . . . No other voice, Indian or white, has as full a command of the overall data of Indian history or affairs, and no other voice has the moral force, the honesty, to admit mistakes and to redress them, or the edge to bite through the layers of soft tissue, through the stereotypes, myths, and outright lies, to the bone, to the bone marrow, of Indian affairs. (Dunsmore, 411)

Deloria was born in Martin, South Dakota. He served in the Marine Corps between 1954 and 1956 before he earned a B.S. degree at Iowa State University in 1958 and a B.D. at the Lutheran School of Theology in 1963. After that, Deloria served as executive director of the National Congress of American Indians.

Early in his life as an activist, Deloria channeled his intellectual efforts into legal studies, entering the University of Colorado Law School in 1967. The same year, he was a member of the Board of Inquiry on Hunger and Malnutrition. While serving on this board, he found black children in the Mississippi Delta eating red clay to deal with hunger (Dunsmore, 412).

Deloria's academic preparation also includes a substantial amount of theology and political science as well as law; the scope of his work is so broad that he could be cross-listed on half dozen faculties at most universities. Deloria's written work, including fifteen books and nearly a hundred major articles by 1998, stresses a common theme, according to Dunsmore, that sin is a major element in American history, and that "the sinners are those who have stolen and desecrated the land" (Dunsmore, 413).

Deloria quotes Curley, a Crow chief, who is best known to history as one of the scouts for George Armstrong Custer at the Little Bighorn in 1876. Curley is not known as a great Native American philosopher, but his words, spoken in 1912, evoke memories of Tecumseh, Sea'thl, and Black Elk:

> The soil you see is not ordinary soil—it is the dust of the blood, the flesh and the bones of our ancestors. We fought and bled and died to keep other Indians from taking it, and we fought and bled and died helping the whites. You will have to dig down through the surface before you find nature's earth, as the upper portion is Crow. The land as it is, is my blood and my dead; it is consecrated; and I do not want to give up any portion of it. (Dunsmore, 415)

As early as the 1950s, Deloria, like Felix Cohen, was engaging in criticism of the Indian Claims Commission, arguing that it was a device by which to avoid treaty issues, not solve them. He pointed out that laws and regulations announced as "help" to Indians often perpetuated colonialism. Historically, Deloria argued, the rights of Native Americans have trailed those of other social groups in the United States. For example, slavery of Alaska Natives was not outlawed until 1886, two decades after the Civil War.

Deloria has won a broad audience among a wide variety of people for asserting, with a sharp wit, contradictions in the general cant of contemporary American life. For example, in *We Talk, You Listen* (1970), Deloria recalled a conversation with a non-Indian who asked him, "What did you [Native Americans] do with the land when you had it?" Deloria said that he did not understand the ecological irony of that question until later, when he discovered that the Cuyahoga River running through Cleveland was inflammable. So many combustible pollutants were being dumped into the river that the inhabitants had to take special precautions during the summer to avoid accidentally setting it on fire. "After reviewing the argument of my non-Indian friend," wrote Deloria, "I decided that he was probably correct. Whites had made better use of the land. How many Indians could have thought of creating an inflammable river?" (Deloria, *We Talk*, 9).

Deloria defines the differences between European and Native American views of the land this way:

> The tribal-communal way of life, devoid of economic competition, views land as the most vital part of man's existence. It is THEIRS. It supports them, tells them where they live, and defines HOW they live. Land does not have the simple sentimentality of purple mountains majesty. . . . Rather it provides a center of the universe for the group that lives on it. As such, the people who hold land in this way always have a home to go to. Their identity is secure. They live with it and do not abstract themselves from it and live off it. (Deloria, *We Talk*, 175)

Jousting with missionaries, Deloria in his many speeches sometimes condenses half a millennium of history in North America into one sentence: when the missionaries came, they had the Book, and Indians had the land. Now, Deloria says, they have the land and Indians have the Book.

Deloria calls for adaptation of Native American land ethics to a general non-Indian society that finds itself faced with the environmental damage pursuant to two thousand years of multiplying and subduing the earth:

> [A]merican society could save itself by listening to tribal people. While this would take a radical reorientation of concepts and values, it would be well worth the effort. The land-use philosophy of Indians is so utterly simple that it seems stupid to repeat it: man must live with other forms of life on the land and not destroy it. The implications of this philosophy are very far-reaching for the contemporary political and economic system. Reorientation would mean that public interest, indeed the interest in the survival of humanity as a species, must take precedent over special economic interests. Now the laugh is ours. After four centuries of gleeful rape, the white man stands a mere generation away from extinguishing life on this planet. (Deloria, *We Talk*, 189, 195)

During the late twentieth century, Deloria continued to write a number of books and articles in scholarly journals that often took issue with Eurocentric interpretations of reality. His early books, such as *Custer Died for Your Sins* (1969), *We Talk, You Listen* (1970), and *Of Utmost Good Faith* (1971), continued to spread to new, younger audiences.

In all of his works, Deloria has asserted Native American rights of occupancy to the land. Under international law, according to Deloria, Native American nations possess an equitable title of occupancy over lands upon which they lived, "and this occupancy was not to be disturbed except by voluntary and lawful sales of lands to the European country claiming the legal title to the area in question" (Lyons, et al. 283).

Deloria's writings also compare the metaphysics of Native American and European points of view, especially in legal and religious matters. In *God Is Red*, he contrasts Native American religion's melding of life with a concept of sacred place to the artifices of Christianity and other "Near Eastern" religions. Deloria compares the nature of sacredness in each perceptual realm. His discussion of sacredness also examines ecological themes in Native American religions. Deloria also compares the ways in which each culture perceives reality—Europeans seeing time as lineal and history as a progressive sequence of events; most Native American cultures as neither of these. Christianity usually portrays God as a humanlike being, often meddlesome and vengeful, whereas many Native American religions place supreme authority in a great spirit or great mystery symbolizing the life forces of nature.

To Deloria, the great mystery of Sioux theology becomes an ecological metaphor as he explains ways in which Native American theologies weave a concept of cycles into life, reinforcing reverence for the land and the remains of ancestors buried in it, contrasted to Europeans' ability to move from place to place without regard for location until the reality of the American land and its often-unwritten history begins to absorb them. Deloria's beliefs are not his alone; they may be read in a historical context provided by Luther Standing Bear, Chief Sea'thl, and other Native American leaders whose thoughts have been examined in earlier chapters.

Deloria points out that many Native Americans and non-Indians have trouble communicating because, even today, their perceptual realms are different:

> The fundamental factor that keeps Indians and non-Indians from communicating is that they are speaking about two entirely different perceptions of the world. Growing up on an Indian reservation makes one acutely aware of the mysteries of the universe. Medicine men practicing their ancient ceremonies perform feats that amaze and puzzle the rational mind. The sense of contentment enjoyed by older Indians in the face of a lifetime's experience of betrayal, humiliation and paternalism stuns the outside observer. It often appears that Indians are immune to the values which foreign institutions have forced them to confront. Their minds remain fixed on other realities. (Deloria, *Metaphysics*, vii)

Ernst Cassirer, who is cited approvingly by Deloria, wrote that for tribal peoples, "nature becomes one great society, the society of life. Man is not endowed with an outstanding rank in this society. He is part of it, but he is in no respect higher than any other member" (Cassirer, 83). Comments Deloria: "All species, all forms of life, have equal status before the presence of the universal power to which they are subject. The religious requirement for all life-forms is thus harmony, and this requirement holds for every species, ours included" (Deloria, *Metaphysics*, 153–154).

Deloria provides a trenchant critique of "progress" and "civilization," two connotatively loaded words that have propelled the expansion of European lifeways around the earth, two words that are usually invested by European-descended thinkers with connotations of uncontested goodness or, if not goodness, at least of inevitability.

> In recent years, we have come to understand what progress is. It is the total replacement of nature by an artificial technology. Progress is the absolute destruction of the real world in favor of a technology that creates a comfortable way of life for a few fortunately situated people. Within our lifetime the difference between the Indian use of land and the white use of land will become crystal clear. The Indian lived with his land. *The white destroyed his land. He destroyed the planet earth.* (Hughes, 136; emphasis in original)

For more than three decades, Deloria has been a leading national spokesperson for a Native American intellectual movement toward sovereignty and redefinition of many assumptions that have contributed to oppression of Native Americans. In person, Deloria is known for his sharp wit. Addressing 500 students at Boise State University on February 27, 1998, he jested about nineteenth-century psuedoscientific assumptions that Europeans were the most intelligent race because they had the largest skulls. That was before "the discovery that Apaches had something like 100 cc's more cranial capacity than Harvard professors," Deloria joked (Etlinger, 1-B).

Entering his late sixties by the end of the 1990s, Deloria often walked with a cane. When people asked him about it, he was prone to say that he had "been bitten by a rabid Republican and got a staph infection" (Wilitz, 1). In a complaint about the left-leaning nature of the professoriate, Vincent Carroll, editorial-page editor of Denver's *Rocky Mountain News*, pointed out, with a straight face that Deloria might find downright funny, that Deloria was the only registered Republican among the faculty of the History Department at the University of Colorado at Boulder (Carroll, A-22).

A consummate observer of academic rituals, Deloria has been a continuing critic of research methods often employed by scholars investigating Native American peoples:

> My original complaint against researchers is that they seem to derive all the benefits and bear no responsibility for the ways in which their findings are used. In making this accusation, I said that scholars should be required to put something back into the Indian community, preferably some form of financial support so the community can do some things it wants to do. (Deloria, "Commentary," 457)

Deloria's fifteen books (by 1998) have taken issue with dominant assumptions in many areas, among them theories on evolution as well as assumptions that Native Americans' oral histories are less reliable than European-style written documents. Deloria's outspoken stances have earned him a number of different responses, from e-mails accusing him of being a bigot to lines of people at conferences who hug him and have their pictures taken with him.

Deloria has many critics. John C. Whittaker, writing in the *Skeptical Inquirer*, said that Deloria's fifteeenth book, *Red Earth, White Lies* (1995), is "a wretched piece of Native American creationist claptrap that has all the flaws of the Biblical creationists he disdains" (Whittaker, 47). Throughout his life, Deloria has been a sharp critic of many theories that have often assumed the status of revealed truth among many non-Indian academics. One of these is the assumption that Native Americans populated the Western Hemisphere solely by crossing a land bridge from Siberia.

> Scientists, and I use the word as loosely as possible, are committed to the view that Indians migrated to this country over an imaginary Bering Straits bridge, which

comes and goes at the convenience of the scholar requiring it to complete his or her theory. Initially, at least, Indians are [said to be] homogenous. But there are also eight major language families within the Western Hemisphere, indicating to some scholars that if Indians followed the trend that can be identified in other continents, then the migration went from east to west; tourists along the Bering straits were going *to* Asia, not migrating *from* it. (Deloria, "Indigenous").

While some scholars debate whether Native Americans really had a religious ethic that viewed the earth as mother, contemporary Native American religious and intellectual leaders continue to use the image with a frequency that evokes the rhetoric of Tecumseh and Black Elk. Deloria, who is arguably the father of the late-twentieth-century intellectual renaissance in Native America, has been arguing ecological views of history for more than three decades with a rising sense of urgency as environmental crises intensify around the world. The stakes, in Deloria's analysis, include the future of humanity (as well as other animals) as viable species on an increasingly sullied earth.

"It will take a continuing protest from an increasingly large chorus," writes Deloria, "to reprogram the psychology of American society so that we will not irreversibly destroy the land we live on" (Deloria, *God Is Red*, 2). His sense of urgency at the speed of environmental deterioration during the last years of the twentieth century is palpable: "Only a radical reversal of our attitudes toward nature can help us" (Deloria, *God Is Red*, 2). "Nor do I look forward to paying the penalties that Mother Earth must now levy against us in order for Her to survive" (Deloria, *God Is Red*, 3).

It remains for us now to learn once again that we are part of nature, not a transcendent species with no responsibilities to the natural world. As we face the twenty-first century, the next decade will be the testing ground for this proposition. We may well become one of the few species in this vast universe that has permanently ruined our home. (Deloria, *God Is Red*, 3)

Oren Lyons (b. 1930)

Like Vine Deloria, Jr., Oren Lyons (Turtle Clan Onondaga) is an ideological descendant of the Native American leaders (Tecumseh, Sea'thl, and others) whose voices were raised during previous centuries against the reduction of indigenous land base and culture as Indians were forced through the gauntlet of assimilation and dispossession. Both also have been spokespersons for the reassertion of Native American identity during the late twentieth century.

Lyons, whose Onondaga name is Joagquisho, became known worldwide during the last half of the twentieth century as an author, publisher, and crisis negotiator, as well as a spokesperson for the Haudenosaunee (Iroquois) in several world forums. He is also an accomplished graphic artist as well as a renowned lacrosse player and coach. In addition, Lyons is a professor of Native American studies at the State University of New York at Buffalo.

"When you talk about Lacrosse, you talk about the lifeblood of the Six Nations," says Lyons, faithkeeper of the Haudenosaunee Grand Council at Onondaga and an all-American lacrosse player as a goalkeeper when he was a student at Syracuse University in the late 1950s (Lipsyte, 28). On the 1957 Syracuse University team, Lyons played lacrosse with Jim Brown, later a celebrated professional football player. Lyons' father also was a

---

Oren Lyons. © Marcia Keegan

well-known goalkeeper. In 1990, Lyons organized an Iroquois national team that played in the world lacrosse championships in Australia.

Lyons was educated in art at Syracuse University (1954–1958). After his graduation from college, Lyons enjoyed a successful career as a commercial artist at Norcross Greeting Cards in New York City for more than a decade (1959–1970). Lyons began as a paste-up artist at Norcross; in a dozen years at the firm, he worked his way up to head planning director for seasonal lines.

In 1970, Lyons abandoned his career in greeting cards and returned home to the Onondaga Territory, where he was condoled (installed) as faithkeeper of the Iroquois Grand Council. Lyons also was part of a negotiating team from the Iroquois Confederacy that helped resolve the 1990 standoff between Mohawks and authorities at Kanesatake (Oka), Quebec. The confederacy's negotiators came to occupy a crucial middle ground between the Warriors and Canadian officials during the months of negotiations that preceded the use of armed force by the Canadian army and police at Kanesatake and Kahnawake. The Iroquois negotiators urged both sides to concentrate on long-term solutions to problems brought to light by the summer's violence. They recommended a fair land-rights process in Canada, the creation of viable economic bases for the communities involved in the crisis, and the recognition of long-standing (but often-ignored) treaty rights, including border rights.

Lyons also has been involved in a number of other Iroquois-rights issues, most notably the return of wampum belts to the confederacy by the state of New York. He has spoken on behalf of the Haudenosaunee in several international forums, including the United Nations. Lyons also is known as an author, notably as lead author of *Exiled in the Land of the Free* (1992).

Lyons also has been active in uniting religious peoples of differing traditions. On April 28, 1997, Lyons took part in an interfaith service at Saint Bartholomew's Church in New York City in support of the United Nations with leaders from Christian, Jewish, Buddhist, Sikh, Jainist, Islamic, and Hindu clergy. One aim of the service was to diminish international tensions based on religious differences.

Lyons has faced harsh attacks by independent merchants in the Iroquois Confederacy for his belief that some of their profits should go back to the nations in which they do business. This criticism reached a peak in the late winter of 1998 when Lyons and other supporters of the traditional council burned and bulldozed four smoke shops on Onondaga Territory. Lyons and other members of the council have long maintained that sovereignty is a collective right to be exercised by a governing body, not a license to make profits because merchants on Native American territories may avoid paying New York State sales tax.

"Who represents the sovereignty of the United States?" Lyons and coauthor John C. Mohawk asked in *Cultural Survival Quarterly* (Lyons and Mohawk, 58). "Is it the New York Yankees? Bloomingdales? the Los Angeles *Times*? William F. Buckley?" Just as private enterprises do not speak for the United States, wrote Lyons and Mohawk, private Iroquois business-people cannot exercise national sovereignty as individuals, especially when it is used as a cover for socially debasing activities such as smuggling illegal drugs.

When freebooting smugglers used some of their profits to establish gambling houses at Akwesasne (St. Regis) in the late 1980s, for example, Lyons and Mohawk argued that owners of the casinos and bingo halls were crippling Mohawk sovereignty rather than exercising it. "Common sense dictates," they wrote, "that the gambling operators are the greatest threat to Mohawk sovereignty," (Lyons and Mohawk, 59). Lyons also has been a longtime opponent of Native American dependence on gambling for economic development. "Gaming has run its course before and each time it goes bust," Lyons has said. "Poor people are the ones who gamble. It's like chewing on your own wrist" (Slackman, A-8).

A key concept of Native America's resurgence is a concept of sovereignty and self-determination, a desire to define identity vis-a-vis the smothering hand of federal strictures sewn into the "wardship" system of the Bureau of Indian Affairs. "Sovereignty," writes Lyons, "is the act thereof. . . . The action of a people in a territory, the ability and willingness of a people to defend that territory, and the recognition of that ability by other nations.

Lyons' construction of humankind's position vis-à-vis the rest of nature has traditional Native American roots. The defining point for Lyons, as for Tecumseh, is the land as the basis and sustainer of a people's collective relationship with the earth in a mutually dependent web of life. Lyons also shares the view of many Native Americans, past and present, that "in our perception all life is equal, and that includes the birds, animals, things that grow, things that swim" (Vecsey and Venables, 173).

Like their forebears before the twentieth century, Native American leaders in the late twentieth century invoke the image of "mother earth." Lyons, for example, told the United Nations at the opening of the Year of Indigenous Peoples (1993):

> Indeed, the Seed is the the Law of Life. It is the Law of Regeneration. Within the seed is the mysterious force of life and creation. Our mothers nurture and guard that seed and we respect and love *I-hi-do'hah*, our Mother Earth, for the same spiritual work and mystery. . . . When we walk upon Mother Earth, we always plant our feet carefully because we know the faces of our future generations are looking up at us from beneath the ground. (Lyons, "Opening Address")

Lyons is reflecting the same view of the natural world as Chief Joseph, Black Elk, Sea'thl, and other nineteenth-century Native American leaders when he expresses a spirit of equality with all of creation. He opened a working session of the United Nations Working Group on Indigenous Peoples during 1997 by asking whether the United Nations represents only human beings or all life on the earth:

> I do not see a delegation for the four-footed. I see no seat for the eagle. We forget and we consider ourselves superior, but we are after all a mere part of the creation. And we must continue to understand where we are. We stand between the mountain and the ant, somewhere and only there, as part and parcel of the creation. (Lyons, "Opening Remarks")

The Haudenosaunee have an enduring relationship with the United Nations. During the organization's early years, a delegation of Haudenosaunee chiefs visited its headquarters in New York City, usually about once a year, drawing parallels between the world body and their own "league of nations." Since 1977, Lyons and other indigenous representatives have approached the United Nations to speak on behalf of the natural world. Lyons speaks for trees that cannot flee the chainsaw. He speaks on behalf of salmon, herring, tuna, and haddock killed in their spawning beds by runoff from eroded hillsides. "We had alarming news from the Four Directions about fish, wildlife and birds, contaminated, sick and disappearing. And today we continue to speak on their behalf. Today, they are more endangered than ever, and if anything, their conditions are worse. . . . As long as you make war against *Etenoha* (Mother Earth), there can never be peace" (Lyons, "Opening Remarks").

Chief Arvol Looking Horse, the nineteenth keeper of the Lakotas' Sacred White Buffalo Calf Pipe, evoked a similar image in 1998, using words that sound like those of Black Elk. Looking Horse was taught the words by oral tradition, however, rather than through John Neihardt's *Black Elk Speaks*.

> As a keeper of a sacred bundle, I ask for prayers for Global Healing. Our Mother Earth is suffering. Her wonderful gift of water, trees, and air is being abused. Her children, the two-legged, the four-legged, those that swim, crawl, and fly are being annihilated. . . . Our relatives, the animal nations, reflect our well-being. What happens to them, happens to us. . . . The prophecies tell us it is time to begin mending the Sacred Hoop and begin global healing by working towards world peace and harmony. (Looking Horse, "Invitation")

In the environmental critique of Lyons, Deloria, and others, there is a sense of urgency because the exploitive reach of the conquest, in its broadest sense, during the late twentieth century has reached the size, scale, and ability to destroy the natural balance of the earth's ecology, for the first time in human history, on a planetwide scale.

Lyons has sounded warnings in a number of international environmental forums. The venues differ, but the message is always similar: "We were told that there would come a time when we would not find clean water to wash ourselves, to cook our foods, to make our medicines, and to drink." Today Lyons peers into the future with great apprehension. "We were told that there would come a time when, tending our gardens, we would pull up our plants and the vines would be empty. Our precious seed would begin to disappear. . . . Can we withstand another 500 years of 'sustainable development?' I don't think so" (Lyons, "Address"). "It is not too late," Lyons told the United Nations General Assembly. "We still have options. We need the courage to change our values to the regeneration of families, the life that surrounds us" (Lyons, "Address").

At the Constitutional Sovereignty Summit during June 1995, Lyons created a stir in Washington, D.C., at the front desk of the Vista Hotel (which was best known locally as the hotel in which Mayor Marion Barry was arrested for buying crack cocaine) when he tried to register without a credit card. It took some doing, but the hotel's desk was finally persuaded to accept the good faith and credit of the Lummi Nation, the conference's main organizers. Later, Lyons explained some of the other practical problems created by exercising sovereignty: for example, it takes a talented travel agent to get a visa to the Czech Republic on a Haudenosaunee passport.

"Shut down the reservations, and you'll have a meeting at the White House," said Oren Lyons, speaking during the conference's first panel (Johansen, "Sovereignty Summit," 79). Uncharacteristically angry, Lyons said that he was tired of attending conferences at which sovereignty was discussed in theory. "We go to conferences to discuss sovereignty because we haven't got it," he said. One major indication of sovereignty, Lyons said, is that it is practiced. "You do not ask the colonizer to recognize it." Lyons proposed that Indian nations declare July 5 "Native American Sovereignty Day" and close their borders "to show whose land it is" (Johansen, "Sovereignty Summit," 79). The question of land tenure is never far from Lyons' thoughts; in his speeches he reiterates repeatedly that "land is the issue. Land has *always* been the issue with indigenous peoples" (Lyons, "Ethics,"; emphasis added).

Lyons returned to the podium early during the second day of the Sovereignty Summit to describe the structure and principles of the Iroquois Confederacy and ways in which it shaped the founding of the United States. He reflected on the anger behind his words the day before, but did not recant them. He seemed worried about offending more moderate members of the audience, but then said, "I am getting to the age where I don't give a damn" (Johansen, "Sovereignty Summit," 79).

Several times, speakers suggested redefining American federalism more along the lines of the Iroquois Confederacy with respect to diversity and respect for women. "A lot of the problems in the world can be related directly to men's reluctance to engage women in governance," said Lyons.

"In Iroquois society, women's opinions are sought" (Johansen, "Sovereignty Summit," 80).

Lyons has become a social and political activist on a worldwide scale. For example, he has spoken out against policies of the World Bank that have an adverse impact on indigenous peoples, usually through the backing of development projects that impinge on traditional lifeways by destroying environmental balance and stimulating in-migration of nonindigenous peoples. Lyons cites from a statement by Survival International dated September 20, 1994:

> The World Bank and the IMF make decisions every day that affect the lives of hundreds of thousands of tribal peoples. The tribes are hardly, if ever, consulted. In the last fifty years the World Bank has approved projects that have had catastrophic results for indigenous people worldwide. According to the Bank's own figures, by 1996 it will have evicted 4 million people, many of them tribal. (Lyons, "Ethics")

Present World Bank policy excludes the participation of indigenous peoples of North America, a policy that Lyons believes is particularly uninformed, insensitive, and debilitating to American Indian nations' requirements for capital from sources that affirm their sovereignty and self-determination. Migration into the "underdeveloped" regions of some nations, such as the Amazon Valley of Brazil, lightens the burden on governments overwhelmed with demands for relief from the social pressures of unemployment and poverty. The immigrants, desperate from poverty, have little regard for fragile indigenous communities living in what Lyons calls "the last reaches of the natural ecosystems of the world" (Lyons, "Ethics"). Lyons believes that the World Bank favors short-term economic growth based on consumption over the futures of the world's few surviving indigenous peoples, who "will have to pay for the market-driven forces of greed" (Lyons, "Ethics"). During his consultations with World Bank officials, Lyons often poses questions of authority: "From whence do you derive your authority when you determine projects impacting indigenous peoples and lands? Is there in the lexicon of your organization a 'moral' standard for indigenous peoples and their lands? Are there moral and ethical standards for any lands and natural resources?" (Lyons, "Ethics").

While Lyons has been meeting with World Bank officials, the organization's own internal inspectors have been confirming what he has been saying. The inspectors recommended that the bank remedy the environmental and social damage wrought by a series of projects it financed in the Brazilian Amazon during the 1980s. Four years after the bank launched that effort, known as PLANAFLORO, deforestation had actually increased to "high historical levels" of nearly 450,000 hectares per year, the agency's inspection panel said in a new report to the executive board. "Analysis of satellite imagery . . . done under the project demonstrates that, contrary to project objectives, deforestation during the period 1993–1996 has increased considerably," the report stated. "Although there's been much progress in demarcating reserves and establishing the legal title of Amerindians [to local lands] these are largely ignored. There's no policing, and lots of encroachment" (Aslam, "Environment/Brazil").

Lyons said that indigenous peoples have long been victims of development projects throughout the world. This occurs consistently, because indigenous peoples live in so-called undeveloped or underdeveloped territories. The natural resources, lands, and water are the targets of development that can take many different forms. The extraction of oil, gold, other minerals, timber, or water results in a fundamental change in the natural environment in which indigenous peoples have culturally and physically adapted for thousands of years. Lyons, in a 1995 statement to World Bank officials, maintained that water is life. "People migrate to water and people live by water for its sustenance," Lyons said.

> Projects funded by the World Bank have been notorious for negative impacts on indigenous peoples' lives and aboriginal lands. . . . We have been impacted by the mining of gold, uranium, and other minerals, [as well as] roads and highways built to access raw materials which not only remove minerals and destroy forests and fragment habitat for living creatures, but also provide access to land-hungry individuals coming from deprived circumstances in deteriorating infrastructures of overpopulated cities and urban wastelands. These people bring with them a fierce instinct for survival coupled with racism. (Lyons, "Ethics")

Lyons acknowledges that prior criticism of the World Bank has had an effect. The World Bank's Vice Presidency for Environmentally Sustainable Development and its Division for Social Policy and Resettlement have undertaken several initiatives in recent years to improve the bank's approach toward indigenous peoples. The bank has begun social assessments to better identify indigenous peoples and other minority communities in the countries where the bank has an active lending program. In Latin America, several training workshops have been held with indigenous peoples to strengthen their capacities to engage in designing development programs for the benefit of their own communities.

> We would like to encourage the Bank to continue in this direction. We believe that small loans and direct funding to communities and indigenous peoples is a positive step for empowering indigenous peoples and others at the grass-roots level. This process will engage their genius for their own development. It empowers indigenous peoples in poverty-stricken communities immediately. (Lyons, "Ethics,")

Lyons believes that human beings can be productive and supportive of nature, or they can be parasites. "Right now we are parasites," Lyons argues. We are, by sheer numbers and behavior, extinguishing other life forms. "The natural law says that no one entity can grow unchecked," Lyons believes. "There are forces that will check this unbridled growth, such as disease and lack of food and water. Privilege will not prevail. There can be no peace as long as you make war on Mother Earth" (Lyons, "Ethics").

Lyons also has spoken out against the Human Genome Diversity Project, which aims to preserve DNA cell lines of indigenous populations before these populations or their cell lines become extinct either through intercultural marriage or through the demise of the population in question. The Human Genome Diversity Project seeks to collect samples of blood, saliva, cells, hair roots, and other biological materials from 500 indigenous populations. Lyons has said that indigenous peoples were never consulted in the design of the project.

Equally troubling to Lyons is the legal patenting of some gene types by corporations. When in this process do people cease to own their own bodies? Lyons asks. What does it mean, practically, ethically, and legally, for an indigenous person to consent to give DNA samples to the Human Genome Diversity Project? Does this consent open the doors for others to patent sequences of his or her DNA? How would one know if part of one's DNA sequence has been patented at some point in the future? What recourse would one have nationally and internationally if one discovered that part of his or her DNA was subsequently patented?

Senator Slade Gorton (b. 1928)

Like President Andrew Jackson in the 1830s, Senator Henry Dawes in the 1880s, and Termination sponsor Senator Arthur V. Watkins in the 1950s, Senator Slade Gorton, Republican of Washington State, during the 1980s and 1990s became a leading national advocate of legislative measures to disassemble the remaining Native American land base. Gorton, a member of the New England fishing family of the same name whose Gorton's frozen products are sold in grocery stores nationwide, moved to Seattle from Chicago in 1953. He married Sally Clark of Selah, Washington, in 1958. By the late 1990s, they had three children and seven grandchildren. Gorton served in the U.S. Army from 1946 to 1947. He was in the U.S. Air Force Reserve, where he reached the rank of colonel, from 1956 to 1981.

In 1958, Gorton began his political career as a Washington state representative; he went on to serve as state house majority leader. In 1968, Gorton was elected attorney general of Washington State, in which position he argued fourteen cases before the Supreme Court. In June 1980, he received the Wyman Award as Outstanding Attorney General in the United States, and in 1982, he was elected to the U.S. Senate.

Senator Gorton's proposals to abrogate treaties with Native Americans were defeated in the U.S. Senate during the middle 1990s. Native American

---

Senator Slade Gorton. Courtesy Office of Senator Slade Gorton leaders credited Indian organizing and a Senate leadership that understands the historic importance of the treaties.

One Gorton initiative, to tax profits from Indian casinos, was narrowly defeated in the Senate during the spring of 1997 after a General Accounting Office study disclosed that only a few reservations have had casino windfalls. Ten casinos generated almost half the $7 billion in annual revenues generated by Indian tribes (with a net income of $1.6 billion a year), according to the GAO. Nearly all of them are located close to major urban areas that supply a large number of non-Indian gamblers. Most reservations in rural areas have small gaming operations or none at all. Gorton has complained that Indians are using their treaty rights as a shield against civil lawsuits and to make tax-free profits from casinos, as well as sales of cigarettes and other goods. The tribes have replied that they have the same protection against civil lawsuits as state, federal, and county governments.

During the summer of 1997, Gorton's treaty-busting activity emerged from the Senate in the form of two "riders" on a $13 billion appropriations bill for the Interior Department.

Gorton is chairman of the Senate Interior Appropriations Subcommittee, which oversees the budget of the Bureau of Indian Affairs. He used a special privilege of his office, the "chairman's mark," to insert his riders after public debate on the spending bill.

One of the riders required Native American nations to waive their sovereign immunity in exchange for $767 million in federal funds designated for tribal operations, a figure representing half the operating budgets of 550 Native American governmental entities. Gorton's second rider would have denied federal funds to Indian tribes that make more than a certain amount of money from gambling or other forms of economic development. This measure stemmed from a belief that reservation residents have become suddenly rich, despite the fact that unemployment for Native Americans was still about 15 percent in the late 1990s, more than three times the national average for non-Indians. "I find nothing in any Indian treaty that says they must be continually supported by the federal taxpayers," said Gorton (Johansen, "Slade," 4). When Gorton called treaty-based sovereign immunity "an anachronism," he may not have realized that the same language was used by President Andrew Jackson in 1830 to support the Removal Act, which legally authorized the forced removal of tens of thousands of Native Americans from their homes.

The *New York Times* on August 31, 1997, editorially condemned Gorton's proposals as "reprehensible" changes in basic law that, if enacted, "would undercut tribal sovereignty and hurt some tribes financially" (Johansen, "Slade," 4). The *Times* editorial said that Gorton's riders were "profoundly ahistorical" because they ignored the treaties. Interior Secretary Bruce Babbitt called Gorton's measures "financial blackmail" (Johansen, "Slade," 4).

Representatives of more than a hundred tribes met in Washington, D.C., during early September 1997 to forge strategies to deal with Gorton's riders. The same week, President Bill Clinton also pledged to veto the bill if Gorton's riders were not stripped from it. Even some Senate Republicans argued that Gorton's riders, if enacted, would not survive legal testing. Senator John McCain, chairman of the Senate Indian Affairs Committee, opposed the riders on grounds that they denied the validity of treaties and were part of "a rising anti-Indian movement in the Congress" based on assumed Indian affluence from gambling operations. McCain said: "The treaties are clear in what they say. . . . [They] were written in exchange for a significant portion of America" (Johansen, "Slade," 4).

Senator Ben Nighthorse Campbell, who at one time had pledged that the riders would pass over his dead body, played a major role with Senators Daniel Inouye and McCain as the Senate defeated Section 120 (the operations-funds measure) and changed Section 118 so that it would not penalize native nations and tribes. On September 16, 1997, the day that Gorton's measures went down to defeat, W. Ron Allen, chairman of the National Congress of American Indians (NCAI) as well as chair of the Jamestown S'Klallam tribe in Gorton's home state of Washington, said, "Today, Indian Country earned a major victory in the protection and preservation of our way of life. . . . Today, Senator Gorton realized that his extreme proposals were out of step with his colleagues in the Senate and most Americans who believe in protecting the rights of Indian tribes" (Johansen, "Slade," 4).

Gorton's riders reflect his tactics at home, especially with regard to the Lummi. Gorton has supported white homeowners near Bellingham, on northern Puget Sound, who live on the Lummi Reservation and use roughly 70 percent of its water. When the Lummis announced plans to cut water supplies to the whites, Gorton retaliated by introducing a special measure in the U.S. Senate (which failed to pass) designed to cut the Lummis' federal appropriations by half.

Gorton's proposal to abrogate sovereign immunity surfaced in the Senate again during early 1998. Gorton claimed substantial support from many of his constituents, especially in the densely populated Puget Sound corridor, where many of Washington State's twenty-seven tribal governments have been flexing their economic muscles with fisheries, smoke shops, casinos, and other initiatives. Many of the small reservations in the Puget Sound area lie adjacent to non-Indian suburbs, where some of the residents have complained that such things as the Puyallups' video billboards and a Muckleshoot 20,000-seat amphitheater violate local regulations, providing what the *Seattle Times* called "a recipe for conflict" (Mapes, B-1).

As has been the case since the first European landings in North America, the main ingredient in this recipe for conflict has been differing perceptions of who has the right to use the land, and how it should be used. Gorton's measure would allow tribal governments to be sued over these developments. Native governments' immunity from such suits stems from Chief Justice John Marshall's findings during the 1830s that Indian nations possess a form of limited sovereignty. In practice, this has meant that reservations have governing authority largely parallel to that of cities and counties, which are generally not allowed to exercise jurisdiction over native lands.

"We're acting like governments? Well, excuse us!" said Allen. "[A]s long as Indians are attractive for the community, giving them artistry or character, or dancing or basket-weaving, then it's 'Oh, these are our Indians,' almost like property. You don't recognize us as a fellow citizen, or an equal government" (Mapes, B-1). Gorton's proposal would "render Indian tribes impotent to protect their lands, resources, cultures, and future generations," said Allen (Knickerbocker, 1). A large number of lawsuits could bankrupt smaller tribal governments.

Many Native American leaders fear that Gorton's attack on sovereign immunity is only the first stage of a campaign to eliminate tribal governments entirely by undermining their economic bases. One related conflict pits state governments against Native American nations and tribes within their borders that do not collect sales taxes, an annual total of about $100 million in New York State, where state attempts to collect sales taxes have led to clashes between Indian merchants and police and the closure of some major highways for days at a time. Nationally, the states contend that they were being deprived, in 1998, of $1 billion a year in unpaid taxes.

Gorton's attempts to dismember what remains of the Native American land base bring to mind past attempts, such as allotment and termination. Historically, each of these proposals has tried to get around historical circumstances sketched by *Indian Country Today* publisher Tim Giago: "Indian nations gave up millions of acres of land for perpetual funds to educate their children, for health care and other rights, and for the right to run their own governments" (Knickerbocker, 1).

Joe de la Cruz, former NCAI president and chairman of the Quinault nation on Washington's Pacific coast, laughed out loud at Gorton's assertions that the law, as now interpreted, gave Indians a superior position in American society. "If this country's history was laid down for a United Nations committee," said de la Cruz, "this country could not live the shame down" (Mapes, B-1). Gorton retorted: "I don't think society is helped by grievances that are 150 years old. After a while, [they] should get over it" (Mapes, B-1). Gorton in April 1998 said that his bill did not have enough support to pass the U.S. Senate, but "some kind of legislation is inevitable" (Mapes, B-1).

Gorton's most recent attempt to place Native Americans between a legal rock and a financial hard place is the latest in nearly three decades of crusading by him, first as attorney general of Washington in the 1970s) and then as a U.S. senator, to enact into law Gorton's belief that treaties make Native Americans "supercitizens" with rights denied other Americans. Gorton steadfastly denies that he is still rubbing his wounds from Washington State fishing-rights battles, during which the federal government and Indian tribes soundly defeated his attorney general's office, culminating in Supreme Court affirmation of the 1974 "Boldt decision" (see the Appendix), which reserved up to half the salmon returning to Puget Sound for Native American use.

REFERENCES

Aslam, Abid. "Environment/Brazil: World Bank to Overhaul Amazon Project." Interpress service, April 18, 1997. http://edvmix3.ub.tu-berlin.de/lists/native-1/199704/19970423.html.

Carroll, Vincent. "Republican Professors? Sure, There's One." *Wall Street Journal*, May 11, 1998, A-22.

Cassirer, Ernst. *An Essay on Man*. New Haven, CT: Yale University Press, 1944.

Cohen, Felix. "Americanizing the White Man." *American Scholar* 21:2 (1952): 171–191.

———. *The Legal Conscience: Selected Papers of Felix S. Cohen*. Ed. Lucy Kramer Cohen. New Haven, CT: Yale University Press, 1960.

Deloria, Vine, Jr. "Commentary: Research, Redskins, and Reality." *American Indian Quarterly* 15:4 (Fall 1991): 457–468.

———. *God Is Red: A Native View of Religion*. 2nd ed. Golden, CO: North American Press/Fulcrum, 1992.

———. "Indigenous Peoples' Literature." http://www.indians.org/welker/vine.htm.

———. *The Metaphysics of Modern Existence*. San Francisco: Harper & Row, 1979.

———. *Red Earth, White Lies: Native Americans and the Myth of Scientific Fact*. New York: Scribner, 1995.

———. *We Talk, You Listen: New Tribes, New Turf*. New York: Macmillan, 1970.

Dunsmore, Roger. "Vine Deloria, Jr." In *Handbook of Native American Literature*, ed. Andrew Wiget, 411–415. New York: Garland Publishing, 1996.

Etlinger, Charles. "Indian Scholar Blows Holes in Theories: Deloria Says Lazy Scientists Adjust Facts to Fit Ideas." *Idaho Statesman*, February 28, 1998, 1-B.

Hughes, J. Donald. *American Indian Ecology*. El Paso: Texas Western Press, 1983.

Johansen, Bruce E. "Slade Gorton's Latest." *Native Americas* 14:3 (Fall 1997): 3–4.

———. "Sovereignty Summit." *Akwesasne Notes*, n.s. 1:3/4 (Fall 1995): 78–81.

Knickerbocker, Brad. "Tribal Nations Fight Challenges to Their Sovereignty." *Christian Science Monitor*, April 3, 1998, p. 1.

Lipsyte, Robert. "Lacrosse: All-American Game." *New York Times Sunday Magazine*, June 15, 1986, 28.

Looking Horse, Arvol. "Invitation to World Peace and Prayer Day, June 21, 1998, at Pipestone, Minnesota." http://www.peaceday.org/0621.htm.

———. "Ethics and Spiritual Values, and the Promotion of Environmentally Sustainable Development: 50 Years of the World Bank, over 50 Tribes Devastated." October 3, 1995. http://www.ratical.com/ratville/OrenLyons.html#development.

Lyons, Oren. "Haudenosaunee Faithkeeper, Chief Oren Lyons Addressing Delegates to the United Nations Organization [which] Opened 'The Year of the Indigenous Peoples' (1993) in the United Nations General Assembly Auditorium, United Nations Plaza, New York City, December 10, 1992." http://www.ratical.com/many_worlds/6Nations/OLatUNin92.html.

———. "Opening Address for the Year of Indigenous Peoples, United Nations, New York City, 1993." http://www.indians.org/walker/onondaga.htm.

———. "Opening Remarks." Working Group on Indigenous Peoples, United Nations, Geneva, Switzerland. Document E/CN.4/Sub.2/1997/14. 15th Session, July 28–August 1, 1997. http://www.docip.org/anglais/update_en/up_en_19_20.html#opst.

Lyons, Oren, and John C. Mohawk. "Sovereignty and Common Sense." *Cultural Survival Quarterly* 17:4 (Winter 1994): 58–60.

Lyons, Oren, John Mohawk, Vine Deloria, Jr., Laurence Hauptman, Howard Berman, Donald A. Grinde, Jr., Curtis Berkey, and Robert Venables. *Exiled in the Land of the Free: Democracy, Indian Nations, and the U.S. Constitution.* Santa Fe, NM: Clear Light, 1992.

Mapes, Lynda V. "Backlash for Tribal Immunity—Debate over Move to End Sovereign Status." *Seattle Times*, April 5, 1998, B-1.

Moquin, Wayne, comp. *Great Documents in American Indian History*. New York: Praeger, 1973.

Slackman, Michael. "A Pot of Gold: State Casinos Foreseen as Cash Cow." *Newsday*, August 31, 1996, A-8.

Vecsey, Christopher, and Robert W. Venables, eds. *American Indian Environments: Ecological Issues in Native American History*. Syracuse, NY: Syracuse University Press, 1980.

Whittaker, John C. "Red Earth, White Lies: Native Americans and the Myth of Scientific Fact." *Skeptical Inquirer* 1:21 (January 11, 1997): 47.

Wilitz, Teresa. "An Anniversary Celebration: Native American Author Exults in Gadfly Role at Newberry Conference." *Chicago Tribune*, September 15, 1997, Tempo 1.

APPENDIX: BRIEF BIOGRAPHIES

Anderson, Wallace ("Mad Bear"), Tuscarora, 1927–1985. Wallace "Mad Bear" Anderson was one of the most noted Native American rights activists in the 1950s, before the general upsurge in Native American self-determination efforts in the 1960s. Anderson later evolved into a noted spokesperson for Native American sovereignty in international forums. *Further Reading*: Anderson, Wallace (Mad Bear). "The Lost Brother: An Iroquois Prophecy of Serpents." In *The Way: An Anthology of American Indian Literature*, ed. Shirley Hill Witt and Stan Steiner. New York: Vintage, 1972. Wilson, Edmund. *Apologies to the Iroquois*. New York: Farrar, Straus & Cudahy, 1960.

Big Foot (Spotted Elk), Miniconjou Sioux, c. 1820–1890. Big Foot was the leader of the band of Sioux (some accounts say Cheyennes as well) who took the brunt of the casualties at the Wounded Knee massacre in December 1890. Troops opened fire from four Hotchkiss guns, breech-loading cannons that hurled 3.2-inch explosive shells. They also used small arms, killing more than 200 people, including Big Foot, who died from a bullet in his head. *Further Reading*: Brown, Dee. *Bury My Heart at Wounded Knee*. New York: Holt, Rinehart & Winston, 1970. Jensen, Richard E., R. Eli Paul, and John E. Carter. *Eyewitness at Wounded Knee*. Lincoln: University of Nebraska Press, 1991.

Black Kettle (Moketavato), Southern Cheyenne, c. 1800–1868. Born in the Black Hills, Black Kettle became a leading chief of the Southern Cheyennes before his people were massacred at Sand Creek in 1864. Four years later, he was killed in the Washita massacre by George Armstrong Custer's Seventh Cavalry. *Further Reading:* Hoig, Stan. *The Sand Creek Massacre.* Norman: University of Oklahoma Press, 1961. Scott, Robert. *Blood at Sand Creek: The Massacre Revisited.* Caldwell, ID: Caxton Printers, 1994.

Boldt, George Hugo, 1903–1984. On February 12, 1974, U.S. District Court Judge George Boldt ruled that Indians were entitled to an opportunity to catch as many as half the fish returning to off-reservation sites that had been the "usual and accustomed places" when treaties were signed with Puget Sound Indian tribes in the 1850s. The case became an object of major controversy between Indians and commercial and sports fishermen. *Further Reading*: American Friends Service Committee. *Uncommon Controversy: Fishing Rights of the Muckleshoot, Puyallup, and Nisqually Indians.* Seattle: University of Washington Press, 1970. Brown, Bruce. *Mountain in the Clouds.* New York: Simon & Schuster, 1982.

Brant, Joseph (Thayendanegea), Mohawk, 1743–1807. Joseph Brant was the son of Aroghyiadecker (Nicklaus Brant), who was prominent on the New York frontier during the mid-1700s as an Iroquois leader and an ally of the British in the American Revolution. Braut led Mohawks from the United States to Canada after the Revolutionary War, and was one of the Iroquois' most prominent speakers during that era. His grandfather Sa Ga Yean Qua Prah Ton was one of the four "American kings" who were invited to London to visit Queen Anne's court in 1710. *Further Reading*: Edmunds, R. David, ed. *American Indian Leaders: Studies in Diversity.* Lincoln: University of Nebraska Press, 1980. Kelsay, Isabel Thompson. *Joseph Brant, 1743–1807.* Syracuse, NY: Syracuse University Press, 1984. Waters Frank. *Brave Are My People: Indian Heroes Not Forgotten.* Santa Fe, NM: Clear Light, 1993.

Campbell, Ben Nighthorse, Northern Cheyenne, b. 1933. Ben Nighthorse Campbell was elected to the U.S. House of Representatives from Colorado in 1986 and in 1992 became the first Native American to serve in the U.S. Senate since Charles Curtis nearly a century earlier. At the same time, Campbell also was a member of the traditional Council of 44 in his Northern Cheyenne homeland in Montana. In March 1995, Campbell resigned from the Democratic Party and joined the Republicans. *Further*

Reading: Viola, Herman J. *Ben Nighthorse Campbell: An American Warrior*. New York: Orion Books, 1993.

Cody, William (Buffalo Bill), 1846–1917. An Indian fighter in his early life, William Cody ("Buffalo Bill") adapted to the end of the Plains Indian wars by presenting some of his former enemies as star attractions in his Wild West Show. The show, with Sitting Bull, Black Elk, and other notable Native Americans, toured large urban areas of the eastern seaboard as well as Western Europe. *Further Reading*: Sell, Henry B., and Victor Weybright. *Buffalo Bill and the Wild West*. New York: Oxford University Press, 1955.

Cornplanter (John O'Bail), Seneca, c. 1735–1836. Cornplanter was a major Iroquois leader of the late eighteenth century; he figured importantly in the shifting alliances that accompanied the American Revolution and became a personal friend of George Washington through the Tammany Society, a group that observed the fusion of European and Native American cultures in America. *Further Reading*: Parker, Arthur Caswell. *Notes on the Ancestry of Cornplanter*. Rochester, NY: Lewis H. Morgan Chapter, 1927. Stone, William L. (William Leete). *Life and Times of Red-Jacket, or Sa-go-ye-wat-ha: Being the Sequel to the History of the Six Nations*. New York: Wiley & Putnam, 1841.

Costo, Rupert, Cahuilla, 1906–1989. As a football player in the 1920s at Haskell Institute and Whittier College, where he played with future president Richard M. Nixon, Rupert Costo early in life demonstrated his athletic and intellectual aptitudes to the Indian and non-Indian world. From the 1930s to the 1950s, he was active in national and tribal politics, serving both as a vocal critic of the Indian New Deal in the 1930s and tribal chairman of the Cahuillas in the 1950s. Upon his retirement, Costo and his wife, Jeannette Henry Costo (Eastern Cherokee), founded the San Francisco–based American Indian Historical Society in 1964. *Further Reading*: Costo, Rupert, and Jeannette Henry. *Indian Treaties: Two Centuries of Dishonor*. San Francisco: Indian Historian Press, 1977. Costo, Rupert, and Jeannette Henry Costo. *Natives of the Golden State, the California Indians*. San Francisco: Indian Historian Press, 1995.

Crazy Horse (Tashunka Witco), Oglala Lakota, c. 1842–1877. Crazy Horse, a daring military strategist, was a major leader of the Lakotas during the final phases of the Plains Indian wars in the last half of the nineteenth century. Alone among the leaders of the Plains Indian wars, he never signed a treaty with the United States and repudiated the idea of reservation life until his violent death at the young age of about thirty-five. Crazy Horse never wore European-style clothing, and his photograph was never taken. To Oglala Lakotas and to many other Native American people generally, his memory has become the essence of resistance to European colonization. *Further Reading*: Ambrose, Stephen E. *Crazy Horse and Custer*. New York: New American Library, 1986. Sandoz, Mari. *Crazy Horse: The Strange Man of the Oglalas*. New York: Alfred A. Knopf, 1942.

Crook, George, 1828–1890. As commander of the U.S. Army in the area around Omaha, Nebraska, General George Crook was so upset at the treatment of the Ponca Standing Bear and his band that he agreed to be the target of a lawsuit (*Standing Bear v. Crook*, 1879) that became the first legal ruling in the United States to extend the right of habeas corpus to American Indians. The case was decided in Omaha federal court by Judge Elmer Dundy. *Further Reading*: Tibbles, Thomas Henry. *The Ponca Chiefs: An Account of the Trial of Standing Bear*. Ed. Kay Graber. 1880. Lincoln: University of Nebraska Press, 1972.

Dawes, Henry, 1816–1903. U.S. Senator Henry Dawes of Massachusetts was the principal author of legislation (the Allotment Act, passed in 1887) designed to break down common landholdings among Indians and replace them with individual tracts. The idea, born of late-nineteenth-century non-Indian "reform" efforts, was designed to transform Indians into self-sufficient farmers. *Further Reading*: Josephy, Alvin M., Jr. *The Indian Heritage of America*. New York: Bantam, 1969. Nabokov, Peter, ed. *Native American Testimony*. New York: Viking, 1991.

Deganawidah, Huron, fl. 1100–1150. The Iroquois Confederacy was founded by the Huron prophet Deganawidah, who is called "the Peacemaker" in oral discourse among many Iroquois. Deganawidah enlisted the aid of a speaker, Aionwantha (sometimes called Hiawatha), to spread his vision of a united Haudenosaunee (Iroquois) confederacy. *Further Reading*: Gibson, John Arthur. *Concerning the League: The Iroquois League Tradition as Dictated in Onondaga by John Arthur Gibson*. 1912. Ed. and trans. Hanni Woodbury. Memoir 9. Winnipeg: Algonquian and Iroquoian Linguistics, 1992. Wallace, Paul A. W. *The White Roots of Peace*. Santa Fe, NM: Clear Light, 1994.

Deskaheh (Levi General), Cayuga, 1873–1925. Deskaheh was Tadadaho (speaker) of the Iroquois Grand Council at Grand River, Ontario, in the early 1920s, when Canadian authorities closed the traditional longhouse, which had been asserting independence from Canadian jurisdiction. The Canadian authorities proposed to set up a governmental structure that would answer to its Indian-affairs bureaucracy. When Canadian police were about to arrest him, Deskaheh traveled to the headquarters of the League of Nations in Geneva, Switzerland, with an appeal for support from the international community. *Further Reading*: Akwesasne Notes, ed. *A Basic Call to Consciousness*. 1978. Rooseveltown, NY: Akwesasne Notes, 1986. Johansen, Bruce E., and Donald A. Grinde, Jr. *The Encyclopedia of Native American Biography*. New York: Henry Holt, 1997.

Dundy, Elmer S., 1830–1896. Elmer S. Dundy was the federal judge in Omaha who ruled during 1879 in the case of the Ponca Standing Bear that Indians must be treated as "people" under U.S. law. The ruling implicitly denied the U.S. Army's presumed right to relocate individual Native Americans against their will. The ruling was written by Dundy to apply only to Standing Bear's people. If it had applied to all Native Americans, the army would have been legally enjoined from pursuing the last years of the Plains Indian wars. *Further Reading*: Massey, Rosemary, and the Omaha Indian Center. *Footprints in Blood: Standing Bear's Struggle for Freedom and Human Dignity*. Omaha: American Indian Center of Omaha, 1979. Tibbles, Thomas Henry. *The Ponca Chiefs: An Account of the Trial of Standing Bear*. Ed. Kay Graber. 1880. Lincoln: University of Nebraska Press, 1972.

Echohawk, Walter Pawnee b. 1948. As senior staff attorney with the Native American Rights Fund for many years, Walter Echohawk earned a reputation as one of the best-known attorneys in the United States in cases involving the disposition of human remains and burial artifacts. He was one of the leaders behind a major effort to return such remains and artifacts from museums and historical societies to Native American people. Echohawk, who has served on the Pawnee Supreme Court, also has litigated cases concerned with religious freedom, water rights, prisoners' rights, and treaty rights. *Further Reading*: Echo-Hawk, Walter, and C. Echo-Hawk. *Battlefields and Burial Grounds: The Indian Struggle to Protect Ancestral Graves in the United States*. Minneapolis: Lerner Publications, 1994. Vicki Quade. "Who Owns the Past? How Native American Indian Lawyers Fight for Their Ancestors' Remains and Memories." *Human Rights* 16:3 (1989): 24–29, 53–55.

Engels, Friedrich, 1820–1895. The authors of *The Communist Manifesto* found themselves to be overly Eurocentric after they became acquainted with the social and political system of the Iroquois. When the *Manifesto* was originally published in 1848, Karl Marx and Friedrich Engels wrote,

"The history of all hitherto existing societies is the history of class struggles." In the 1888 edition of the *Manifesto*, Engels added a footnote qualifying that statement to take into account information on prehistoric societies with which he and the recently deceased Marx had become acquainted during the ensuing four decades. Engels inherited Marx's copious notes on Lewis H. Morgan's *Ancient Society* (1877) and, after Marx's death, authored *The Origin of the Family, Private Property, and the State.* Studying Morgan's account of "primitive" societies, with the Iroquois being his cornerstone, Engels provided what he believed to be an egalitarian, classless model of society that also provided justice between the sexes. Having discovered the "mother-right gens," Engels could scarcely contain himself: "It has the same significance for the history of primitive society as Darwin's theory of evolution has for biology, and Marx's theory of surplus value for political economy. . . . *The mother-right gens has become the pivot around which this entire science turns*" (Engels, 3:201, emphasis added). *Further Reading*: Engels, Friedrich. *The Origin of the Family, Private Property, and the State, in Light of the Researches of Lewis H. Morgan.* 1886. In *Selected Works*. London: Lawrence & Wishart, 1968. Grinde, Donald A., Jr., and Bruce E. Johansen. *Exemplar of Liberty: Native America and the Evolution of Democracy.* Los Angeles: UCLA American Indian Studies Center, 1991.

Geronimo (Gokhlayeh, Goyathlay), Chiricahua Apache, c. 1825–1909. The man the Spanish would come to call Geronimo was born along the upper Gila River, very likely on the Arizona side of the New Mexico–Arizona border. Taklishim, his father, was a Chiricahua, as was his mother Juana, although she had been a captive among the Mexicans during childhood. In his youth, Geronimo served under the Chiricahua leaders Cochise and Mangas Coloradas. While Geronimo was not a hereditary chief, his reputation among the Apaches increased due to his bravery and prowess in battle. In 1858, Mexicans killed his wife, mother, and three children, causing Geronimo to dislike Mexicans intensely and mount campaigns against them for revenge. Geronimo also was a respected medicine man. *Further Reading*: Adams, Alexander B. *Geronimo: A Biography*. New York: Putnam, 1971. Debo, Angie. *Geronimo: The Man, His Time, His Place.* Norman: University of Oklahoma Press, 1976.

Handsome Lake (Ganeodiyo), Seneca, c. 1733–1815. The religion of Handsome Lake, which began as a series of visions in 1799, combined Quaker forms of Christianity with Native American traditions. Its influence is still strongly felt among the traditional Iroquois, who often call the Code of Handsome Lake "the Longhouse Religion." His personal name was Ganeodiyo; "Handsome Lake," a reference to Lake Ontario, is one of the fifty chieftainship lines of the Iroquois Confederacy. Handsome Lake was a half-brother of the Seneca chief Cornplanter and an uncle of Red Jacket. *Further Reading*: Thomas, Chief Jacob (Jake) [Cayuga], with Terry Boyle. *Teachings from the Longhouse*. Toronto: Stoddart, 1994. Wallace, Anthony F. C. *The Death and Rebirth of the Seneca*. New York: Alfred A. Knopf, 1970.

Hiawatha (Aionwantha), Mohawk, fl. 1100–1150. The Iroquois Confederacy was formed by the Huron prophet Deganawidah, who is called "the Peacemaker" in oral discourse among Iroquois. Deganawidah enlisted the aid of a speaker, Hiawatha (sometimes called Aionwantha), to spread his vision of a united Haudenosaunee confederacy because he stuttered so badly he could hardly speak. *Further Reading*: Howard, Helen A. "Hiawatha: Co-founder of an Indian United Nations." *Journal of the West* 10:3 (1971): 428–438. Wallace, Paul A. W. "The Return of Hiawatha." *Quarterly Journal of the New York State Historical Association* 29:4 (1948): 385–403.

Jefferson, Thomas, 1743–1826. Thomas Jefferson, as George Washington's secretary of state during the 1790s, found that affairs of state often concerned the many Native American nations that bordered the new United States. Before his service as secretary of state, Jefferson authored *Notes on the State of Virginia*, with its detailed accounts of native peoples. Jefferson might have written the most detailed compilation of American Indian languages of his time. His notes, saved for his attention after his service as president ended, were stolen by thieves and dumped in the Potomac River while they were being shipped from the federal capital to Jefferson's home. *Further Reading*: Jefferson, Thomas. *Notes on the State of Virginia*. 1784. New York: Harper & Row, 1984.

LaDuke, Winona, Mississippi Band Anishinabe, b. 1959. Winona LaDuke has become one of the foremost environmental advocates in Native America during the last quarter of the twentieth century. She lectures, writes, and presses authorities for answers on issues from the Navajo uranium mines and Hydro-Quebec's construction sites at James Bay to toxic-waste sites on Native Alaskan and Canadian land along the Arctic Ocean. LaDuke is a daughter of Vincent LaDuke, who was an Indian activist in the 1950s, and Betty LaDuke, a painter. She was educated at Harvard University in the late 1970s. In the early 1980s, she moved to the White Earth Ojibwa Reservation at Round Lake, Minnesota. LaDuke became involved in protests of environmental racism and in recovery of Native American land base. *Further Reading*: LaDuke, Winona. *Last Standing Woman*. Stillwater, MN: Voyageur Press, 1997. LaDuke, Winona. "Native Economies in Native Hands." *Wildfire* 4:4 (Fall 1989): 68–69.

Leschi, Nisqually, c. 1825–1858. Chief Leschi was one of the principal leaders in the Yakima War, which comprised armed resistance during 1855 and 1856 to treaties negotiated by Washington territorial governor Isaac Stevens. The guerrilla war at one point spilled westward over the Cascades in a raid on the Puget Sound settlement of Seattle, after which Leschi was caught and hanged. *Further Reading*: Emmons, Della Gould. *Leschi of the Nisquallies*. Minneapolis: T. S. Denison, 1965.

Looking Glass (Allalimya Takanin), Nez Perce, c. 1822–1877. As a war chief with Chief Joseph the Younger's band of Nez Perces, Looking Glass led the band through much of its Long March in 1877. At first, Looking Glass was the principal chief of a Nez Perce band that was not allied with Joseph. Looking Glass's village was attacked by U.S. troops looking for Joseph's "hostiles," after which his people joined them on their Long March. *Further Reading*: Joseph, Chief [In-mut-too-yah-lat-lat]. "An Indian's View of Indian Affairs." *North American Review* 128 (April 1879): 415–433. Josephy, Alvin M., Jr. *The Nez Perce Indians and the Opening of the Northwest*. New Haven, CT: Yale University Press, 1965.

Mather, Cotton, 1663–1728. A Puritan minister, Cotton Mather was an intellectual antagonist of Roger Williams. While Williams believed that ownership of American land rested with its original inhabitants, Mather argued that the Christian God had opened the land for settlement by his chosen people, the Puritans. Mather had no knowledge of how disease travels and no inkling of the fact that the Europeans themselves had brought the pathogens that depopulated much of the New England countryside. *Further Reading*: Lincoln, Charles Henry, ed. *Narratives of the Indian Wars, 1675–1699*. New York: C. Scribner's Sons, 1913. Silverman, Kenneth. *The Life and Times of Cotton Mather*. New York: Harper & Row, 1984.

McLaughlin, James, 1842–1923. James McLaughlin, the Indian agent at Standing Rock who made Sitting Bull's life miserable during the late years of the chief's life, published his memoirs in 1910 under the title *My Friend the Indian*. The book's dedication leaves no doubt of McLaughlin's professed belief in the wildly paradoxical assumption of his time that the best

Indian is a vanishing one: "To my friend the Indian, whose good parts survive as a monument over the graves of a vanishing race" (McLaughlin, frontispiece). "The Caucasian had wheeled the [railroad] car of progress up to the border of Indian land," writes McLaughlin, "and had been compelled to halt until the red man had been coerced, cajoled, or compelled to get out of the way" (McLaughlin, 1). *Further Reading*: McLaughlin, James. *My Friend the Indian.* 1910. Seattle: Superior Publishing Co., 1970. Utley, Robert M. *The Lance and the Shield: The Life and Times of Sitting Bull.* New York: Henry Holt, 1993.

Osceola (Asi-yahola, Bill Powell, Talcy), Seminole, c. 1803–1838. Osceola, whose name was derived from *asi-yahola*, meaning "black drink crier," was born on the Talapoosa River near the border of Alabama and Georgia. His mother was Polly Copinger, a Creek woman, and she married William Powell, a white man. Osceola became the Seminoles' best-known leader during several decades of running warfare with the U.S. Army in southern Florida. *Further Reading*: Johansen, Bruce E., and Donald A. Grinde, Jr. *The Encyclopedia of Native American Biography.* New York: Henry Holt, 1997. Waters, Frank. *Brave Are My People: Indian Heroes Not Forgotten.* Santa Fe, NM: Clear Light, 1993.

Parker, Arthur (Gawasowaneh), Seneca, 1881–1955. Arthur Parker, whose Iroquois name means "big snowsnake," became one of history's leading Native Americans in anthropology and museum directorship. Born on the Cattaraugus Senecas Reservation, the one-quarter-blood Parker was a grandnephew of Ely S. Parker, secretary to Ulysses S. Grant, as well as a distant relative of the Iroquois prophet Handsome Lake. Parker held several important museum positions in New York State and published many volumes on Iroquois ethnology and other matters. *Further Reading*: Fenton, William N. "Editor's Introduction." In *Parker on the Iroquois*, ed. William N. Fenton, 1–47. Syracuse: Syracuse University Press, 1968. Thomas, W. Stephen. "Arthur Caswell Parker: 1881–1955: Anthropologist, Historian, and Museum Pioneer." *Rochester History* 18:3 (1955): 1–20.

Parker, Ely (Donehogawa), Seneca, 1828–1905. Col. Ely Parker was secretary to General Ulysses S. Grant; he wrote the surrender ending the Civil War that General Robert E. Lee signed at Appomattox. After the Civil War, Parker became the first Native American U.S. commissioner of Indian affairs after Grant was elected president. *Further Reading*: Armstrong, William N. *Warrior in Two Camps: Ely S. Parker, Union General and Seneca Chief.* Syracuse, NY: Syracuse University Press, 1989. Parker, Arthur C.

The Life of General Ely S. Parker: Last Grand Sachem of the Iroquois and General Grant's Military Secretary. Buffalo: Buffalo Historical Society, 1919.

Parker, Quanah, Comanche, 1845–1911. Born at Cedar Lake, Texas, in May 1845, Quanah Parker was a strong and brave leader of the Comanches. His mother, Cynthia Ann Parker, was captured on May 19, 1836, during a raid on white settlements by Comanches; she was nine years old at the time. Quanah Parker grew up in two swiftly changing worlds, the culture of his Comanche father and that of his European-American mother, as he led his people in a series of wars on the southern Plains, then helped to guide them through reservation life. *Further Reading*: Hagan, William T. *Quanah Parker: Comanche Chief*. Norman: University of Oklahoma Press, 1993. Neeley, Bill. *The Last Comanche Chief: The Life and Times of Quanah Parker*. New York: J. Wiley, 1995.

Paxton Boys. The Paxton Boys were European-American vigilantes who preyed on Christianized Indians in Pennsylvania during the early 1760s. After one attack, Benjamin Franklin denounced the Paxton Boys' actions in such strident terms that their supporters voted him out of the Pennsylvania Assembly. *Further Reading*: Franklin, Benjamin. "A Narrative of the Late Massacres in Lancaster County of a Number of Indians, Friends of This Province, by Persons Unknown." In *The Papers of Benjamin Franklin*, ed. Leonard W. Labaree, 11:42–52. New Haven, CT: Yale University Press, 1959.

Peltier, Leonard (Anishinabe), b. 1944. An activist in the American Indian Movement during the 1973 confrontation at Wounded Knee, Leonard Peltier was caught in a shootout with Federal Bureau of Investigation agents and state police at the Jumping Bull Compound on the Pine Ridge Indian Reservation during June 1975. He was later convicted of killing two FBI agents, Jack Williams and Ronald Coler. The trial, which was held in Fargo, North Dakota, Federal District Court in 1977, has since become the focus of an international protest movement aimed at winning Peltier's release from prison. *Further Reading*: Johansen, Bruce E. "Peltier and the Posse." *Nation*, October 1, 1977, 304–307. Matthiessen, Peter. *In the Spirit of Crazy Horse*. New York: Viking, 1983.

Pierce, Maris Bryant (Ha-dya-no-doh, Swift Runner), Seneca, 1811–1874. Following the American Revolution, the Senecas who remained in the United States were faced with reconstructing lives shattered by the punitive raids of John Sullivan in 1779. The destitution of the area contributed to the rise of Handsome Lake's prophecy and to the land-rights activities of Maris Bryant Pierce. Pierce fought efforts to convince Senecas to cede all of their lands in New York and move westward. His primary focus was the 1838 Treaty of Buffalo Creek. *Further Reading*: Pierce, Maris Bryant. "Address on the Present Condition and Prospects of the Aboriginal Inhabitants of North America." In *Indian Lives*, ed. L. G. Moses and Raymond Wilson. Norman: University of Oklahoma Press, 1968. Vernon, H. A. "Maris Bryant Pierce: The Making of a Seneca Leader." In *Indian Lives*, ed. L. G. Moses and Raymond Wilson. Norman: University of Oklahoma Press, 1968.

Plenty Coups (Aleek-chea-ahoosh), Crow, 1848–1932. Plenty Coups, whose Crow name meant "many achievements," was the principal chief of the Crows during the latter stages of the Plains Indian wars. He spearheaded the Crow strategy to cooperate with the U.S. Army in its pursuit of the Cheyennes, Sioux, Arapahoes, and other "hostiles." His Crows provided scouts for George Armstrong Custer in his loss at the Little Bighorn in 1876 and mourned his death. *Further Reading*: Hamilton, Charles, ed. *Cry of the Thunderbird*. Norman: University of Oklahoma Press, 1972. Linderman, Frank. *Plenty-Coups: Chief of the Crows*. 1930. Lincoln: University of Nebraska Press, 1962.

Pontiac (Ponteach), Ottawa, c. 1720–1769. Pontiac, after whom General Motors named an automobile model, tried to erect a Native American confederacy that would block European-American immigration into the Old Northwest. During the spring of 1763, a general uprising was planned by the combined forces of the Ottawas, Hurons, Delawares, Senecas, and Shawnees. On May 9, each tribe was to attack the closest English fort. Pontiac's plan was betrayed to the commander of the British fort at Detroit by an Ojibwa woman named Catherine, to whom he had made love. Pontiac laid siege to the fort at Detroit, and other members of the alliance carried out their respective roles, but an appeal to the French fell on deaf ears, since they had been defeated. After a siege that lasted through the winter and into the spring of 1764, the fort received outside reinforcements, tipping the balance against Pontiac after fifteen months. *Further Reading*: Hays, Wilma P. *Pontiac: Lion in the Forest*. Boston: Houghton Mifflin, 1965. Peckham, Howard H. *Pontiac and the Indian Uprising*. Chicago: University of Chicago Press, 1961.

Riel, Louis David (the younger), Metis/Cree, 1844–1885. Louis Riel was the leader of the most substantial Native American uprising on the Canadian frontier, a conflict that illustrated the complexities of clashing cultures. Riel was only one-eighth Native American, but was representative of a large number of Canadians, the offspring of French traders, usually men, and Native American women. These mixed bloods, called "Metis," form a substantial part of Canadian Native American populations. *Further Reading*: Flanagan, Thomas. *Louis "David" Riel, Prophet of the New World*. Toronto: University of Toronto Press, 1979. MacEwan, Grant. *Metis Makers of History*. Saskatoon, Saskatchewan: Western Producer Prairie Books, 1981.

Schuyler, Peter (Quider), 1657–1724. Peter Schuyler was one of Britain's foremost Indian agents. "Quider," the name used to recognize him among the Iroquois, also was an Iroquois name used for the British government in Albany. It was based on a Mohawk pronunciation of "Peter." In 1678, Schuyler was appointed British representative to the Iroquois Confederacy. Schuyler kept the Iroquois from uniting against the English in support of the French in King William's War, 1689–1697. Schuyler was Albany's first mayor after it was incorporated in 1686. He also served as acting governor of New York in 1719 and 1720, shortly before his death. In 1710, Schuyler invited four Mohawks, including Hendrick, to the court of Queen Anne in London as part of a diplomatic offense to win Iroquois alliance from the French. The fact that all four were Mohawks was not coincidental, for the Mohawks were the best-known of the five Iroquois nations to the English, the keepers of the eastern door of the longhouse, which opened at the British trading post of Albany. *Further Reading*: Bond, Richmond P. *Queen Anne's American Kings*. Oxford: Clarendon Press, 1952.

Schuyler, Philip, 1733–1804. Grandnephew of Peter Schuyler, the first British Indian agent to the Iroquois, Philip Schuyler was born into a family that became one of the wealthiest in America and probably the richest in Albany after Peter Schuyler was appointed the city's first mayor in 1686. Philip Schuyler fought in the French and Indian War (1754–1763) and became a major general in the Continental Army during the American Revolution. He was a member of the Board of Indian Commissioners. Schuyler served as U.S. representative from New York in 1789–1791 and 1797–1798; his daughter Elizabeth married Alexander Hamilton. *Further Reading*: Gerlach, Don R. *Philip Schuyler and the American Revolution in New York, 1733–1777*. Lincoln: University of Nebraska Press, 1964. Graymont, Barbara. *The Iroquois in the American Revolution*. Syracuse, NY: Syracuse University Press, 1972.

Stanton, Elizabeth Cady, 1815–1902. Elizabeth Cady Stanton referred to the influence of Iroquois women in national councils and to the fact that their society was descended through the female line. Stanton made a case for sexual equality based on the Iroquois model:

> In closing, I would say that every woman present must have a new sense of dignity and self respect, feeling that our mothers, during long periods in the long past, have been the ruling power and that they used that power for the best interests of humanity. As history is said to repeat itself, we have every reason to believe that our turn will come again[.] It may not be for woman's supremacy, but for the as yet untried experiment of complete equality, when the united thought of man and woman will inaugurate a just government, a pure religion, a happy home, a civilization at last in which ignorance, poverty and crime will exist no more. Those who watch already behold the dawn of the new day. (Grinde and Johansen 232)

Further Reading: Grinde, Donald A., Jr., and Bruce E. Johansen. *Exemplar of Liberty: Native America and the Evolution of Democracy*. Los Angeles: UCLA American Indian Studies Center, 1991. Stanton, Elizabeth Cady. "The Matriarchate or Mother-Age." *National Bulletin* [National Council of Women] 1:5 (February 1891). Wagner, Sally Roesch. *The Untold Story of the Iroquois Influence on Early Feminists*. Aberdeen, SD: Sky Carrier Press, 1996.

Thoreau, Henry David, 1817–1862. During the 1840s and 1850s, Henry David Thoreau compiled roughly 2,800 pages (500,000 words) of handwritten notes in eleven notebooks on Native American lifeways, history, and culture, which comprise "probably the largest body of knowledge on American Indian culture in the nineteenth century" (Fleck, 3). Despite all his thinking, note taking, and professed empathy for Native Americans in some of his nature writings, Thoreau's attitude toward allotment seemed to vary little from the mainstream "reformer" rhetoric popularized by Helen Hunt Jackson, beginning almost half a century before publication of her *Century of Dishonor*: "For the Indian there is no safety but in the plow. If he would not be pushed into the Pacific, he must seize hold of a plowtail and let go his bow and arrow, his fish-spear and rifle. This is the only Christianity that will save him" (Sayre, 21). *Further Reading*: Fleck, Richard F., ed. *The Indians of Thoreau: Selections from the Indian Notebooks*. Albuquerque: Hummingbird Press, 1974. Sayre, Robert F. *Thoreau and the American Indians*. Princeton, NJ: Princeton University Press, 1977.

Thorpe, James Francis, Sauk/Fox, 1888–1953. Born near Prague, Oklahoma, during 1888 of Irish, French, Sauk/Fox, and Potawatomi descent, James Francis Thorpe (Wathohuck, "The Bright Path") was an outstanding college and professional football player and a gold-medal Olympic athlete. Some sports historians have called him one of the greatest athletes of any era. Thorpe's mother was a granddaughter of the Sauk leader Black Hawk. Thorpe was an all-American college football player in 1911 and 1912, when Coach Glenn S. ("Pop") Warner turned Carlisle Indian School into a national football power. Thorpe won letters in ten sports besides football while at Carlisle: baseball, track, boxing, wrestling, lacrosse, gymnastics, swimming, hockey, handball, and basketball. He also was a prize-winning marksman and excelled at golf. Thorpe represented the United States at the 1912 Olympics in Stockholm, where he won both the decathlon and the pentathlon, the first time the same person had ever won both events in an Olympic Games. King Gustav of Sweden called him the greatest athlete in the world. The gold medals were taken from Thorpe later when it was discovered that he had played professional baseball for a short time in 1911, violating Olympic rules. The medals were returned to Thorpe's family at the 1984 Summer Olympics in Los Angeles. Thorpe played professional baseball between 1913 and 1919 for the New York Giants and Boston Braves. In the 1920s, he began another professional sports career in football with the Chicago Cardinals and other teams. Thorpe also recruited an all-Indian team, the Oorang Indians, for the fledgling National Football League. *Further Reading*: Hirschfelder, Arlene, and Martha Kreipe de Montano. *The Native American Almanac.* New York: Prentice Hall, 1993. Wheeler, Robert W. *Jim Thorpe, World's Greatest Athlete.* Norman: University of Oklahoma Press, 1979.

BIBLIOGRAPHY

INTRODUCTION

Armstrong, Virginia Irving. *I Have Spoken: American History through the Voices of the Indians*. Athens, OH: Swallow Press, 1984.

Black, Nancy B., and Bette S. Weidman, eds. *White on Red: Images of the American Indian*. Port Washington, NY: Kennikat Press, 1976.

Boas, Franz. *Contributions to the Ethnology of the Kwakiutl*. Columbia University Contributions to Anthropology, 3. New York: Columbia University Press, 1925.

Brandon, William. *The American Heritage Book of Indians*. New York: Dell, 1964.

Cornell, George. "Native American Perceptions of the Environment." *Northeast Indian Quarterly* 7:2 (Summer 1990): 3–13.

Cronon, William. *Changes in the Land: Indians, Colonists, and the Ecology of New England*. New York: Hill & Wang, 1983.

Deloria, Vine, Jr. "Comfortable Fictions and the Struggle for Turf: An Essay Review of James Clifton, *The Invented Indian: Cultural Fictions and Government Policies*." *American Indian Quarterly* 16:3 (1992): 397–410.

Fenton, William N. *The Great Law and the Longhouse: A Political History of the Iroquois Confederacy*. Norman: University of Oklahoma Press, 1998.

Gill, Sam. *Mother Earth: An American Story*. Chicago: University of Chicago Press, 1987.

Hughes, J. Donald. *American Indian Ecology*. El Paso: Texas Western Press, 1983.

Iverson, Peter. "Taking Care of the Earth and Sky." In *America in 1492: The World of the Indian Peoples before the Arrival of Columbus*, ed. Alvin Josephy, Jr. New York: Alfred A. Knopf, 1992.

Josephy, Alvin, Jr. *The Patriot Chiefs: A Chronicle of American Indian Leadership*. New York: Viking, 1961.

Martin, Calvin. *Keepers of the Game*. Berkeley: University of California Press, 1978.

Miller, Jay, Colin G. Calloway, and Richard A. Sattler, comps. *Writings in Indian History, 1985–1990*. Norman: University of Oklahoma Press, 1995.

Moquin, Wayne, ed. *Great Documents in American Indian History*. New York: Praeger, 1973.

Nabokov, Peter, ed. *Native American Testimony*. New York: Viking, 1991.

Nabokov, Peter, and Dean Snow. "Farmers of the Woodlands." In *America in 1492: The World of the Indian Peoples before the Arrival of Columbus*, ed. Alvin Josephy, Jr. New York: Alfred A. Knopf, 1992.

Olson, James S., and Raymond Wilson. *Native Americans in the Twentieth Century*, Urbana: University of Illinois Press, 1984.

Porter, Tom. New York State Assembly hearings, "Crisis at Akwesasne." Day 1 (Ft. Covington, NY), July 24, 1990, transcript, 24–28.

Russo, Kurt, ed. *Our People, Our Land: Reflections on Common Ground*. Bellingham, WA: Lummi Tribe and Kluckhohn Center, 1992.

Schoolcraft, Henry Rowe. *Travels in the Central Portions of the Mississippi Valley: Comprising Observations on Its Mineral Geography, Internal Resources, and Aboriginal Population*. New York: Collins & Hannay, 1825.

Standing Bear, Luther. *Land of the Spotted Eagle*. Lincoln: University of Nebraska Press, 1978.

Starna, William A. [Review of Vecsey and Venables, *American Indian Environments*.] *American Anthropologist* 84 (1982): 468.

Toelken, Barre, "Seeing with a Native Eye: How Many Sheep Will It Hold?" In *Seeing with a Native Eye: Essays on Native American Religion*, ed. Walter Holden Capps. New York: Harper Forum Books, 1976.

Tucker, Glenn. *Tecumseh: Vision of Glory*. Indianapolis: Bobbs-Merrill, 1956.

Underhill, Ruth. *Red Man's Religion: Beliefs and Practices of the Indians North of Mexico*. Chicago: University of Chicago Press, 1965.

Vecsey, Christopher, and Robert W. Venables. eds. *American Indian Environments: Ecological Issues in Native American History*. Syracuse, NY: Syracuse University Press, 1980.

Vogel, Virgil J. *This Country Was Ours: A Documentary History of the American Indian*. New York: Harper & Row, 1972.

Waters, Frank. *Brave Are My People: Indian Heroes Not Forgotten*. Santa Fe, NM: Clear Light, 1993.

ROGER WILLIAMS AND METACOM

Axtell, James. *The European and the Indian: Essays in the Ethnohistory of Colonial North America*. New York: Oxford University Press, 1981.

Bourne, Russell. *The Red King's Rebellion: Racial Politics in New England, 1675–1678*. New York: Atheneum, 1990.

Brockunier, Samuel H. *The Irrepressible Democrat: Roger Williams*. New York: Ronald Press, 1940.

Calloway, Colin, ed. *The World Turned Upside Down: Indian Voices from Early America*. Boston: Bedford Books/St. Martin's Press, 1994.

Chapin, Howard M. *Sachems of the Narragansetts*. Providence: Rhode Island Historical Society, 1931.

Chupack, Henry. *Roger Williams*. New York: Twayne, 1969.

Cook, Sherburne F. "Interracial Warfare and Population Decline among the New England Indians." *Ethnohistory* 20:1 (Winter 1973): 1–24.

Covey, Cyclone. *The Gentle Radical: A Biography of Roger Williams*. New York: Macmillan, 1966.

Davis, Jack L. "Roger Williams among the Narragansett Indians." *New England Quarterly* 43:4 (December 1970): 593–604.

Dorr, Henry Crawford. "The Narragansetts." *Rhode Island Historical Society Collections* 7 (1885): 187–188.

Drake, Samuel G. *Biography and History of the Indians of North America*. 11th ed. Boston: Sanborn, Carter & Bazin, 1857.

Ernst, James. *Roger Williams and the English Revolution*. Rhode Island Historical Society Collections 24:1. Providence, 1931.

———. *Roger Williams: New England Firebrand*. New York: Macmillan, 1932.

Giddings, James L. "Roger Williams and the Indians." Typescript, Rhode Island Historical Society, [1957].

Grinde, Donald A., Jr., and Bruce E. Johansen. *Exemplar of Liberty: Native America and the Evolution of Democracy*. Los Angeles: UCLA American Indian Studies Center, 1991.

Guild, Reuben Aldridge. *Footprints of Roger Williams*. Providence: Tibbitts & Preston, 1886.

Howe, George. *Mount Hope: A New England Chronicle*. New York: Viking Press, 1959.

Josephy, Alvin, Jr. *The Patriot Chiefs: A Chronicle of American Indian Leadership*. New York: Viking, 1961.

Kennedy, J. H. *Jesuit and Savage in New France*. New Haven, CT: Yale University Press, 1950.

Labaree, Benjamin W. *America's Nation-Time, 1607–1789*. Boston: Allyn & Bacon, 1972.

Leach, Douglas E. *Flintlock and Tomahawk: New England in King Philip's War*. 1958. New York: W. W. Norton, 1966.

Miller, Perry. *Roger Williams: His Contribution to the American Tradition*. Indianapolis: Bobbs-Merrill Co., 1953.

Morgan, Edmund. *Roger Williams: The Church and the State*. New York: Harcourt, Brace & World, 1967.

Parrington, Vernon Louis. *Main Currents in American Thought*. New York: Harcourt, Brace & Co., 1927.

Poteat, Edwin M. "Roger Williams Redivivus." Speech at the Northern Baptist Convention, Atlantic City, NJ, May 1940. Unpaginated typescript in the archives of the Rhode Island Historical Society, Providence.

Rider, Sidney S. *The Lands of Rhode Island As They Were Known to Caunounicus and Miantunnomu When Roger Williams Came in 1636*. Providence: the author, 1904.

Salisbury, Neal. *Manitou and Providence: Indians, Europeans, and the Making of New England, 1500–1643*. New York: Oxford University Press, 1982.

Savelle, Max. "Roger Williams: A Minority of One." In *The American Story*, ed. Earl S. Miers. Great Neck, NY: Channel Press, 1956.

Slotkin, Richard, and James K. Folsom, eds. *So Dreadfull a Judgment: Puritan Responses to King Philip's War, 1676–1677*. Middletown, CT: Wesleyan University Press, 1978.

Steele, Ian. *Warpaths: Invasions of North America*. New York: Oxford University Press, 1994.

Straus, Oscar S. *Roger Williams: The Pioneer of Religious Liberty*. New York: Century Co., 1894.

Swan, Bradford F. "New Light on Roger Williams and the Indians." *Providence Sunday Journal Magazine*, November 23, 1969, 14.

Waters, Frank. *Brave Are My People: Indian Heroes Not Forgotten*. Santa Fe, NM: Clear Light, 1993.

Williams, Roger. *The Complete Writings of Roger Williams*. New York: Russell & Russell, 1963.

———. *A Key into the Language of America*. 1643. Providence: Rhode Island and Providence Plantations Tercentenary Committee, 1936.

Winslow, Ola Elizabeth. *Master Roger Williams*. New York: Macmillan, 1957.

Wood, William. *New England's Prospect*. 1635. Amherst: University of Massachusetts Press, 1977.

HENDRICK, CANASSATEGO, BENJAMIN FRANKLIN, AND RED JACKET

Alden, John R. "The Albany Congress and the Creation of the Indian Superintendencies." *Mississippi Valley Historical Review* 27:2 (September 1940): 193–210.

Aquila, Richard. *The Iroquois Restoration: Iroquois Diplomacy on the Colonial Frontier, 1701–1754*. Detroit: Wayne State University Press, 1983.

Armstrong, Virginia Irving. *I Have Spoken: American History through the Voices of the Indians*. Athens, OH: Swallow Press, 1984.

Ashton, John. *Social Life in the Reign of Queen Anne*. London: Chatto & Windus, 1882.

Atkinson, Theodore. "Memo Book of My Journey as One of the Commissioners to the Six Nations, 1754." Manuscript Division, Library of Congress.

Bigelow, John, ed. *Autobiography of Benjamin Franklin*. Philadelphia: Lippincott, 1868.

Bond, Richmond. *Queen Anne's American Kings*. Oxford: Clarendon Press, 1952.

Bonomi, Patricia U. *A Factious People: Politics and Society in Colonial New York*. New York: Columbia University Press, 1971.

Boyd, Julian P. "Dr. Franklin: Friend of the Indian." 1942. In *Meet Dr. Franklin*, ed. Roy N. Lokken, 239–245. Philadelphia: Franklin Institute Press, 1981.

———. ed. *Indian Treaties Printed by Benjamin Franklin, 1736–1762*. Philadelphia: Historical Society of Pennsylvania, 1938.

Boyer, Abel. *The History of the Reign of Queen Anne, Digested into Annals: Year the Ninth*. 189–191. London: Thomas Ward, 1711.

Calloway, Colin, ed. *The World Turned Upside Down: Indian Voices from Early America*. Boston: Bedford Books/St. Martin's Press, 1994.

Colden, Cadwallader. *The History of the Five Indian Nations of Canada*. 2 vols. 1765. New York: New Amsterdam Book Co., 1902.

Colonial Records of Pennsylvania 6:98. Harrisburg: Theo. Fenn & Co., 1851.

Commager, Henry Steele. *Documents of American History*. 7th ed. New York: Appleton-Century-Crofts, 1963.

Crèvecoeur, J. Hector St. John. *Letters from an American Farmer*. 1782. New York: E. P. Dutton & Co., 1926.

Downes, Randolph C. *Council Fires on the Upper Ohio: A Narrative of Indian Affairs in the Upper Ohio Valley until 1795*. Pittsburgh: University of Pittsburgh Press, 1940.

Evans, Lewis. "Brief Account of Pennsylvania." In *Lewis Evans*, ed. Lawrence H. Gipson. Philadelphia: Historical Society of Pennsylvania, 1939.

Franklin, Benjamin. "Remarks Concerning the Savages of North-America." In *Franklin Writings*, ed. Lemay. 969–970. Cited in Robert W. Venables. "The Founding Fathers: Choosing to be Romans." *Northeast Indian Quarterly* 6: 4 (Winter 1989): 30–55.

———. "Rules Established for a Club in Philadelphia." Benjamin Franklin Papers, Reel 11, Library of Congress, Washington, DC.

Gibson, Arrell M. *The American Indian: Prehistory to the Present*. Lexington, MA: D. C. Heath, 1980.

Gipson, Lawrence H. "The Drafting of the Albany Plan of Union: A Problem in Semantics." *Pennsylvania History* 26:4 (October 1959): 292–316.

Grinde, Donald A., Jr. *The Iroquois and the Founding of the American Nation*. San Francisco: Indian Historian Press, 1977.

Grinde, Donald A., Jr., and Bruce E. Johansen. *Exemplar of Liberty: Native America and the Evolution of Democracy*. Los Angeles: UCLA American Indian Studies Center, 1991.

Hamilton, Charles, ed. *Cry of the Thunderbird*. Norman: University of Oklahoma Press, 1972.

Hamilton, Milton. *Sir William Johnson, Colonial American, 1715–1763*. Port Washington, NY: Kennikat Press, 1976.

Harrison, Samuel Alexander. *Memoir of Lieut. Col. Tench Tilghman*. New York: Arno Press, 1971.

Hunt, George T. *The Wars of the Iroquois*. Madison: University of Wisconsin Press, 1940.

Jacobs, Wilbur R. *Wilderness Politics and Indian Gifts*. Lincoln: University of Nebraska Press, 1966.

Jennings, Francis. *The Ambiguous Iroquois Empire: The Covenant Chain Confederation of Indian Tribes with English Colonies from Its Beginnings to the Lancaster Treaty of 1744*. New York: W. W. Norton, 1984.

Jennings, Francis, ed.; William N. Fenton, joint ed.; Mary A. Druke, associate ed.; David R. Miller, research ed. *The History and Culture of Iroquois Diplomacy: An Interdisciplinary Guide to the Treaties of the Six Nations and Their League*. Syracuse, NY: Syracuse University Press, 1985.

Johansen, Bruce E. "The Forgotten Founders: Benjamin Franklin, the Iroquois, and the Rationale for the American Revolution." *Four Winds* 2:4 (1982): 9–13.

———. *Forgotten Founders: Benjamin Franklin, the Iroquois, and the Rationale for the American Revolution*. Ipswich, MA: Gambit, 1982.

Jones, Louis Thomas. *Aboriginal American Oratory: The Tradition of Eloquence among the Indians of the United States*. Los Angeles: Southwest Museum, 1965.

Katz, Stanley N. *Newcastle's New York: Anglo-American Politics, 1732–1753*. Cambridge, MA: Belknap Press of Harvard University Press, 1968.

Kelsay, Isabel Thompson. *Joseph Brant, 1743–1807*. Syracuse, NY: Syracuse University Press, 1984.

Labaree, Leonard W., ed. *The Autobiography of Benjamin Franklin*. New Haven, CT: Yale University Press, 1964.

———. *The Papers of Benjamin Franklin*. New Haven, CT: Yale University Press, 1959–1998.

Leder, Lawrence H., ed. *The Livingston Indian Records, 1666–1723*. New York: Earl M. Coleman, 1979.

Marshe, Witham. *Lancaster in 1744: Journal of the Treaty at Lancaster in 1744, with the Six Nations*. Annotated by William H. Egle. Lancaster, PA: New Era Steam and Job Print Press, 1884.

Mathur, Mary E. Fleming. "Tiyanoga of the Mohawks: Father of the United States." *Indian Historian* 3:2 (Spring 1970): 59–62, 66.

McAnear, Beverly. "Personal Accounts of the Albany Congress of 1754." *Mississippi Valley Historical Review* 39:4 (1953): 727–746.

McIlwain, Charles H., ed. *Wraxall's Abridgement of the New York Indian Records, 1678–1751*. Cambridge, MA: Harvard University Press, 1915.

Moquin, Wayne, ed. *Great Documents in American Indian History*. New York: Praeger, 1973.

Morley, Henry, ed. *The Spectator*. London: George Routledge & Sons, 1891.

Newbold, Robert C. *The Albany Congress and Plan of Union of 1754*. New York: Vantage Press, 1955.

Norton, Thomas E. *The Fur Trade in Colonial New York, 1686–1776*. Madison: University of Wisconsin Press, 1974.

O'Callaghan, E. B., ed. *The Documentary History of the State of New-York*. 4 vols. Albany: Weed, Parsons & Co., 1849–1851.

———. *Documents Relative to the Colonial History of the State of New-York*. Vol. 6. Albany: Weed, Parsons, 1853–1887.

Parker, Arthur C. *The Constitution of the Five Nations*. Albany: New York State Museum, 1916.

Ritchie, Robert C. *The Duke's Province: A Study of New York Politics and Society, 1664–1691*. Chapel Hill: University of North Carolina Press, 1977.

Rosenstiel, Annette. *Red and White: Indian Views of the White Man, 1492–1982*. New York: Universe Books, 1983.

Rossiter, Clinton. "The Political Theory of Benjamin Franklin." In *Benjamin Franklin: A Profile*, ed. Esmond Wright. New York: Hill & Wang, 1970.

Shebbeare, John. *Lydia, or Filial Piety*. 3 acts. 1755. New York: Garland Publishing, 1974.

Smyth, Albert H., ed. *The Writings of Benjamin Franklin.* 10 vols. New York: Macmillan Co., 1905–1907.

"Society of St. Tammany, Constitution and Roll of Members." Manuscript Division, New York Public Library.

Spectator, no. 50, April 27, 1711.

Swift, Jonathan. *Journal to Stella*, ed. Harold Williams. Oxford: Clarendon Press, 1948.

Tatler, no. 171, May 13, 1710.

"To Our Great Queen, April, 1710," and "The Four Indian Sachems Letter to Rt. Honourable Lord's of Her Majesty's Council" [April 1710]. Schuyler Indian Papers, Box 13, Manuscript Division, New York Public Library.

Trelease, Allen W. *Indian Affairs in Colonial New York: The Seventeenth Century.* Ithaca, NY: Cornell University Press, 1960.

Venables, Robert W., ed. *The Six Nations of New York: The 1892 United States Extra Census Bulletin.* Ithaca, NY: Cornell University Press, 1995.

Wallace, Paul A. W. *Indians in Pennsylvania.* Harrisburg: Pennsylvania Historical and Museum Commission, 1961.

———. *The White Roots of Peace.* Philadelphia: University of Pennsylvania Press, 1946.

LITTLE TURTLE, TECUMSEH, WILLIAM HENRY HARRISON, AND BLACK HAWK

Armstrong, Virginia Irving. *I Have Spoken: American History through the Voices of the Indians.* Athens, OH: Swallow Press, 1984.

Beckhard, Arthur J. *Black Hawk.* New York: Julian Messner, 1957.

Black Hawk. *Life of Ma-ka-tai-me-she-kia-kiak, or Black Hawk, Dictated by Himself.* Boston: N.p., 1834.

Calloway, Colin, ed. *The World Turned Upside Down: Indian Voices from Early America.* Boston: Bedford Books/St. Martin's Press, 1994.

Carter, Harvey Lewis. *The Life and Times of Little Turtle: First Sagamore of the Wabash.* Urbana: University of Illinois Press, 1987.

Clark, Peter [Dooyentate]. *Origin and Traditional History of the Wyandotts.* Toronto: N.p., 1870.

Drake, Benjamin F. *Life of Tecumseh and His Brother the Prophet with a Historical Sketch of the Shawanoe Indians.* Cincinnati, OH: E. Morgan & Co., 1841. Reprint. New York: Arno Press and New York Times, 1969.

Eckert, Allan W. *A Sorrow in Our Heart: The Life of Tecumseh.* New York: Bantam, 1992.

Edmunds, R. David. *The Shawnee Prophet.* Lincoln: University of Nebraska Press, 1983.

———. *Tecumseh and the Quest for Indian Leadership.* Boston: Little, Brown, 1984.

Eggleston, Edward. *Tecumseh and the Shawnee Prophet: Including Sketches of George Rogers Clark, Simon Kenton, William Henry Harrison, Cornstalk, Blackhoof, Bluejacket, the Shawnee Logan, and Others Famous in the Frontier Wars of Tecumseh's Time.* New York: Dodd, Mead & Company, 1880.

Esarey, Logan, ed. *Messages and Letters of William Henry Harrison*. Indianapolis: Indiana Historical Commission, 1922.

Gill, Sam. *Mother Earth: An American Story*. Chicago: University of Chicago Press, 1987.

Green, James A. *William Henry Harrison: His Life and Times*. Richmond, VA: Garrett & Massie, 1941.

Hagan, William T. *The Sac and Fox Indians*. Norman: University of Oklahoma Press, 1958.

Hamilton, Charles, ed. *Cry of the Thunderbird*. Norman: University of Oklahoma Press, 1972.

Hubbard, J. Niles. *An Account of Sa-go-ye-wat-ha, or Red Jacket, and His People, 1750–1830*. Astoria, NY: J. C. & A. L. Fawcett, 1990.

Jackson, Donald, ed. *Black Hawk: An Autobiography*. Urbana: University of Illinois Press, 1964.

Johansen, Bruce E., and Donald A. Grinde, Jr. *The Encyclopedia of Native American Biography*. New York: Henry Holt, 1997.

Jones, Louis Thomas. *Aboriginal American Oratory: The Tradition of Eloquence among the Indians of the United States*. Los Angeles: Southwest Museum, 1965.

Josephy, Alvin, Jr. *The Patriot Chiefs: A Chronicle of American Indian Leadership*. New York: Viking, 1961.

Manypenny, George W. *Our Indian Wards*. Cincinnati: Robert Clarke & Co., 1880.

Moquin, Wayne, ed. *Great Documents in American Indian History*. New York: Praeger, 1973.

Nabokov, Peter, ed. *Native American Testimony*. New York: Viking, 1991.

Oskison, John M. *Tecumseh and His Times: The Story of a Great Indian*. New York: G. P. Putman's Sons, 1938.

Parker, Arthur C. *Red Jacket: Last of the Seneca*. New York: McGraw-Hill, 1952.

Porter, C. Fayne. *Our Indian Heritage: Profiles of 12 Great Leaders*. Philadelphia: Chilton, 1964.

Red Jacket. *A Long-Lost Speech of Red Jacket*. Ed. J. W. Sanborn. Friendship, NY: N.p., 1912.

Rosenstiel, Annette. *Red and White: Indian Views of the White Man, 1492–1982*. New York: Universe Books, 1983.

Schoolcraft, Henry Rowe. *Travels in the Central Portions of the Mississippi Valley: Comprising Observations on Its Mineral Geography, Internal Resources, and Aboriginal Population*. New York: Collins & Hannay, 1825.

Stone, Jana, ed. *Every Part of This Earth Is Sacred: Native American Voices in Praise of Nature*. San Francisco: HarperCollins, 1993.

Stone, William L. The *Life and Times of Sa-go-ye-wat-ha, or Red-Jacket*. Albany, NY: Munsell, 1866.

Sugden, John. *Tecumseh: A Life*. New York: Henry Holt, 1998.

Tebbel, John, and Keith Jennison. *The American Indian Wars*. New York: Bonanza Books, 1960.

Thornbrough, Gayle. *Letter Book of the Indian Agency at Fort Wayne, 1809–1815*. Indianapolis: Indiana Historical Society, 1961.

Thwaites, Reuben Gold. *The Story of the Black Hawk War*. Madison, WI: State Historical Society of Wisconsin, 1892.
Tucker, Glenn. *Tecumseh: Vision of Glory*. Indianapolis: Bobbs-Merrill, 1956.
Vanderwerth, W. C., ed. *Indian Oratory*. Norman: University of Oklahoma Press, 1971.
Vecsey, Christopher, and Robert W. Venables, eds. *American Indian Environments: Ecological Issues in Native American History*. Syracuse, NY: Syracuse University Press, 1980.
Waters, Frank. *Brave Are My People: Indian Heroes Not Forgotten*. Santa Fe, NM: Clear Light, 1993.
Winger, Otho. *The Last of the Miamis: Little Turtle*. North Manchester, IN: Lawrence W. Shultz, 1968.
Young, Calvin M. *Little Turtle (Me-she-kin-no-quah): The Great Chief of the Miami Indian Nation*. 1917. Evansville, IN: Unigraphic, 1972.

ANDREW JACKSON, SEQUOYAH, JOHN ROSS, AND JOHN MARSHALL

Baker, Leonard. *John Marshall: A Life in Law*. New York: Macmillan, 1974.
Barsh, Russel, and James Henderson. *The Road: Indian Tribes and Political Liberty*. Berkeley: University of California Press, 1980.
Beveridge, Albert J. *The Life of John Marshall*. Vol. 1, *Frontiersman, Soldier, Lawmaker, 1755–1788*. Boston: Houghton Mifflin, 1916.
Black, Nancy B., and Bette S. Weidman, eds. *White on Red: Images of the American Indian*. Port Washington, NY: Kennikat Press, 1976.
Brandon, William. *The American Heritage Book of Indians*. New York: Dell, 1964.
Cherokee Nation v. Georgia, 5 Peters 1 (1831).
Cohen, Felix. *The Legal Conscience: Selected Papers of Felix S. Cohen*. Ed. Lucy Kramer Cohen. New Haven, CT: Yale University Press, 1960.
Cole, Donald B. *The Presidency of Andrew Jackson*. Lawrence: University Press of Kansas, 1993.
Collier, John. *Indians of the Americas*. New York: New American Library, 1947.
Corkran, David H. *The Cherokee Frontier: Conflict and Survival, 1740–62*. Norman: University of Oklahoma Press, 1962.
Coulter, Robert T., and Steven M. Tullberg. "Indian Land Rights." In *The Aggressions of Civilization*, ed. Sandra L. Cadwalader and Vine Deloria, Jr., 185–214. Philadelphia: Temple University Press, 1984.
Debo, Angie. *And Still the Waters Run*. Princeton, NJ: Princeton University Press, 1940.
Deloria, Vine, Jr., ed. *American Indian Policy in the Twentieth Century*. Norman: University of Oklahoma Press, 1985.
Drinnon, Richard. *Facing West: The Metaphysics of Indian-hating and Empire-building*. New York: Schocken Books, 1990.
Garland, Hamlin. "The Final Council of the Creek Nation." In *Hamlin Garland's Observations on the American Indian, 1895–1905*, ed. Lonnie E. Underhill and Daniel F. Littlefield, Jr., 184–192. Tucson: University of Arizona Press, 1976.

Hall, Ted Byron. *Oklahoma, Indian Territory.* Fort Worth, TX: American Reference Publishers, 1971.

Hobson, Charles F. *The Great Chief Justice: John Marshall and the Rule of Law.* Lawrence: University Press of Kansas, 1996.

Jahoda, Gloria. *The Trail of Tears.* New York: Holt, Rinehart & Winston, 1975.

Johnson v. MacIntosh, 8 Wheaton 543 (1823).

Maxwell, Amos D. *The Sequoyah Constitutional Convention.* Boston: Meador, 1953.

MoNickle, D'Arcy. *Native American Tribalism.* New York: Oxford University Press, 1973.

———. *They Came Here First: The Epic of the American Indian.* Philadelphia: J. B. Lippincott Co., 1949.

Moquin, Wayne, ed. *Great Documents in American Indian History.* New York: Praeger, 1973.

Moulton, Gary E. *John Ross: Cherokee Chief.* Athens: University of Georgia Press, 1978.

Norgren, Jill. *The Cherokee Cases: The Confrontation of Law and Politics.* New York: McGraw-Hill, 1996.

O'Brien, Sharon. *American Indian Tribal Governments.* Norman: University of Oklahoma Press, 1989.

Rogin, Michael Paul. *Fathers and Children: Andrew Jackson and the Subjugation of the American Indian.* New York: Alfred A. Knopf, 1975.

Satz, Ronald N. *American Indian Policy in the Jacksonian Era.* Lincoln: University of Nebraska Press, 1975.

Smith, Jean Edward. *John Marshall: Definer of a Nation.* New York: Henry Holt, 1996.

Stannard, David. *American Holocaust: Columbus and the Conquest of the New World.* Oxford: Oxford University Press, 1992.

Strickland, Rennard. *The Indians in Oklahoma.* Norman: University of Oklahoma Press, 1980.

Tebbel, John W. *The Compact History of the Indian Wars.* New York: Hawthorn Books, 1966.

Thornton, Russell. "Cherokee Population Losses during the Trail of Tears: A New Perspective and a New Estimate." *Ethnohistory* 31:4 (1984): 289–300.

Tocqueville, Alexis de. *Democracy in America.* Trans. Henry Reeve. New York: Century Co., 1898.

U.S. Congress. *Report of the Select Committee to Investigate Matters Connected with Affairs in the Indian Territory with Hearings, November 11, 1906–January 9, 1907.* 59th Cong., 2nd sess. Senate Report 5013, pts. 1 and 2. 2 vols. Washington, DC: U.S. Government Printing Office, 1907.

Van Every, Dale. *Disinherited: The Lost Birthright of the American Indian.* New York: William Morrow & Co., 1966.

Venables, Robert. "Revisiting 1984" [review essay]. *Native Americas* 13:1 (Spring 1996): 60–62.

Wallace, Anthony F. C. *The Long, Bitter Trail: Andrew Jackson and the Indians.* New York: Hill & Wang, 1993.

Washburn, Wilcomb E., ed. *The American Indian and the United States: A Documentary History.* New York: Random House, 1973.

Weeks, Philip. *Farewell, My Nation: The American Indian and the United States, 1820–1890.* Arlington Heights, IL: Harlan Davidson, 1990.
Wheaton, Henry. *Elements of International Law.* 8th ed. Ed. Richard Henry Dana, Jr. Boston: Little, Brown, 1866.
Wilkinson, Charles F. *American Indians, Time, and the Law: Native Societies in a Modern Constitutional Democracy.* New Haven, CT: Yale University Press, 1987.
Worcester, Donald E., ed. *Forked Tongues and Broken Treaties.* Caldwell, ID: Caxton Printers, 1975.
Worcester v. Georgia, 31 U.S. (6 Peters) 515, 560 (1832).
Wright, J. Leitch. *The Only Land They Knew: The Tragic Story of the American Indians in the Old South.* New York: Fres Press, 1981.
Wright, Ronald. *Stolen Continents: The America's through Indian Eyes since 1492.* Boston: Houghton Mifflin, 1992.

CHIEF JOSEPH, OLIVER O. HOWARD, SITTING BULL, GEORGE ARMSTRONG CUSTER, RED CLOUD, AND STANDING BEAR (PONCA)

Armstrong, Virginia Irving. *I Have Spoken: American History through the Voices of the Indians.* Athens, OH: Swallow Press, 1984.
Beal, Merrill D. *"I Will Fight No More Forever."* Seattle: University of Washington Press, 1963.
Black, Nancy B, and Bette S. Weidman. *White on Red: Images of the American Indian.* Port Washington, NY: Kennikat Press, 1976.
Brandon, William. *The American Heritage Book of Indians.* New York: Dell, 1964.
Brininstool, E. A. *Fighting Indian Warriors.* New York: Bonanza Books, 1953.
Brown, Mark H. *The Flight of the Nez Perce.* Lincoln: University of Nebraska Press, 1982.
Calloway, Colin, ed. *Our Hearts Fell to the Ground: Plains Indian Views of How the West Was Lost.* Boston: Bedford Books/St. Martin's Press, 1996.
Carpenter, John A. *Sword and Olive Branch: Oliver Otis Howard.* Pittsburgh: University of Pittsburgh Press, 1964.
Chalmers, Harvey. *The Last Stand of the Nez Perce.* New York: Twayne, 1962.
Custer, George Armstrong. *My Life on the Plains.* Ed. Milo Milton Quaife. Lincoln: University of Nebraska Press, 1952.
Davis, Russell, and Brent Ashabranner. *Chief Joseph: War Chief of the Nez Perce.* New York: McGraw-Hill, 1962.
DeVoto, Bernard. *Across the Wide Missouri.* Boston: Little, Brown, 1947.
Dugan, Bill. *Sitting Bull.* San Francisco: HarperCollins, 1994.
Dunsmore, Roger. *Earth's Mind.* Albuquerque: University of New Mexico Press, 1997.
Edmunds, R. David, ed. *American Indian Leaders: Studies in Diversity.* Lincoln: University of Nebraska Press, 1980.
Fee, Chester. *Chief Joseph: The Biography of a Great Indian.* New York: Wilson-Erickson, Inc., 1936.
Giago, Tim. "Book Lacks Lakota View." *Indian Country Today*, August 4, 1993, 4.

Gidley, Mick. *Kopet: A Documentary Narrative of Chief Joseph's Last Years*. Seattle: University of Washington Press, 1981.

Gill, Sam. *Mother Earth: An American Story*. Chicago: University of Chicago Press, 1987.

Haines, Francis. *Red Eagles of the Northwest: The Story of Chief Joseph and His People*. Portland, OR: Scholastic Press, 1993.

Hamilton, Charles, ed. *Cry of the Thunderbird*. Norman: University of Oklahoma Press, 1972.

Hayes, Robert G. *A Race at Bay: New York Times Editorials on "the Indian Problem, 1860–1900*. Carbondale: Southern Illinois University Press, 1997.

Howard, Helen A. *War Chief Joseph*. Caldwell, ID: Caxton Publishers, 1941.

Howard, Helen A., and Dan L. McGrath. *War Chief Joseph*. Caldwell, ID: Caxton, 1952.

Howard, Oliver Otis. *Famous Indian Chiefs I Have Known*. 1908. Lincoln: University of Nebraska Press, 1989.

———. *Nez Perce Joseph: An Account of His Ancestors, His Lands, His Confederates, His Enemies, His Murders, His War, His Pursuit and Capture*. 1881. Boston: Lee & Shepard, 1900.

Hyde, George E. *Red Cloud's Folk: A History of the Oglala Sioux Indians*. Norman: University of Oklahoma Press, 1967.

———. *A Sioux Chronicle*. Norman: University of Oklahoma Press, 1956.

Jackson, Helen Hunt. *A Century of Dishonor: A Sketch of the United States Government's Dealings with Some of the Indian Tribes*. Boston: Roberts Bros., 1888. Reprint. St. Clair Shores, MI: Scholarly Press, 1972.

Jones, Louis Thomas. *Aboriginal American Oratory: The Tradition of Eloquence among the Indians of the United States*. Los Angeles: Southwest Museum, 1965.

Joseph, Chief [In-mut-too-yah-lat-lat]. "An Indian's View of Indian Affairs." *North American Review* 128 (April 1879): 415–433.

Josephy, Alvin M., Jr. *The Nez Perce Indians and the Opening of the Northwest*. 1965. Lincoln: University of Nebraska Press, 1979.

———. *The Patriot Chiefs: A Chronicle of American Indian Leadership*. New York: Viking, 1961.

Larson, Robert W. *Red Cloud: Warrior-Statesman of the Lakota Sioux*. Norman: University of Oklahoma Press, 1997.

Lavender, David. *Let Me Be Free*. San Francisco: HarperCollins, 1992.

MacMurray, J. W. "The 'Dreamers' of the Columbia River Valley, in Washington Territory." *Transactions of the Albany Institute* (1887): 247–248.

Marquis, Thomas B. *A Warrior Who Fought Custer*. Minneapolis: Midwest Co., 1931.

Massey, Rosemary, and the Omaha Indian Center. *Footprints in Blood: Standing Bear's Struggle for Freedom and Human Dignity*. Omaha: American Indian Center of Omaha, 1979.

Mathes, Valerie Sherer. "Dr. Susan LaFlesche Picotte: The Reformed and the Reformer." In *Indian Lives*, ed. L. G. Moses and Raymond Wilson. Albuquerque: University of New Mexico Press, 1985.

———. "Helen Hunt Jackson and the Ponca Controversy." *Montana: The Magazine of Western History* 39:1 (Winter 1989): 42–53.

McLaughlin, James. *My Friend the Indian*. 1910. Seattle: Superior Publishing Co., 1970.

Milner, Richard. "Red Cloud." In *The Encyclopedia of Evolution*, 386–387. New York: Henry Holt Reference Books, 1993.

Moquin, Wayne, ed. *Great Documents in American Indian History*. New York: Praeger, 1973.

Nabokov, Peter, ed. *Native American Testimony*. New York: Viking, 1991.

Olson, James C. *Red Cloud and the Sioux Problem*. Lincoln: University of Nebraska Press, 1965.

Powers, William K. *Indians of the Northern Plains*. New York: G. P. Putnam's Sons, 1969.

Rosenstiel, Annette. *Red and White: Indian Views of the White Man, 1492–1982*. New York: Universe Books, 1983.

Stannard, David. *American Holocaust: Columbus and the Conquest of the New World*. New York: Oxford University Press, 1992.

Stone, Jana, ed. *Every Part of This Earth Is Sacred: Native American Voices in Praise of Nature*. San Francisco: HarperCollins, 1993.

Tibbles, Thomas Henry. *The Ponca Chiefs: An Account of the Trial of Standing Bear*. Ed. Kay Graber. 1880. Lincoln: University of Nebraska Press, 1972.

Tiller, Veronica E. Velarde, ed. *Tiller's Guide to Indian Country: Economic Profiles of American Indian Reservations*. Albuquerque: BowArrow Publishing, 1996.

Utley, Robert M. *Cavalier in Buckskin: George Armstrong Custer and the Western Military Frontier*. Norman: University of Oklahoma Press, 1988.

———. *The Lance and the Shield: The Life and Times of Sitting Bull*. New York: Henry Holt, 1993.

Vanderwerth, W. C., ed. *Indian Oratory: Famous Speeches by Noted Indian Chieftains*. Norman: University of Oklahoma Press, 1971.

Vestal, Stanley. *Sitting Bull: Champion of the Sioux*. 1932. Norman: University of Oklahoma Press, 1957.

Vogel, Virgil J. *This Land Was Ours: A Documentary History of the American Indian*. New York: Harper & Row, 1972.

Waters, Frank. *Brave Are My People: Indian Heroes Not Forgotten*. Santa Fe, NM: Clear Light, 1993.

Weaver, Jace, ed. *Defending Mother Earth: Native American Perspectives on Environmental Justice*. Maryknoll, NY: Orbis Books, 1996.

Wilson, Dorothy Clarke. *Bright Eyes: The Story of Susette La Flesche, an Omaha Indian*. New York: McGraw-Hill, 1974.

Winik, Lyric Wallwork. " 'We're Doing It Because We Think It's Right.' " *Parade Magazine*, June 15, 1997, 4–6.

Wood, H. Clay. *The Status of Young Joseph and His Band of Nez-Perce Indians*. Portland, OR: The Dept. from WorldCAT. 1876.

SEA'THL, BLACK ELK, AND LUTHER STANDING BEAR

Anderson, Eva Greenslit. *Chief Seattle*. Caldwell, ID: Caxton, 1950.

Armstrong, Virginia Irving. *I Have Spoken: American History through the Voices of the Indians*. Athens, OH: Swallow Press, 1984.

Arrowsmith, William. "Speech of Chief Seattle, January 9, 1855." *Arion* 8 (1969): 461–464.

Bagley, Clarence B. "Chief Seattle and Angeline." *Washington Historical Quarterly* 22 (1931): 243–275.

———. *History of Seattle from the Earliest Settlement to the Present Time*. 3 vols. Chicago: S. J. Clarke, 1916.

Black Elk. *Black Elk Speaks: Being the Life Story of a Holy Man of the Oglala Sioux/as Told through John G. Neihardt (Flaming Rainbow)*. 1932. Lincoln: University of Nebraska Press, 1979.

———. *Black Elk Speaks: Being the Life Story of a Holy Man of the Oglala Sioux as Told through John G. Neihardt*. 1932. Lincoln: University of Nebraska Press, 1979.

———. *The Sacred Pipe: Black Elk's Account of the Seven Rites of the Oglala Sioux, Recorded and Edited by Joseph Epes Brown*. 1953. Norman: University of Oklahoma Press, 1967.

Black Elk, Wallace H., and William S. Lyon. *Black Elk: The Sacred Ways of a Lakota*. San Francisco: Harper & Row, 1990.

Brown, Dee. *Bury My Heart at Wounded Knee*. New York: Holt, Rinehart & Winston, 1970.

Calloway, Colin, ed. *Our Hearts Fell to the Ground: Plains Indian Views of How the West Was Lost*. Boston: Bedford Books/St. Martin's Press, 1996.

Carter, Harvey Lewis. *The Life and Times of Little Turtle: First Sagamore of the Wabash*. Urbana: University of Illinois Press, 1987.

Chalmers, Harvey. *The Last Stand of the Nez Perce*. New York: Twayne, 1962.

Churchill, Ward. "A Little Matter of Genocide: Sam Gill's *Mother Earth*, Colonialism, and the Appropriation of Indigenous Spiritual Tradition in Academia." In *Fantasies of the Master Race: Literature, Cinema, and the Colonization of American Indians*, ed. M. Annette Jaimes, 187–213. Monroe, ME: Common Courage Press, 1992.

Cornell, George. "Native American Perceptions of the Environment." *Northeast Indian Quarterly* 7:2 (Summer 1990): 3–13.

Curtis, Natalie. *The Indian's Book*. New York: Harper & Brothers, 1907.

Deloria, Vine, Jr. "Comfortable Fictions and the Struggle for Turf: An Essay Review of James Clifton, *The Invented Indian: Cultural Fictions and Government Policies. American Indian Quarterly* 16:3 (1992): 397–410.

DeMallie, Raymond J., ed. *The Sixth Grandfather: Black Elk's Teachings Given to John G. Neihardt*. Lincoln: University of Nebraska Press, 1984.

Dunsmore, Roger. *Earth's Mind*. Albuquerque: University of New Mexico Press, 1997.

Fadden, John Kahionhes. Personal correspondence with author, March 31, 1998, in author's files.

Fenton, William N. *The Great Law and the Longhouse: A Political History of the Iroquois Confederacy*. Norman: University of Oklahoma Press, 1998.

Fleck, Richard F., ed. *The Indians of Thoreau: Selections from the Indian Notebooks*. Albuquerque: Hummingbird Press, 1974.

Forbes, Jack D., ed. *The Indian in America's Past*. Englewood Cliffs, NJ: Prentice-Hall, 1964.

Furtwangler, Albert. *Answering Chief Seattle*. Seattle: University of Washington Press, 1997.

Gibson, Arrell Morgan. *The American Indian: Prehistory to the Present*. Lexington, MA: D. C. Heath, 1980.

Gill, Sam. *Mother Earth: An American Story*. Chicago: University of Chicago Press, 1987.

———. *Native American Religions: An Introduction*. Belmont, CA: Wadsworth, 1982.

Gorman, Carl N. "Navajo Vision of Earth and Man." *Indian Historian* 6 (Fall 1973): 19–22.

Griffin-Pierce, Trudy. *Earth Is My Mother, Sky Is My Father: Space, Time, and Astronomy in Navajo Sandpainting*. Albuquerque: University of New Mexico Press, 1992.

Hamilton, Charles, ed. *Cry of the Thunderbird*. Norman: University of Oklahoma Press, 1972.

Harner, Michael J. *The Jivaro: People of the Sacred Waterfalls*. New York: Natural History Press, 1972.

Hayes, Robert G. *A Race at Bay: New York Times Editorials on "the Indian Problem," 1860–1900*. Carbondale: Southern Illinois University Press, 1997.

Holler, Clyde. *Black Elk's Religion: The Sun Dance and Lakota Catholicism*. Syracuse, NY: Syracuse University Press, 1995.

Howard, O. O. *Famous Indian Chiefs I Have Known*. 1908. Lincoln: University of Nebraska Press, 1989.

Hughes, J. Donald. *American Indian Ecology*. El Paso: Texas Western Press, 1983.

Iverson, Peter. "Environmental History and Native Americans: A Comment." In *Environmental History: Critical Issues in Comparative* Perspective, ed. K. E. Bailes; 288–292. Lanham, MD: University Press of America, 1985.

Jahner, Elaine A. "Lakota Genesis: The Oral Tradition." In *Sioux Indian Religion: Tradition and Innovation*, ed. Raymond J. DeMallie and Douglas R. Parks. Norman: University of Oklahoma Press, 1987.

James, Jewell Praying Wolf. In *Our People, Our Land: Perspectives on the Columbus Quincentenary,* ed. Kurt Russo. 32–36. Bellingham, WA: Kluckhohn Center and Lummi Tribe, 1992.

Jocks, Christopher. "Response: American Indian Religious Traditions and the Academic Study of Religion." *Journal of the American Academy of Religion* 66:1 (1997): 169–176.

Jones, Malcolm. "Just Too Good to Be True: Another Reason to Beware of False Eco-Prophets." *Newsweek*, May 4, 1992, 68.

Joseph, Chief [In-mut-too-yah-lat-lat]. "An Indian's View of Indian Affairs." *North American Review* 128 (April 1879): 415–433.

Kaiser, Rudolf. "Chief Seattle's Speech(es): American Origins and European Receptions." In *Recovering the Word: Essays on Native American Literature*, ed. Brian Swann and Arnold Krupat. 497–536. Berkeley: University of California Press, 1887.

Kluckhohn, Clyde, and Dorothea Leighton. *The Navaho*. Rev. ed. by Lucy H. Wales and Richard Kluckhohn. Garden City, NY: Anchor Books/Doubleday, 1962.

MacMurray, J. W. "The 'Dreamers' of the Columbia River Valley, in Washington Territory." *Transactions of the Albany Institute* (1887): 247–248.

McLuhan, T. C., ed. *Touch the Earth: A Self-Portrait of Indian Existence*. New York: Outerbridge & Dienstfrey, 1971.

McNab, Miriam. "What Evidence Is There That Western Indians Were Conservationists?" *Native Studies Review* 1:1 (1984): 96–107.

Moquin, Wayne, ed. *Great Documents in American Indian History*. New York: Praeger, 1973.

Morgan, Lewis H. *League of the Ho-de-no-saunee or Iroquois*. Ed. Herbert M. Lloyd. New York: Burt Franklin, 1901. 2 vols.

Murúa, Martin de. *Historia de origen y genealogía real de los reyes Incas del Perú*. 1590. Cited in Irene Silverblatt. *Moon, Sun, and Witches: Gender Ideologies and Class in Inca and Colonial Peru*. Princeton, NJ: Princeton University Press, 1987.

Nabokov, Peter, ed. *Native American Testimony*. New York: Viking, 1991.

Neihardt, Hilda. *Black Elk and Flaming Rainbow: Personal Memories of the Lakota Holy Man and John Neihardt*. Lincoln: University of Nebraska Press, 1995.

Olson, Paul A., ed. *The Struggle for the Land: Indigenous Insight and Industrial Empire in the Semiarid World*. Lincoln: University of Nebraska Press, 1990.

Palmer, Rose A. *The North American Indians: An Account of the American Indians North of Mexico, Compiled from the Original Sources*. Washington, DC: Smithsonian Institution, 1929.

Paper, Jordan. "Through the Earth Darkly: The Female Spirit in Native American Religions." In *Religion in Native North America*, ed. Christopher Vecsey, 3–19. Moscow: University of Idaho Press, 1990.

Penn, William S., ed. *As We Are Now: Mixblood Essays on Race and Identity*. Berkeley: University of California Press, 1997.

Powers, Marla N. *Oglala Women: Myth, Ritual, and Reality*. Chicago: University of Chicago Press, 1986.

Rice, Julian, "Black Elk." In *Handbook of Native American Literature*, ed. Andrew Wiget, 211–216. New York: Garland Publishing, 1996.

———. *Black Elk's Story: Distinguishing Its Lakota Purpose*. Albuquerque: University of New Mexico Press, 1991.

Rosenstiel, Annette. *Red and White: Indian Views of the White Man, 1492–1982*. New York: Universe Books, 1983.

Sayre, Robert F. *Thoreau and the American Indians*. Princeton, NJ: Princeton University Press, 1977.

Schwarz, Douglas O. "Plains Indian Influences on the American Environmental Movement: Ernest Thompson Seton and Ohiyesa." In *The Struggle for the Land: Indigenous Insight and Industrial Empire in the Semiarid World*, ed. Paul A. Olson, 273–288. Lincoln: University of Nebraska Press, 1990.

Smith, Dr. Henry A. "Early Reminiscences. Number Ten. Scraps from a Diary. Chief Seattle—a Gentleman by Instinct—His Native Eloquence, etc., etc." *Seattle Star*, October 29, 1887, n.p.

Standing Bear, Luther. *Land of the Spotted Eagle*. 1928. Lincoln: University of Nebraska Press, 1978.

———. *My People the Sioux*. 1933. Ed. E. A. Brininstool. Lincoln: University of Nebraska Press, 1975.

Starna, William A. [Review of Vecsey and Venables, *American Indian Environments.*] *American Anthropologist* 84 (1982): 468.

Steltenkamp, Michael F. *Black Elk: Holy Man of the Oglala*. Norman: University of Oklahoma Press, 1993.

Stone, Jana, ed. *Every Part of This Earth Is Sacred: Native American Voices in Praise of Nature*. San Francisco: HarperCollins, 1993.

Stuart, George E. "Maya Heartland Under Siege." *National Geographic*, November 1992, 94–107.

Suquamish Museum. *The Eyes of Chief Seattle*. Seattle: University of Washington Press, 1985.

Utley, Robert M. *The Lance and the Shield: The Life and Times of Sitting Bull*. New York: Henry Holt, 1993.

Vanderwerth, W. C., ed., *Indian Oratory: Famous Speeches by Noted Indian Chieftains*. Norman: University of Oklahoma Press, 1971.

Vecsey, Christopher, and Robert W. Venables, eds. *American Indian Environments: Ecological Issues in Native American History*. Syracuse, NY: Syracuse University Press, 1980.

Vogel, Virgil J. *This Country Was Ours: A Documentary History of the American Indian*. New York: Harper & Row, 1972.

Walker, James R. *Lakota Myth*. Ed. Elaine A. Jahner. Lincoln: University of Nebraska Press, 1983.

Waters, Frank. *Brave Are My People: Indian Heroes Not Forgotten*. Santa Fe, NM: Clear Light, 1993.

———. "Neihardt and the Vision of Black Elk." In *A Sender of Words: Essays in Memory of John G. Neihardt*, ed. Vine Deloria, Jr., 12–24. Salt Lake City: Howe Brothers, 1984.

Weaver, Jace, ed. *Defending Mother Earth: Native American Perspectives on Environmental Justice*. Maryknoll, NY: Orbis Books, 1996.

White, Richard. "American Indians and the Environment." *Environmental Review* 9 (1985): 101–103.

HELEN HUNT JACKSON, L. FRANK BAUM, AND RICHARD HENRY PRATT

Allen, Paula Gunn. *The Sacred Hoop: Recovering the Feminine in American Indian Traditions*. Boston: Beacon Press, 1986.

Banning, Evelyn. *Helen Hunt Jackson*. New York: Vanguard Press, 1973.

Barrows, William. *The Indian's Side of the Indian Question*. Boston: D. Lothrop Co., 1887.

Barsh, Russel, and James Henderson. *The Road: Indian Tribes and Political Liberty*. Berkeley: University of California Press, 1980.

Black, Nancy B., and Bette S. Weidman, eds. *White on Red: Images of the American Indian*. Port Washington, NY: Kennikat Press, 1976.

Brown, Judith K. "Economic Organization and Position of Women among the Iroquois." *Ethnohistory* 17:3–4 (Summer–Fall 1970): 151–167.

Calloway, Colin, ed. *Our Hearts Fell to the Ground: Plains Indian Views of How the West Was Lost.* Boston: Bedford Books/St. Martin's Press, 1996.

Carr, Lucien. *The Social and Political Position of Women among the Huron-Iroquois Tribes.* Salem, MA: Salem Press, 1884.

Churchill, Ward. *From a Native Son: Selected Essays in Indigenism, 1985–1995.* Boston: South End Press, 1996.

Cohen, Felix. *The Legal Conscience: Selected Papers of Felix S. Cohen.* Ed. Lucy Kramer Cohen. New Haven, CT: Yale University Press, 1960.

Custer, George A. *My Life on the Plains.* Ed. Milo Milton Quaife. Lincoln: University of Nebraska Press, 1952.

Deloria, Vine, Jr., and Clifford Lytle. *American Indians, American Justice.* Austin: University of Texas Press, 1983.

Earle, Neil. *The Wonderful Wizard of Oz in American Popular Culture: Uneasy in Eden.* Lewiston, NY: Edwin Mellen Press, 1993.

Edmunds, R. David. *Tecumseh and the Quest for Indian Leadership.* Boston: Little, Brown, 1984.

Engels, Friedrich. *The Origin of the Family, Private Property, and the State, in Light of the Researches of Lewis H. Morgan.* 1886. In *Selected Works.* London: Lawrence & Wishart, 1968.

Fleck, Richard F., ed. *The Indians of Thoreau: Selections from the Indian Notebooks.* Albuquerque: Hummingbird Press, 1974.

Gage, Matilda Joslyn. *Woman, Church, and State.* 1893. Watertown, MA: Persephone Press, 1980.

Greeley, Horace. *An Overland Journey, from New York to San Francisco in the Summer of 1859.* 1860. New York: Knopf, 1964.

Grinde, Donald A., Jr., and Bruce E. Johansen. *Exemplar of Liberty: Native America and the Evolution of Democracy.* Los Angeles: UCLA American Indian Studies Center, 1991.

Hagan, William T. *Theodore Roosevelt and Six Friends of the Indian.* Norman: University of Oklahoma Press, 1997.

Hayes, Robert G. *A Race at Bay: New York Times Editorials on "the Indian Problem." 1860–1900.* Carbondale: Southern Illinois University Press, 1997.

Hoxie, Frederick E. *A Final Promise: The Campaign to Assimilate the Indians, 1880–1920.* Lincoln: University of Nebraska Press, 1984.

Jackson, Helen Hunt. *A Century of Dishonor: A Sketch of the United States Government's Dealings with Some of the Indian Tribes.* Boston: Roberts Bros., 1888. Reprint. St. Clair Shores, MI: Scholarly Press, 1972.

Jacobs, Paul, and Saul Landau, with Eve Pell. *To Serve the Devil.* Vol. I, *Native and Slaves.* New York: Random House, 1971.

Jefferson, Thomas. *Notes on the State of Virginia.* 1784. Ed. William Peden. Chapel Hill: University of North Carolina Press, 1955.

Jensen, Richard E., R. Eli Paul, and John E. Carter. *Eyewitness at Wounded Knee.* Lincoln: University of Nebraska Press, 1991.

Johansen, Bruce E. "L. Frank Baum's Call to Genocide." *Native Americas* 14:1 (Spring 1997): 9.

———. "Taking Indians for a Ride: The BIA's Missing $2.4 Billion." *Native Americas* 14:1 (Spring 1997): 14–23.

Kinney, J. P. *A Continent Lost—A Civilization Won: Indian Land Tenure in America.* 1937. New York: Arno Press, 1975.

Landsman, Gail. "Portrayals of the Iroquois in the Woman Suffrage Movement." Paper presented at the Annual Conference on Iroquois Research, Rensselserville, NY, October 8, 1988.

Leupp, Francis E. *The Indian and His Problem.* New York: Charles Scribner's Sons, 1910. Reprint. New York: Johnson Reprint Corp., 1970.

Manypenny, George W. *Our Indian Wards.* Cincinnati: Robert Clarke & Co., 1880.

Marx, Karl, and Freidrich Engels. *Selected Works.* New York: International Publishers, 1968.

Mathes, Valerie Sherer. "Helen Hunt Jackson: A Legacy of Indian Reform." *Essays and Monographs in Colorado History* 4 (1986): 25–58.

———. *Helen Hunt Jackson and Her Indian Reform Legacy.* Austin: University of Texas Press, 1990.

———. "Helen Hunt Jackson and the Ponca Controversy." *Montana: The Magazine of Western History* 39:1 (Winter 1989): 42–53.

May, Antoinette. *Helen Hunt Jackson: A Lonely Voice of Conscience.* San Francisco: Chronicle Books, 1987.

McLaughlin, James. *My Friend the Indian.* 1910. Seattle: Superior Publishing Co., 1970.

McLaughlin, Michael R. "The Dawes Act, or Indian General Allotment Act of 1887: The Continuing Burden of Allotment." *American Indian Culture and Research Journal* 20:2 (1996): 59–105.

Meriam, Lewis. *The Problem of Indian Administration.* Baltimore: Johns Hopkins Press, 1928.

Moquin, Wayne, ed. *Great Documents in American Indian History.* New York: Praeger, 1973.

Morgan, Lewis Henry. *Ancient Society.* New York: Henry Holt, 1877.

———. *League of the Ho-de-no-sau-nee, or Iroquois.* 1851. New York: Dodd, Mead, 1922.

Morris, Roy, Jr. *Sheridan: The Life and Wars of General Phil Sheridan.* New York: Crown, 1992.

National Resources Board, Land Planning Committee. *Indian Land Tenure, Economic Status, and Population Trends.* Washington, DC: U.S. Government Printing Office, 1935.

O'Brien, Sharon. *American Indian Tribal Governments.* Norman: University of Oklahoma Press, 1989.

Palmer, Rose A. *The North American Indians: An Account of the American Indians North of Mexico, Compiled from the Original Sources.* Washington, DC: Smithsonian Institution, 1929.

Pommersheim, Frank. *Braid of Feathers: American Indian Law and Contemporary Tribal Life.* Berkeley: University of California Press, 1995.

Pratt, Richard Henry. *Battlefield and Classroom: Four Decades with the American Indian, 1867–1904.* Ed. Robert M. Utley. 1964. Lincoln: University of Nebraska Press, 1987.

Prucha, Francis Paul, ed. *Americanizing the American Indians: Writings by the*

"Friends of the Indian," 1830–1900. Cambridge, MA: Harvard University Press, 1973.

Ramsay, Allan. *Thoughts on the Origin and Nature of Government*. Cited in Staughton Lynd. *Intellectual Origins of American Radicalism*. New York: Pantheon Books, 1968.

Reilly, Hugh. "Treatment of Native Americans by the Frontier Press: An Omaha, Nebraska, Case Study." M.A. Thesis, University of Nebraska at Omaha, 1997.

Riley, Glenda. *Women and Indians on the Frontier, 1825–1915*. Albuquerque: University of New Mexico Press, 1984.

Sayre, Robert F. *Thoreau and the American Indians*. Princeton, NJ: Princeton University Press, 1977.

Snake, Reuben. *Reuben Snake, Your Humble Serpent: Indian Visionary and Activist*, as told to Jay C. Fikes. Santa Fe, NM: Clear Light, 1996.

Stanton, Elizabeth Cady. "The Matriarchate or Mother-Age." *National Bulletin* [National Council of Women] 1:5 (February 1891).

Stanton, Elizabeth Cady, Susan B. Anthony, and Matilda Joslyn Gage, eds. *History of Woman Suffrage*. 6 vols. Salem, NH: Ayer Co., 1985.

Tibbles, Thomas Henry. *The Ponca Chiefs: An Account of the Trial of Standing Bear*. Ed. Kay Graber. 1880. Lincoln: University of Nebraska Press, 1972.

Tucker, Robert C., ed. *The Marx-Engels Reader*. New York: W. W. Norton, 1972.

Tyler, S. Lyman. *A History of Indian Policy*. Washington, DC: Bureau of Indian Affairs, 1973.

Vogel, Virgil J. *This Country Was Ours: A Documentary History of the American Indian*. New York: Harper & Row, 1972.

Wagner, Sally Roesch. "The Iroquois Confederacy: A Native American Model for Non-sexist Men." *Changing Men*, Spring-Summer 1988, 32–33.

———. *The Untold Story of the Iroquois Influence on Early Feminists*. Aberdeen, SD: Sky Carrier Press, 1996.

Washburn, Wilcomb. *The Assault on Indian Tribalism: The General Allotment Law (Dawes Act) of 1887*. Philadelphia: J. B. Lippincott, 1975.

Waters, Frank. *Brave Are My People: Indian Heroes Not Forgotten*. Santa Fe, NM: Clear Light, 1993.

Whitaker, Rosemary. *Helen Hunt Jackson*. Boise, ID: Boise State University, 1987.

Wilkinson, Charles F. *American Indians, Time, and the Law: Native Societies in a Modern Constitutional Democracy*. New Haven, CT: Yale University Press, 1987.

FELIX COHEN, VINE DELORIA, JR., OREN LYONS, AND SLADE GORTON

Aslam, Abid. "Environment/Brazil: World Bank to Overhaul Amazon Project." Interpress service, April 18, 1997. http://edvmix3.ub.tu-berlin.de/lists/native-1/199704/19970423.html.

Carroll, Vincent. "Republican Professors? Sure, There's One." *Wall Street Journal*, May 11, 1998, A-22.

Cassirer, Ernst. *An Essay on Man*. New Haven, CT: Yale University Press, 1944.

Churchill, Ward. *Struggle for the Land: Indigenous Resistance to Genocide, Ecocide, and Expropriation in Contemporary North America.* Monroe, ME: Common Courage Press, 1993.

Cohen, Felix. "Americanizing the White Man." *American Scholar* 21:2 (1952): 171–191.

———. *Ethical Systems and Legal Ideals.* 1933. Westport, CT: Greenwood Press, 1976.

———. *Handbook of Federal Indian Law.* Washington, DC: Interior Department, 1942.

———. *The Legal Conscience: Selected Papers of Felix S. Cohen.* Ed. Lucy Kramer Cohen. New Haven, CT: Yale University Press, 1960.

Cohen, Morris R., and Felix S. Cohen. *Readings in Jurisprudence and Legal Philosophy.* Boston: Little Brown, 1951.

Colorado River Native Nations Alliance, Press Release, February 14, 1998, in author's files.

Deloria, Vine, Jr. *Behind the Trail of Broken Treaties.* 1974. Austin: University of Texas Press, 1985.

———. "Commentary: Research, Redskins, and Reality." *American Indian Quarterly.* 15:4 (Fall 1991): 457–468.

———. *Custer Died for Your Sins: An Indian Manifesto.* Norman: University of Oklahoma Press, 1988.

———. *God Is Red: A Native View of Religion.* 2nd ed. Golden, CO: North American Press/Fulcrum, 1992.

———. *The Indian Affair.* New York: Friendship Press, 1974.

———. "Indigenous Peoples' Literature." http://www.indians.org/welker/vine.htm.

———. *The Metaphysics of Modern Existence.* San Francisco: Harper & Row, 1979.

———. *Red Earth, White Lies: Native Americans and the Myth of Scientific Fact.* New York: Scribner, 1995.

———. *We Talk, You Listen: New Tribes, New Turf.* New York: Macmillan, 1970.

———. ed. *American Indian Policy in the Twentieth Century.* Norman: University of Oklahoma Press, 1985.

Deloria, Vine, Jr., and Clifford Lytle. *American Indians, American Justice.* Austin: University of Texas Press, 1983.

———. *The Nations Within.* New York: Pantheon, 1984.

Dunsmore, Roger, "Vine Deloria, Jr.," In *Handbook of Native American Literature,* ed. Andrew Wiget, 411–415. New York: Garland Publishing, 1996.

Etlinger, Charles. "Indian Scholar Blows Holes in Theories: Deloria Says Lazy Scientists Adjust Facts to Fit Ideas." *Idaho Statesman,* February 28, 1998, 1-B.

Hasse, Larry J. "Termination and Assimilation: Federal Indian Policy, 1943 to 1961." Ph.D. dissertation, Washington State University, 1974. Ann Arbor, MI: University Microfilms.

Haynes, V. Dion. "Mojave Desert Indians Fighting to Stop Dump." *Chicago Tribune,* March 22, 1998. C-3.

Hughes, J. Donald. *American Indian Ecology.* El Paso: Texas Western Press, 1983.

Johansen, Bruce E. "Slade Gorton's Latest." *Native Americas* 14:3 (Fall 1997): 3–4.

———. "Sovereignty Summit." *Akwesasne Notes*, n.s. 1:3/4 (Fall 1995): 78–81.

———. "Taking Indians for a Ride: The BIA's Missing $2.4 Billion." *Native Americas* 14:1 (Spring 1997): 14–23.

Knickerbocker, Brad. "Tribal Nations Fight Challenges to Their Sovereignty." *Christian Science Monitor*, April 3, 1998, 1.

Lipsyte, Robert. "Lacrosse: All-American Game." *New York Times Sunday Magazine*, June 15, 1986, 28.

Looking Horse, Arvol. "Invitation to World Peace and Prayer Day, June 21, 1998, at Pipestone, Minnesota." http://www.peaceday.org/0621.htm.

Lyons, Oren. "Ethics and Spiritual Values, and the Promotion of Environmentally Sustainable Development: 50 Years of the World Bank, Over 50 Tribes Devastated." October 3, 1995. http://www.ratical.com/ratville/OrenLyons.html #development.

———. "Haudenosaunee Faithkeeper, Chief Oren Lyons Addressing Delegates to the United Nations Organization [which] Opened 'The Year of the Indigenous Peoples' (1993) in the United Nations General Assembly Auditorium, United Nations Plaza, New York City, December 10, 1992." http://www.ratical.com/many_worlds/6Nations/OLatUNin92.html.

———. "Opening Address for the Year of Indigenous Peoples, United Nations, New York City, 1993." http://www.indians.org/walker/onondaga.htm.

———. "Opening Remarks." Working Group on Indigenous Peoples United Nations, Geneva, Switzerland. Document E/CN.4/Sub.2/1997/14. 15th Session, July 28–August 1, 1997. http://www.docip.org/anglais/update_en/up_en19_20.html#opst.

Lyons, Oren, and John C. Mohawk. "Sovereignty and Common Sense." *Cultural Survival Quarterly* 17:4 (Winter 1994): 58–60.

Lyons, Oren, John Mohawk, Vine Deloria, Jr., Laurence Hauptman, Howard Berman, Donald A. Grinde, Jr., Curtis Berkey, and Robert Venables. *Exiled in the Land of the Free: Democracy, Indian Nations, and the U.S. Constitution.* Santa Fe, NM: Clear Light, 1992.

Mapes, Lynda V. "Backlash for Tribal Immunity—Debate over Move to End Sovereign Status." *Seattle Times*, April 5, 1998, B-1.

McCarthy, Jack. "Tribes' Role Unique in Ward Valley Dispute." *Riverside* [CA] *Press-Enterprise*, February 22, 1998, A-1.

Moquin, Wayne, comp. *Great Documents in American Indian History*. New York: Praeger, 1973.

Murkland, Pat. "Nuclear Dump Foes Vow Not to Move from Desert Site." *Riverside* [CA] *Press-Enterprise*, February 16, 1998, 1.

Nabokov, Peter, ed. *Native American Testimony*. New York: Viking, 1991.

Rice, Julian. *Deer Women and Elk Men: The Lakota Narratives of Ella Deloria.* Albuquerque: University of New Mexico Press, 1992.

Slackman, Michael. "A Pot of Gold: State Casinos Foreseen as Cash Cow." *Newsday*, August 31, 1996, A-8.

Steiner, Stan. *The New Indians*. New York: Harper & Row, 1968.

Vecsey, Christopher, and Robert W. Venables, eds. *American Indian Environments: Ecological Issues in Native American History*. Syracuse, NY: Syracuse University Press, 1980.

Vogel, Virgil J. *This Country Was Ours: A Documentary History of the American Indian*. New York: Harper & Row, 1972.

Warner, Gene. "Chief Sees Pluses in Deal with State." *Buffalo News*, April 13, 1997, 1-B.

Watkins, Arthur V. "Termination of Federal Supervision: The Removal of Restriction over Indian Property and Person." *Annals of the American Academy of Political and Social Science* 311 (May 1957): 47–55.

Whittaker, John C. "Red Earth, White Lies: Native Americans and the Myth of Scientific Fact." *Skeptical Inquirer* 21:1 (January–February 1997): 47–50.

Wilitz, Teresa. "An Anniversary Celebration: Native American Author Exults in Gadfly Role at Newberry Conference." *Chicago Tribune*, September 15, 1997, Tempo 1.

INDEX

About the Author

BRUCE E. JOHANSEN is Robert T. Reilly Professor of Communication and Native American Studies at the University of Nebraska at Omaha. The author of 13 other books, he specializes in the influence of Native American political systems on U.S. political and legal institutions. His other books include *Exemplar of Liberty* (1991, with Donald A. Grinde, Jr.), *Encyclopedia of Native American Legal Traditions* (Greenwood, 1998) and *The Encyclopedia of Native American Economic History* (Greenwood, 1999).